In a Vision of the Night

In a Vision of the Night

JOB, CORMAC McCARTHY, AND THE CHALLENGE OF CHAOS

Philip S. Thomas

BAYLOR UNIVERSITY PRESS

© 2021 by Baylor University Press
Waco, Texas 76798

All Rights Reserved. No part of this publication may be reproduced, stored in a retrieval system, or transmitted, in any form or by any means, electronic, mechanical, photocopying, recording, or otherwise, without the prior permission in writing of Baylor University Press.

Unless otherwise stated, Scripture quotations are from the New Revised Standard Version Bible, copyright 1989, Division of Christian Education of the National Council of the Churches of Christ in the United States of America. Used by permission. All rights reserved.

Cover and book design by Kasey McBeath
Cover art: Shutterstock/Kateryna Zaytseva

The Library of Congress has cataloged this book under ISBN 978-1-4813-1598-2. Library of Congress Control Number: 2021022756

Printed in the United States of America on acid-free paper with a minimum of 30 percent recycled content.

For Elizabeth, Will, and Oliver,
and *in memoriam* Susan Winifred Thomas (1944–1990)

I had to find an explanation other than the real one, which was that we were no more immune to misfortune than anybody else.

William Maxwell, *So Long, See You Tomorrow*

Contents

Preface and Acknowledgments

The untimely death of a loved one. An unexpected and life-altering medical diagnosis. The birth of a child who lies outside the societally mandated definition of "normality." My own experiences of lumbering Behemoth and brutal Leviathan are neither unique nor unusual, but are merely illustrative of the myriad ways in which the waves of unpredictable and inexplicable chaos can break over the shoreline of settled life.

In such circumstances, the cry of "Why me?" is unremarkable, but is ultimately unanswerable from the human perspective. Furthermore, any human attempt to speak for the divine is fraught with considerable risk, to put it mildly.

It was as one of these waves receded that I began to read the fiction of Cormac McCarthy. It soon became apparent that his works, when read alongside the book of Job, could prove generative in circumventing these age-old difficulties. What I found in McCarthy, and also in Job, was the challenge to hold on to hope in apparent hopelessness, to live with meaning when all seems meaningless, and to believe that small kindnesses are not eradicated by painful tragedy.

Any book that offers a reading of Job is likely to be thought of as having fallen into the comforters' errors: flattening all experiences such that they can be covered by a broad generalization; and arrogating to one particular viewpoint a greater degree of authority and gravity than is appropriate. It is for the reader to judge whether or not I have followed the lead of Eliphaz, Bildad, and Zophar in this regard.

Who would have thought that my brother's decision to move house would, through the strange workings of time, have allowed me to study for a PhD in the area from which this book arose? Certainly not me, but I am grateful to Chris and Claire that it did, as well as to Anthony and Jeannie. In Dr. Jon Coutts I found a supervisor who was attentive, interested, and critical, and I am thankful for how he welcomed and encouraged me in my studies. I am also grateful to the faculty and postgraduate students of Trinity College, Bristol, for their warm welcome, insightful questions, and stimulating discussions. Thanks to Cade Jarrell for his support through the writing process, and to all the editorial team at Baylor University Press for their careful editing, attention to detail, and generous help. Finally, the greatest debt of gratitude I have is owed to my wife, Elizabeth, and my teenage children, Will and Oliver, for their indulgence, encouragement, and patience.

Abbreviations

CD	Karl Barth, *Church Dogmatics*, trans. by Geoffrey Bromiley (Edinburgh: T&T Clark, 1956–1975).
TOK	Cormac McCarthy, *The Orchard Keeper* (London: Picador, 1965).
OD	Cormac McCarthy, *Outer Dark* (London: Picador, 1968).
BM	Cormac McCarthy, *Blood Meridian or The Evening Redness in the West* (London: Picador, 1985).
ATPH	Cormac McCarthy, *All the Pretty Horses* (London: Picador, 1992).
TC	Cormac McCarthy, *The Crossing* (London: Picador, 1994).
COTP	Cormac McCarthy, *Cities of the Plain* (London: Picador, 1998).
NCFOM	Cormac McCarthy, *No Country for Old Men* (London: Picador, 2005).
TR	Cormac McCarthy, *The Road* (London: Picador, 2006).
TSL	Cormac McCarthy, *The Sunset Limited* (London: Picador, 2010).
TCo	Cormac McCarthy, *The Counselor* (London: Picador, 2013).

Introduction

TRUE WORDS IN LITERATURE

Since Vereen Bell's 1988 book *The Achievement of Cormac McCarthy* kick-started critical engagement with Cormac McCarthy's literary works, there has been a growing body of scholarly investigation into McCarthy's writings in monographs, edited essay collections, and articles in the excellent *Cormac McCarthy Journal*. The sheer variety of these attests to the fact that his novels and plays offer sustained and profound explorations of various themes. Some of the themes regularly identified in his work and discussed in the literature include nihilism, gnosticism, Platonism, and existential Christianity,[1] and while McCarthy may be influenced by all of these factors—and possibly more—it remains doubtful that he is out to persuade readers of a specific philosophical position. Rather, his books entertain a range of philosophical and ideological vantages that he allows to coexist in mutual interrogation.[2] Thus there is a dialogical current to his work—in style as well as in content—that confronts any reader who expects a unified moral vision with a confounding plurality.[3] However, this dialogical plurality permits multiple avenues of interpretation into the different accounts of ethics, metaphysics and theology that are increasingly recognized as essential components of his novels.[4] In 2000 critic Rick Wallach eagerly anticipated fresh critical examinations of McCarthy's work, stating that he believed "his canon still needs some exemplary treatments from perspectives not yet brought to bear in print."[5] Critics have taken this to heart, and recent essays have investigated the intersection of McCarthy's works with fields as diverse as disability studies, faerie lore, and visual art.[6] There is a seemingly endless generativity to McCarthy's works and their polysemous characters such that the various readings and interpretations mutually illuminate one another and the texts themselves, resisting attempts to impose closure on them. No single reading excludes any other; rather, they generate a polyphonic conversation about the works, stimulating further approaches and insights that are then enfolded into this ongoing colloquy. The present work focuses on one aspect of this generativity and, rather than seeking to critically dissect or rebuff alternative readings of McCarthy's works and characters—although the notes do contain references to specific studies—it examines a selection of McCarthy's work through a "perspective[s] not yet brought to bear," and thereby adds a further voice to the already lively and fascinating chorus of McCarthy criticism.[7] It is a voice that is theological in tone,[8] and, more specifically, it adds to the conversation surrounding the themes, ideas, and language of both McCarthy and the biblical book of Job. The main focus of this study is the book of Job, and McCarthy's works act as a lens through which that book may be encountered. However, in reading Job *through* McCarthy in this way, the book of Job *reflects back* into the reading of McCarthy in a complex hermeneutical relationship of mutual illumination. Thus the influence of Job on McCarthy will be discussed even though the main interest is on how McCarthy might bring insights to a reading of Job.[9]

In the early third century A.D., the North African Christian author and apologist Tertullian asked what Athens had to do with Jerusalem. For Tertullian, theological reflection on Holy Scripture and interaction with Greek philosophy constituted separate disciplines, and the latter could yield no insight into the former. Such a dispiritingly divisive attitude has continued to hold sway in certain theological circles, a fact that was commented on in the 1980s by Ulrich Simon, who characterized some theologians as treating literature "as if novels provided an escape mechanism from serious issues."[10] This was echoed by Stanley Hauerwas' wry observation that "theologians and novelists generally do not mix."[11]

This is a statement tinged with sadness, and it risks presenting too gloomy a view of the situation. There has been a growing awareness of the mutual benefits to both literature and theology of including the other discipline in each one's investigations. Without attempting to give an exhaustive genealogy, since at least the 1960s when Frederick Dillistone and Nathan Scott published important works,[12] there has been a growing awareness of the mutual benefits to both literature and theology of interacting with each other. In subsequent years there has continued to be interest in how these two disciplines interrelate and mutually illuminate.[13] Today, the theologian with literary interests or the literary critic (or just the reader) with theological curiosity has a steadily growing number of books from which to choose. From depictions of the atonement or how wisdom is understood to engagements with authors such as Fyodor Dostoyevsky or Flannery O'Connor, from how the biblical language and style—and therefore its values—have shaped literary works to how authors have deliberately shaped novels to reflect biblical themes, there are many resources available.[14] What these various works share is an assumption that reading literature has an immeasurable value in informing one's faith:

> When we put old ideas and the texts that express them into dialogue with new books and ideas, and, more important, when we put ourselves into dialogue with both—questioning them and being questioned by them—the outcome is a deeper understanding of their ideas and of our own lives. The world becomes for us a richer place that speaks to us more often and more eloquently.[15]

The dynamics of how this occurs have been variously described, and the brief overview that follows is not designed to be a comprehensive survey of the ways in which the literary-theological cake may be cut. For some, theology is grounded in Scripture, but is best illustrated in literature.[16] For others, literature provokes theology by interrogating theology in a concrete and practical way, whereas theology can only ask itself notional or hypothetical questions. Thus literature can reveal the sorts of questions that theology ought to be answering, but rarely does.[17] At the far end of this provocative dynamic, literature can challenge theology by resisting its totalizing perspective.[18] To reverse the direction of flow, it is recognized that theology can influence literature, not least because of the hugely influential place of the Bible in Western literary culture.[19] As such, the biblical narratives continue to inspire contemporary authors: "The author's task, as Thomas Mann saw it, is to open the ancient well and to fill our empty buckets with the waters of the past. The old myths yield the healing springs which may irrigate the parched fields."[20] And the fields *are* parched, argues Simon, and although the world, humanity, and the individual are all in conflict, there is always hope for a better tomorrow. Moreover, it is story that connects the future hope with the present chaos:

> As it entertains and delights, shocks and warns, accuses and challenges, separates and unifies, imprisons and liberates, it reveals us to ourselves, evokes the dimensions of the universe behind ours, and points to the One, always absent and present, immutably transcendent and compassionately with us.[21]

Investigations into literature and theology are, therefore, exercises in intertextuality,[22] for no literary work ever begins from a blank page since it will be shaped by what both the author of the work and the reader who comes to the work and attempts to read it have previously read.[23]

But they are not *only* exercises in intertextuality. In this influencing and inspiring of contemporary authors, there is also a sense in which literature engages in theology. This may sound an alarming note but, nevertheless, it is the case that literary engagements with, and entanglements in, theological issues create a lens through which the reader returns to Scripture, reading it afresh. Robert Alter, in his book on the influence of the King James Version, describes how "the language of the Old Testament in its 1611 English version continued to suffuse the culture even when the fervid faith in Scripture as revelation had begun to fade."[24] But, he continues, American writers did not just channel biblical language. They were engaged in a debate about how the Bible should be interpreted, and they contributed to that same debate by offering readings of, and reflections on, the biblical stories. In essence, these authors were engaged in hermeneutics.[25] And this is not only the case for authors from a confessionally Christian background. Although deliberate submission to Christian tradition may be denied, it is a tradition that has shaped the individual and collective imagination in ways that are hard to shake off.[26] While some writers deliberately plumb the ancient wells of Christian history, it is likely that even those who have disavowed religious belief rationally (for example, George Eliot or Thomas Hardy)[27] retain a sense of it in their imagination, so that "a poem which is deeply endued with Christian doctrine or tradition may be written by a poet who would deny any Christian belief or affiliation."[28]

How does this work theologically, though? The Swiss theologian Karl Barth was famously opposed to any theology that sought to situate a "point of contact" between God and humanity in any place other than the word of God, Jesus Christ. Theology is only possible because of revelation: God has permitted Godself to be known. Barth also believed that the task of "doing" theology, which includes attentive biblical study, careful and sustained dogmatic reflection on the content of those Scriptures, and reflection on how best to communicate this content to the church and the world, was a task that had been given to the church alone.[29] However, Barth also held to a doctrine of divine freedom: God is—and must be—unconstrained by human reason. This means that while the self-revelation of God comes primarily through Jesus Christ's speech in the testimony of the apostles and prophets (i.e., the Scriptures), it is not possible to claim that it *only* comes through them, as he explains when discussing the concept of "true words."[30] This opens up the possibility that insights into the meaning of the scriptural revelation may be given (and it is important for Barth that these insights are a gift, and are not derived from human reason alone; God is unknowable save through God's own self-revelation to God's creation) to those who do not confess belief in that revelation. Or, as Alter puts it, "Once a text, together with the language in which it is cast, has been authoritative, that authority continues to make its force felt in the work of later writers, even those who no longer assent to the original grounds for the authority."[31] Therefore, the theological task can be neither independent of nor "limited by the walls of the Church,"[32] for the church has a theological obligation to enfold the insights and contributions of those outside the church—such as authors of fiction, or poets—within its reflective task. It must do this in a way that is open and yet critically rigorous because these insights (or "true words," in Barth's terminology) should not be equated with the scriptural Word; any truth that they contain is perspectival.[33]

It is on this basis that the present book proceeds. While reading McCarthy and Job together comprises a valuable and intellectually stimulating exercise in intertextuality, it is more than that. It is an investigation into the extent to which McCarthy's fiction displays theological insights that are useful for theological reflection on the book of Job, and on the wider issues contained therein, such as theodicy. It would be easy for the present work to claim both too little and too much. To claim too little would be to read McCarthy and Job as being only "in conversation" and nothing more, while to claim too much would be to attribute to McCarthy an authorial intention to deliberately engage in theological reflection on Job. This work makes no claim that McCarthy is a "Christian author" (whatever the definition of such a person is), merely that he is engaged—whether consciously or no—in a hermeneutical engagement with the Scriptures that have influenced his language and his cultural heritage as a white American of a certain age. Furthermore, it is this book's claim that reading Job through a McCarthyite lens yields genuine insights into the book of Job. Or to put it in Joban language, Elihu's claim that God may speak "in a dream, in a vision of the night" (33:15) is proven true in the case of McCarthy's portentous and baleful fiction.

This book is not intended to be a detailed examination of all of McCarthy's works. It focuses on *Outer Dark*, *Blood Meridian*, the Border Trilogy, *No Country for Old Men*, *The Road*, *The Sunset Limited*, and *The Counselor*. *The Orchard Keeper*, *Child of God*, *The Gardener's Son*, *Suttree*, and *The Stonemason* are mentioned little, if at all. A degree of familiarity with the McCarthy sources—and the book of Job—is assumed, but brief summaries are given that sketch the general shape of the works discussed. It is hoped that these will allow a reader unfamiliar with any particular work to follow the discussion.

1

Of Darkness and Definition

NOT THE WHY BUT THE HOW

> Anybody seeing him all that forewinter long going about the sadder verges of the city might have rightly wondered what his trade was, this refugee reprieved from the river and its fishes. Haunting the streets in a castoff peacoat. Among old men in cubbyhole lunchrooms where life's vagaries were discussed, where things would never be as they had been.[1]

> "He has put my family far from me,
> and my acquaintances are wholly estranged from me.
> My relatives and my close friends have failed me;
> the guests in my house have forgotten me;
> my serving girls count me as a stranger;
> I have become an alien in their eyes." (Job 19:13-15)

A protagonist apparently adrift in a world from which all meaning seems to have been removed, whose agonized attempts to locate some measure of this absented meaning are rebutted and countered by companions who impress on him their own articulations of this chaotic and confusing creation. A seemingly hostile landscape independent of and inimical to human flourishing, populated by a bewildering bestiary and a lurking liminal presence that is seemingly supernatural and almost otherworldly, bristling with barely contained ferocity and unpredictably terrifying savagery from which no one is immune.

A steadily tightening narrative that winds itself to an imagination-assaulting climax followed by a literary silence, and, like the slow exhalation of a held breath, a coda so stylistically different that it stretches to breaking point a sense of superficially confounding tension with all that has preceded it.

This could equally well describe the basic plot of many of Cormac McCarthy's novels or the biblical book of Job. Despite obvious formal differences, the world of McCarthy's novels—whether the Gothic South, the parched Southwest borderlands, or the ashen everywhere of *The Road*—is materially equivalent to the world of the book of Job. Readers who traverse the desolate landscape of McCarthy's fictional terrain will find themselves in moral, existential, and theological terrain reminiscent of the dust and ashes of Uz. Nightmarish and terrifying as McCarthy's novels can be, their world is one in which the reader is faced with questions that echo those with which Job wrestled: How should we attempt to make sense of the world in which we live? Can there be any stay against the threat of chaos, understood as an unpredictable and inexplicable disturbance into human lived experience? How is life to be lived meaningfully in such an unpredictable creation? Ought God to act toward His creatures in a certain manner? It is also a world in which answers to these perennial questions are far from clear. Nevertheless, both the fiction of McCarthy and the book of Job insist that there are answers to these questions. Moreover, it seems that reading McCarthy can help us to apprehend them in the book of Job.

THE SUNSET LIMITED

> Black: Have you ever read it?
> White: I read *The Book of Job*.[2]

In *The Sunset Limited*, McCarthy's "novel in dramatic form," White, the troubled college professor whose suicide attempt has been foiled by Black, the ex-con ex-addict, confesses that he has only read one book of the Bible: the book of Job. This is Chekhov's gun writ large for us, the readers. Why Job? Of all the sixty-six biblical books McCarthy could have chosen, why that one? This Means

Something, and it is the most overt mention of McCarthy's recurring Joban interest.

McCarthy is assuming, probably correctly, that the plot of Job is familiar to many of his readers: Job, an upright man in ancient times, is esteemed as a paragon of piety in the divine council only for one of its number to suggest that this piety presupposes his present prosperity. The Lord allows various tragedies to befall Job's family and then Job himself, yet his piety persists. After this prose prologue the book shifts into poetic dialogues in which Job laments his experiences only to be met by counterarguments from his three comforters—Eliphaz, Bildad, and Zophar—who interpret his misfortunes contrarily. Job rebuts their arguments, which eventually run dry, at which point Elihu, a younger sage, offers his explanation. At the book's close the Lord himself gives two speeches from a whirlwind, interrogating Job about his knowledge and governance of the world and directing him to consider geophysical phenomena and various unusual fauna.[3] Job recants and, returning to prose, the book records the Lord's upbraiding of Job's three friends and Job's subsequent reception of health and parenthood.

By explicitly mentioning Job, McCarthy invites the reader to hold this tale in her mind as she reads the rest of this short novel in dramatic form.[4] McCarthy is encouraging some intertextual reflection within which various questions may be raised and explored: Is White Job? Or is Job Black? Is one of them a comforter to the other? If so, which, and how? Or is the reader Job, and White and Black are both comforters, and so both wrong in what they say? Or should we read one of them as the voice from the whirlwind, addressing the other with glorious finality? As readers we may not know the answers to these questions, but that McCarthy is inviting us to think along these lines seems obvious.

More broadly *The Sunset Limited* overlaps with the book of Job in several ways. Both Black and White are, like Job and his three friends, characters with little or no backstory. As the short dramatic novel unfolds, certain things become clearer. White is someone who is coming to terms with the fact that the world does not exist in the way he had previously thought: "The things I believed in dont exist any more. Its foolish to pretend that they do."[5] This echoes Job's loss of certainty at the world in which he thought he dwelt. Job had imagined that he lived and loved in a world in which God treated people fairly, but his own apparently unfair treatment has shaken that conviction: "Does not calamity befall the unrighteous, and disaster the workers of iniquity?" he asks plaintively (Job 31:3). Apparently not, for they have assailed him, whose blamelessness is undisputed, at least by God and himself, despite the allegations of his "comforters." Later on, Black's language recalls Job 28's poem to wisdom. "At the deep bottom of the mine where the gold is at," says Black, there is neither division between black and white, nor between Jew and Gentile. "There's just the pure ore . . . That you dont think is there."[6] That gold, says Black, is Jesus. The echoes of chapter 28's Hymn to Wisdom resound. In that chapter, miners excavate the ore of gold and silver, iron, and copper, but wisdom—the Fear of the Lord—is not found there. Such wisdom is more precious and valuable than gold, silver, onyx, sapphire, or coral. To be clear, McCarthy is neither exegeting Job nor suggesting that wisdom is acquired, like gold, by strenuous human effort. Rather, he is setting off evocations and allusions to this Joban wisdom by using the Joban language of gold, mines, and ore. The Joban intertext having already been explicitly signaled, the reader is encouraged to ruminate on this irruption of Joban language into Black's idiom and hear the faint suggestion that Black's evangelical faith is no mere wish fulfillment but represents a genuine, deep Fear of the Lord wisdom.

But White will have none of it. He has seen the meaninglessness of life and, like Ivan Karamazov when faced with the cruelty of suffering children, seeks to return his ticket. Toward the end of this medieval morality play in contemporary New York,[7] White explicitly states his lostness: "The truth is that the forms I see have been slowly emptied out. They no longer have any content. They are shapes only. A train, a wall, a world. Or a man. A thing dangling in senseless articulation in a howling void. No meaning to its life. Its words."[8] This is the motivational heart that drove White's suicide attempt: life is meaningless, and in the face of this meaninglessness his liberal education and intellectual prowess count for nothing, for they can explain nothing about how to live in this world. Once again McCarthy tangentially approaches Joban themes: both Job and his friends all assumed that they knew how God governed creation, and each one of them had those assumptions upended and overturned. Job believed that God was acting unjustly, for he, Job, had committed no iniquity. His comforters believed that God was acting justly and Job had been more iniquitous than his vaunted claims allowed. But all were wrong, and the divine speeches serve in part as a rebuke to them all. Yet the book of Job suggests that life may be meaningful even if that meaning is shielded from humanity's understanding in part or in full. To that extent, the book of Job explores many of the same ideas as *The Sunset Limited*'s "philosophical debate concerning the justification for continuing to live in a world of meaningless suffering."[9]

JOB

Job the man is a towering figure in the European—and quite possibly the global—imagination, whether Christian, Jewish, atheist, or Muslim. He is without background and unrooted explicitly in any particular tradition and therefore ripe for co-option by anyone whom his experience tangentially touches. Job appears to be an Everyman, perhaps by deliberate authorial intention: the setting outside Israel, the absence of any specific religious rituals or reference to the Jewish cult, the use of generalized names for the divine rather than the covenant name YHWH all suggest this.[10] Furthermore, the book of Job continues to maintain a perennial appeal to artists, writers, and musicians, who frequently reach for it as inspiration, conversation partner, or intertext.[11]

In Jewish engagement with the book, World War Two marked a decisive turning point.[12] Where earlier interpretation had cast Job as "the most pious Gentile that ever lived" (a viewpoint that continued into medieval times),[13] the modern era's relentless persecution of Jews redefined him. Even before the outrages of World War Two, Job had been cast as an Eastern Jew and so was ripe for use by those seeking symbolic engagement with the horrors of the death camps.[14] Job became the principal interpretive figure of the Holocaust, albeit a troubling one due to his apparent ultimate submission,[15] which led to a reshaping of Job the person so that he might more easily correspond with contemporary attitudes. Whereas the biblical Job clung to God, the contemporary Job turned away from him, unleashing profound antipathy toward God: "Hatred does not develop in the argument but in the turning away, there where all explanation is withheld and the theological investigation of the theodicy has been abandoned."[16] Although the creation of Israel was seen by some as a Joban epilogic reparation, it is nevertheless still the case that, for others, the contemporary Job "loses both sight of the divine dimension and faith in possible reparation."[17] Thus, the Jewish Job of the twenty-first century has become an atheist, and any sense of restitution has gone.[18]

In Christian interpretation, Job the righteous Gentile was Christianized and his significance rested on his prefiguring of Christ's sufferings, his prophetic anticipation of Christ (in the much disputed and textually unclear Job 19:25-27), and his status as a sort of proto-Christian.[19] However, the advent of Gregory the Great's *Morals in Job* (written between A.D. 578 and 595) paved the way for a long line of interlocutors who were attracted to Job because of their own pain and physical suffering.[20] Nor was such an existential attraction limited to bishops, theologians, or—as in Gregory's case—the Pope. Job's voice was well known to the common folk of European Christendom through the medieval Office of the Dead: "His *was* the human voice addressing the mystery of death." Importantly for giving insight into Job's contemporary fascination to those of Abrahamic faith, other faiths, or no faith, "Job continues to have this kind of personal appeal for people who find themselves suffering great and inexplicable sorrow and pain."[21] The book provides not only a pattern for our protests but also a hope that our own grief-stricken complaints to the Almighty may yet be signs of strength, and not failure.[22] People continue to come to Job because in him and in the book that bears his name they find grounds for a hope that their own situations of sorrow may yet be woven into a bigger picture in which some sense of meaning resides.

It is this empathetic quality to Job that explains the book's perennial fascination, for while some religiously aligned people "turn to this text because it's part of a tradition, next up in a lectionary cycle or ritual manual," others, with no religious alignment, "turn to it in grief and confusion, in rage and existential crisis."[23] In our subjective and individualized times Job appeals to the postmodern mind suspicious of dominating narratives precisely because his relationship with God is presented as being on individual terms rather than cast in the language of organized religion. There is no covenant here, no sacred law or prescribed ritual (the sacrifices Job makes in 1:5 give no evidence of being required). It is this rootlessness that allows Job to become the spokesperson and the representative of all who have felt their lives and their assumptions evanescing around them. Thus there is a malleability to the book, a plasticity to Job the man that allows readers to identify with some aspect of his portrayal, whether it is

> Job, the sufferer "without cause," the man whose steadfastness is being tested, man confronting indifference and evil in the world, the pawn between God and Satan, the lonely challenger of divine justice and providence, man undergoing an Odyssey of faith, or personifying the mystery of suffering, or conversely, personifying the futility of asking ultimate questions, man the target of God's unlimited power, or man in poignant struggle with his God.[24]

Job is a book that considers universal themes, for who has not felt—as Job did—the world a coldly unjust crucible? Who has not experienced—as Job did—utterly destabilizing anxiety and dread? Who has not experienced—as Job did—baffling physical or emotional pain and distress? Who has not sought—as Job did—to resist the imposition of speculative "explanations" by well-meaning friends who are just plain wrong? As D. H. Lawrence said: "If you want a story of your own soul, it is perfectly done in the book of Job."[25] It is because of these commonalities that the book of Job continues to be invaluable for, although an ancient text, it "still addresses timely human and societal issues, and . . . can help us address them as well."[26]

What Job Is About

Many people assume—wrongly—that Job deals with the question of why there is suffering in the world. On this reading Job is a test case and a representative for all who suffer. People turn to the book to locate an explanatory "answer" to the question of why there is suffering in the world or a more etiological answer as to why they are suffering. In theological and philosophical terms this approach to the book assumes that it is a theodicy,[27] an attempt to reconcile the fact of evil and suffering in the world with the existence of an all-loving and all-powerful God. Such a view, although mistaken, is understandable given the role of Job's suffering—physical, social, emotional, and spiritual—in kick-starting the dialogues.

However, the book of Job is uninterested in answering this explanatory question of why there is suffering in the world. After all, Job is never given "one least beforehand reason," as Robert Frost puts it. More sharply, in *A Masque of Reason* Frost puts an obviously inadequate explanation in God's mouth:

> I'm going to tell Job why I tortured him
> And trust it won't be adding to the torture.
> I was just showing off to the devil, Job
> As is set forth in chapters One and Two.[28]

Close attention to the text of Job reveals no interest in constructing a general theodicy. Job's complaint is not that there is evil in the world incompatible with the goodness of God but that unpredictability in the world has dismantled *him* when it should not have done: Job complains to Eliphaz that the arrows of the Almighty are in *him*, and the terrors of God are arrayed against *him*, not that the Almighty shoots poisoned arrows in the first place (Job 6:4; cf. 7:20; 16:13). Job asks Bildad why God contends against *him*, not against humanity generally (Job 10:2; cf. 19:8-21). The book shows no interest in any theodicy that overlooks Job's particular situation. That is, it rejects any generalized explanatory answer that disregards the particular questions of the individual situation.[29]

Contemporary theodiceans routinely distinguish between the causes of suffering. First there is natural evil, which befalls human beings without any direct interpersonal agency. Second, there is moral evil, which befalls human beings through the direct agency of another. It is the consequence of human action or inaction and therefore has a moral origin.[30] In contrast, the book of Job is uninterested in distinguishing the causes of suffering into categories of "moral" and "natural" evil as traditional theodicies do. Job befell both "natural" evil—a fire from heaven and a great wind from the desert—and "moral" evil—Sabean and Chaldean raiders—but his complaint does not separate the two. His grief at his situation is regardless of its immediate cause, which is irrelevant for his complaint and his future. This is because the book is primarily interested not in the wherefore but the therefore: neither the explanatory question of why suffering happens nor the etiological one of why Job is suffering but the more pressing pastoral issue of how Job can live with its happening.

Job thought that he understood the world but that understanding has been dismantled. In his final speech he recalls his prior life (chapter 29) and "remembers sweetness, when life was sweet," in Raymond Carver's poignant phrase, from his present situation of chaotic disharmony (chapter 30).[31] Chapter 31's litany of good deeds reads as the complaint of one baffled and directionless, its subtext howling "if I sowed thus and reaped this, then how should I live in the future?" What Job seeks is not an intellectual solution to the *why* question, which is what traditional theodicies usually attempt to provide, but the reassurance that ongoing life is yet possible, and guidance on how to live it. Those who come to Job with the question of "why" foremost in their minds will be repeatedly frustrated by the book's refusal to give any clear answer to the question.

To read Job as a theodicy is a blind alley that lures in the unsuspecting.[32] Therefore, approaching the book with an assumption that its meaning is to do with suffering will inevitably lead to disappointment.[33] Yet that does not deter countless people from assuming that suffering is precisely what Job is about, albeit enmeshed in a forty-two-chapter, apparently repetitive argument ineluctably bogged down in the intransigence of the disputants. They have been led to believe that Job is the biblical explanation of the issue of suffering, so that's the lens through which they read it. But, to read Job through a preconceived lens that assumes its meaning is foreknown is to fail to read it as it is given, and is to fail to see and appreciate other facets of this scriptural gem.

Far from being a degenerating argument that becomes mired in its participants' obduracy, the book is like a steadily progressing spiral staircase that *appears* to cover the same ground over and over again, yet does so from different angles. As it winds ever upward it is leading somewhere, and the destination of this magnificent piece of ancient writing is the divine speeches, which form the book's conclusion and long-awaited climax. Job has long desired God to speak. Initially he fears that God will crush him (9:16-17), but the length of the divine silence is such that this fearfulness is replaced by a confidence that God's reply will indeed attend to his complaint (23:5-6). After the first cycle of speeches Job clearly tells his friends that he wishes to dispute with God, not them (13:3). He cares not whether God or he should speak first: a response is what he seeks (13:22). By the end of the third cycle Job's frustration with God's silence is evident (30:20), exemplified in his insistence that the Almighty answer him (31:35). Thus the whole movement of the book is toward a divine reply. That this is further frustrated by Elihu's interruption only heightens the book's dramatic tension as God's response is again delayed. The whole book, like Job himself, anticipates the divine speeches as providing a new outlook that will cut the Gordian knot of Job's situation and enable him to live out an answer to the question of how to live in the light of this chaos. For them to fail to do so would be literarily inconceivable.

When the speeches do arrive, they strike the reader as circumlocutory and evasive, or as divine bullying that sets Job in his place through a display of divine magnificence against which Job is but nothing. Yet there is more going on within them than this superficial judgment would allow: Job is being invited to see the world anew. Within the book's framework it is evident that the divine speeches evidently communicate *something* to Job, for immediately following them he concludes his complaint, repents, and says no more. But the divine speeches not only bring Job to a place of "repentance," but also they actually impel him to reenter the world that chapter 3's birthday-curse had so exhaustively execrated, as 42:10-17 demonstrates. The epilogue is more than the prologue redux,[34] and the epilogic Job is not merely a restored Job, but is someone who has apprehended something from the divine speeches that leads him to a new understanding of how to live in the world.

AN UNPREDICTABLE WORLD: JOB AND McCARTHY IN CONVERSATION

Job is not a theodicy, for it is neither an explanation of nor a justification for suffering. Likewise McCarthy is wholly *uninterested* in the explanatory questions of theoretical theodicy. Rather, just as

Job's life was derailed by the marauding actions of others—Sabean and Chaldean raiders—so too in McCarthy's novels do we encounter characters whose lives have been similarly upended: Sheriff Bell who knows that somewhere in the West Texan flatlands walks Anton Chigurh, "a true and living prophet of destruction and I dont want to confront him";[35] or Billy Parham, who blames himself for his friend John Grady Cole's death, just as he blamed himself for that of his brother Boyd,[36] and is convinced that "in everything that he'd ever thought about the world and about his life in it he'd been wrong."[37] McCarthy explores how these characters—and many others: Rinthy in *Outer Dark*, the kid in *Blood Meridian*, the boy in *The Road*—live in the light of this calamity and chaos. He is interested in examining the pastoral question of how to live in a world in which the actions of others have consequences that impinge on us, either directly or indirectly. In McCarthy's fiction, such living is a thoroughly risky venture, as evidenced by the unnamed inhabitants of villages and towns who are inexplicably drawn into the whirling violence and chaotic savagery wrought by *Outer Dark*'s grim triune, *Blood Meridian*'s Judge Holden, *No Country for Old Men*'s Anton Chigurh et al. to such devastating end. Life's unpredictability is assumed in McCarthy's fictional worlds and so the questions he asks do not deal with the explanatory concerns ("How did we get here?") but the pastoral ones ("How do we live here?"). This latter question is what the Caborcan asks the priest-hermit in *The Crossing*, and it cannot be answered by the hermit's priestly platitudes because they ignore the particularities of the Caborcan's situation. Thus McCarthy does not believe generalized theodicies that explain *why* people suffer have any part to play in navigating through life. Rather, he returns repeatedly to the question of *how* life is to be lived in the face of unpredictable crisis, and his books explore the worth and value of quiet, "mundane" Christian kindness and the possibility of meaning in life deriving from an awareness of, and gratitude for, one's situated place in sustaining community.

That McCarthy has a recurring interest in Job is increasingly recognized in McCarthy scholarship.[38] As new archival material is researched, this interest becomes ever more apparent. In a 1984 letter to his editor, Albert Erskine, about the book that would be published the following year as *Blood Meridian*, McCarthy admitted that "the historical material is really—to me—little more than a frame work upon which to hang a dramatic inquiry into the nature of destiny and history and the uses of reason and knowledge & the nature of evil and all these sorts of things which have plagued folks since there were folks."[39] This is an extraordinary claim: the blood-spattered plot of *Blood Meridian* and its astonishing prose are mere (!) window dressing to the central philosophical and theological issues with which the book—following the lead of countless other books and poems through the ages—engages. This echoes the views of biblical scholars for whom the questions of the historical provenance of Job as an individual and the book's underlying factuality can become a distraction from the central issue. This tragic tale of one man's suffering is the setting, although not the subject, of the book of Job's argument, which is how to live in a world in which there is unpredictable chaos. Job is not "a book about suffering" but "a book about living." Similarly, McCarthy's novels are not about human depravity and human life gone bad, but about how to live in a world in which such depravity roams about.

However, thematic connections, explicit textual references and a handful of scholarly articles notwithstanding, most critics have not explored this Joban intertext. As readers of Job often fail to see beyond the problem of "suffering," which is a priori assumed to be what the book is "about," so too McCarthy scholars and critics can fail to see beyond those interests that are already assumed to be at play. These are many and various, but routinely narrow down to nihilism and gnosticism.[40]

NIHILISM

From the start of McCarthy criticism, his books have been described as so nihilistic that "the traditional idea of meaning is made obsolete," in his fictional worlds of "mysterious, opaque, and unyielding signification."[41] This nihilism is not a denial of the world's existence or meaning but a claim that the world's meaning and value are utterly obscured, not only to the characters who move through these fictional worlds searching for meaning—even though there is only meaninglessness—but also to the reader as she reads scenes of violence and degradation that receive no apparent authorial censure or explanation. This nihilism is so deep-rooted that McCarthy's texts themselves subvert the very arguments and interpretations that seek to elucidate the thickly drawn textural world that they comprise. Meaning is hard to locate and "the moral and intellectual implications of experience are left intriguingly vague, always eluding the reification of thought."[42] McCarthy's work illustrates this claim by having literal roads that lead not to the neighborhood of meaning, as might be expected, but often to enmiring swamps, as in *Outer Dark*'s last pages:

> Before him stretches a spectral waste out of which reared only the naked trees in attitudes of agony and dimly hominoid like figures in a landscape of the damned. A faintly smoking garden of the dead that tended away to the earth's curve. He tried his foot in the mire before him and it rose in a vulvate welt claggy and sucking. He stepped back. A stale wind blew from this desolation and the marsh reeds and black ferns among which he stood clashed softly like things chained. He wondered why a road should come to such a place.[43]

Other critics have identified a Nietzschean nihilism in *Blood Meridian*'s Judge Holden, who proclaims violence and destruction, in *Cities of the Plain*'s pimp Eduardo, who strips the world of religious mystery and declares it a barren emptiness, and *No Country for Old Men*'s Anton Chigurh, who embraces and embodies the principle of determinism.[44]

The Nietzschean influence is indubitably present, but it is unclear if McCarthy has written these characters in such a way that they reflect, invert, or betray a Nietzschean nihilism.[45] While these Nietzschean ideas are seen in unsympathetic characters, "they are presented in his fiction as potentially accurate descriptions of the world."[46] Meanwhile *No Country for Old Men*'s Sheriff Ed Tom Bell's bewilderment at the failure of his old values to equip him for the contemporary world has been identified as Nietzschean passive nihilism.[47]

Certainly in McCarthy's novels it is true that there is moral barrenness and emptiness and that there are characters who espouse an utterly nihilistic viewpoint. However, a reductive argument that his books are "nihilistic" is an oversimplification. To read *Outer Dark*, for example, as a nadir of nihilism is to fail to see its full richness, which combines nihilism with a mixture of Oedipal and biblical myth.[48] This highlights one of the problems of the charge of nihilism (and of a strongly Nietzschean reading of some of McCarthy's characters), which is that it has pretensions to domination and thereby disallows other readings. It is unlikely that McCarthy has a single authorial voice and, anyway, one of his tropes is to use interpolated tales to offer readers a choice as to which vision of reality they embrace: one in which naked force and brutality reign, or one in which there is some trace of order and morality. Thus there are a range of philosophical and ideological offers in the books, and this sits uneasily with the expectation of a unified moral vision in a work, and so it is unsurprising that the charge of nihilism has stuck. Yet the label of nihilist obscures more than it reveals. Far from being a nihilist, McCarthy "*opposes* the annihilating notion of human insignificance, of nihilism, with the assertion of subjective meaning that is motivated by man's inherent vitality."[49]

GNOSTICISM

Other critics have enthusiastically sought and claimed a gnostic influence in many of McCarthy's works, beginning with this theme's first identification in *Blood Meridian*.[50] Critics have not been slow in scouring McCarthy's other novels for traces of this theme, with one concluding that gnosticism is a key motif forming the worldview of McCarthy's novels, particularly the recurring sense of numinous yet sentient evil that crescendos in *Blood Meridian*'s figure of Judge Holden, who is identified as *the* gnostic demiurge (an inferior creative being):[51]

> A great shambling mutant, silent and serene. Whatever his antecedents he was something wholly other than their sum, nor was there system to divide him back into his origins for he would not go. Whoever would seek out his history through what unraveling of loins and ledger books must stand at last darkened and dumb at the shore of a void without terminus or origin and whatever science he might bring to bear upon the dusty primal matter blowing

> down out of the millennia will discover no trace of any ultimate atavistic egg by which to reckon his commencing.[52]

While critics see *Blood Meridian* as fizzing and sparking with gnosticism, it is McCarthy's second novel, *Outer Dark*—described as "darkest parable" set on a "geographically obfuscated cosmic plateau"—that is the ur-text for gnostic readings.[53] Dianne Luce, in seeking to trace the influences behind McCarthy's Appalachian novels, claims that *Outer Dark* emerges from "a nightmarish dreamworld that derives largely from the myth and symbol systems of ancient gnosticism."[54] She reads the novel's title as referring to the created world, and claims that gnostic thought identified this with darkness, alien both to the Light and to the human spirit.[55] While her reading is admirably well-researched, containing many works that she believes McCarthy may have read, it is problematic. McCarthy's reticence to explain his novels and his preference for letting them convey their own meaning means that Luce can do little more than guess what texts McCarthy used to create his fictional worlds, something that she herself recognizes with her frequent conditional tenses: "McCarthy could . . . have found," "He might have read . . ."[56] She summarizes her approach as hoping that "reading what McCarthy has read, reading about the places he has experienced deeply," will help the reader "to understand what he understands and to see the world in the same contexts as he does."[57] However, we simply cannot know what McCarthy has, or even might have, read. McCarthy admitted to John Sepich that he had read several hundred books while researching and writing *Blood Meridian*, so we may assume that his other novels would have been equally well researched.[58] By one estimate, as far back as 1992 McCarthy owned about seven thousand books.[59]

However, McCarthy is a syncretist and so should not be neatly aligned with any single philosophy, something often overlooked by those critics who appear unable to see beyond gnosticism. *Outer Dark*, while being open to a gnostic reading, does not require one.[60] Such caution is commendable and should be applied to McCarthy's entire corpus, which some have argued has agnosticism—not gnosticism—as the connecting thread.[61]

Owing to the range of philosophical and ideological offers in his books, McCarthy appears to remain agnostic on religious questions, preferring not to resolve them.[62] However, this does not imply that he has no opinion on them. Far more plausible it is that, like the author of Job, he wishes to avoid the simplification of complex issues through the use of dialogism. The dialogical current that flows throughout his work recalls that of Dostoyevsky, and was identified by Mikhail Bakhtin in *The Brothers Karamazov* (one of McCarthy's favorite books), and is something that has also been detected in the book of Job.[63]

McCARTHY AS A GUIDE

The claim that reading McCarthy will enrich our readings of the book of Job is, the thematic and textual connections between McCarthy and Job notwithstanding, nevertheless an unusual one. Why should a contemporary author have valuable insight into Scripture?

It is not as if McCarthy is a theologian, or a biblical scholar, or an author who is writing from a confessionally Christian perspective (such as Marilynne Robinson) or from a place of acknowledged sympathy to Christianity (such as Wendell Berry).[64] Although McCarthy's biography is slender, there is nothing in it that indicates a preoccupation with "questions raised and answered by his lost religious faith."[65] The bare bones of his life are well-known.[66] He was born Charles McCarthy in July 1933 in Providence, Rhode Island, and from the age of four was brought up in Knoxville, Tennessee, where his father was an attorney for the Tennessee Valley Authority. He was raised and educated—with a particular interest in science and engineering while at college[67]—a Roman Catholic, and had a "comfortable upbringing,"[68] from which he enrolled in the University of Tennessee in 1951, leaving in 1953 to join the Air Force.[69] He was stationed in Alaska, where he read voraciously and from where he rejoined the university briefly in 1957, before leaving again without being awarded a degree. He changed his name from Charles to Cormac in the late 1950s, and his first novel was published in 1965. Since then he has been married three times, and has shown a ruthless single-mindedness in pursuing a writing career, regardless of the circumstances in which he might have to live. Stories abound of running out of toothpaste and not being able to afford more, bathing in lakes, subsisting on beans,[70] all of which suggest a complete dedication to the "Spartan simplicity he felt was necessary in order to devote himself fully to writing" by living off award monies and occasional odd jobs.[71] More recently, he has based himself at the Santa Fe Institute (SFI) in New Mexico for many years and is now a trustee.[72] The SFI is an independent research center investigating "big questions" in any and every field, including science, leadership, sustainability, and information theory. Before becoming a trustee, he functioned as a sort of artist-in-residence, who would attend workshops and seminars and proofread texts with ruthless precision for submission to journals or publishers.[73] One of the benefits of being based at the SFI was the anonymity it afforded him—"People here have no idea who I am,"[74] he told a journalist—to write and to *discover*. His friend the late physicist Murray Gell-Mann recalled that "he has a long-standing interest in a great many things and he knows an immense amount about them."[75] McCarthy himself has said that "the most curious thing is incuriosity,"[76] and the SFI allows him to indulge that curiosity, particularly during long mealtime conversations: "I like being around smart, interesting people, and the people who come here are among the smartest, most interesting people on the planet."[77] Often described as famously reclusive—in 1988 one writer remarked that "even if the world wished to beat a path to McCarthy's door, it would be hard-pressed to find it"[78]—this is not a J. D. Salinger–type eremitic withdrawal so much as a disinterest in the machinations of publication industry junkets, interviews, book signings, and tours: "It would be hard to think of a major American writer who has participated less in literary life."[79] In a rare interview in 2007, granted to Oprah Winfrey—of all people—as part of her book club, he spoke of his disinterest in the wide readership that *The Road* had gained him.[80] Reticent is probably a better description of him than reclusive,[81] for he is someone who appears confounded by the world's interest in him.

But it is precisely because McCarthy is clearly someone who would rather think and talk about ideas—"Everything's interesting. I don't think I've been bored in 50 years"[82]—than himself that this Joban correspondence fits so well. McCarthy's letter to Erskine is as close to an authorial admission of intent as it is possible to come for McCarthy scholars, because "one of the topics about which he will not willingly articulate an opinion is his own fiction."[83] Like a true deconstructionist, he is uninterested in how his novels are received and understood. He told Oprah Winfrey that "obviously you can draw conclusions about all sorts of things from reading the book [*The Road*], depending on your taste. It's a pretty simple straightforward story, I think." This is reminiscent of a comment made by Anne DeLisle, his second wife, who recalled how "someone would call up and offer him $2,000 to come speak at a university about his books. And he would tell them that everything he had to say was there on the page."[84]

Exactly what there is on McCarthy's pages is a recurring thematic interest in Job, and it is this interest that motivates the present study. This Joban interest is not unique to McCarthy. Joban questions have bubbled to the surface of the stream of great Western literature many times in its historical flow. From Shakespeare's *King Lear* to Melville's *Moby Dick* and Dostoyevsky's *The Brothers Karamazov*, on to the poems of Robert Frost and Faulkner's *The Sound and the Fury* and beyond, the influence of Job—and the interests of Job—can be felt. All of these authors are either esteemed by McCarthy or their works have been identified as important conversation partners or intertextual sources in his novels.[85] This is not surprising, for McCarthy has stated in an interview that "the ugly fact is books are made out of books. The novel depends for its life on the novels that have been written."[86]

Moreover, these Joban questions are some of the most existentially important that anyone can ask. According to McCarthy, poets write about what they write about because "they know everyone thinks these things are important, and that's why they're talking about them."[87] Such poetic and literary engagements with Job themselves influence the way subsequent generations read the biblical book. "Job is more than the biblical book," argues biblical scholar Choon-Leong Seow, before enumerating different ways in which the Joban story has been "interpreted, retold, and debated," in the arts through various literary means. Rather than detracting from the source text, these imaginative construals "are part and parcel of what people know as Job," such that an interpreter cannot approach the biblical text independent of their influence. They "shape our perception of what is surely one of the most captivating but unsettling stories ever told."[88]

It should not be assumed a priori that such "imaginative construals" will not benefit Christian theological reflection on Scripture, for those outside the Christian faith may have insight into, and understand, texts far better than Christians do.[89] It may be that those who are outside the church, precisely because they have *not* been schooled in reading Scripture so as to see what it is already assumed is there—an answer to the question of suffering in Job, for example—have insights that can benefit the Christian reading of Scripture. It is on this basis that an investigation into how McCarthy's fiction may illumine faithful reading of the scriptural book of Job is legitimated.

Following Barth, whose use of the insights of the existentialists Jean-Paul Sartre and Martin Heidegger in §50 of his *Church Dogmatics* is taken to provide an illustration of how these insights or "true words" may function,[90] there is no need to baptize McCarthy as a "Christian" author (any more than Barth sought to "baptize" Sartre or Heidegger),[91] merely to recognize the importance of the Joban—or, more broadly, Christian—dimension in his fiction. That dimension is not overt but possibly reflects some mystical experience that McCarthy himself has had. McCarthy has suggested that those who have not had firsthand religious experiences cannot understand accounts of other experiences, going on to explain that "the mystical experience is a direct apprehension of reality, unmediated by symbol" and that "our inability to see spiritual truth is the greater mystery."[92] It is telling both that the word "apprehension" is used here, as opposed to "comprehension," as if McCarthy is distinguishing between two ways of understanding, one subjective and affective, the other rational and objective, and that McCarthy apparently believes that there is spiritual truth available that remains unnoticed and so unapprehended. In trying to "comprehend" Job it may be that many Christians have omitted to fully "apprehend" its message. Perhaps McCarthy's fiction might itself aid the reader in apprehending spiritual truth from the world?

THE COUNSELOR AND FOUR DEFINING THEMES

McCarthy's most recent published work of fiction to date, *The Counselor*, provides a helpful introduction to his oeuvre and how it might be useful in apprehending truths contained in the book of Job. Superficially this uncharacteristically pulpy screenplay has little overlap with Job: Job is upright and blameless whereas the eponymous Counselor is anything but, being introduced in McCarthy's most sexually explicit scene.[93] Furthermore, this superficially charming man is soon conducting illicit narcotic deals without his bride's knowledge.[94] Inevitably for both McCarthy's fictional worlds and the narcotics trade, these take a torrid turn for both the Counselor and his new bride, Laura.[95]

However, there are similarities between them: Job lives in Uz (1:1), an undefined everywhere, and *The Counselor* is set in similarly unspecific but recognizable terrain: "High desert grassland, similar to the country around Patagonia Arizona or east of Las Vegas New Mexico."[96] Both men have wealth and status, an unknown history, and both have their lives changed by an encounter with an uncontrollable chaotic force: Job loses his wealth and family to Sabean and Chaldean raiders and desert winds and a fire from heaven (1:13-19), while the Counselor loses his to moral turpitude flowing from the drug trade, which conjoins commerce and gross violence.[97] Its unpredictable chaos is represented by the character of Malkina, the puppeteer pulling the strings that control—directly or indirectly—the marionette figures of the Counselor, Reiner, Westray, and others. In encountering her and the world from which she has emerged and into which she recedes, the hubristic Counselor, who assumed he could enter this selfsame narcotic world, feather his own nest, and tidily exit it in a controlled manner, lays his hand on Leviathan but does not remain unscathed: he will not do so again.[98]

In addition to these Joban parallels, *The Counselor* is a helpful introduction to McCarthy's oeuvre because it contains many tropes and themes that recur throughout his works, which will be discussed in more detail in subsequent chapters: the fruitlessness of philosophical theodicy, which will be explored in relation to *The Crossing*; the place of humanity in creation, which will be investigated by means of *Blood Meridian*; the place of chaotic entities in creation, which recur in *Outer Dark*, *Blood Meridian*, and *No Country for Old Men*; and the possibility of hope amid chaos in *The Road*, *No Country for Old Men*, the Border Trilogy, *Blood Meridian*, and *Outer Dark*.

First, *The Counselor* contains three individuals—not unlike Job's comforters—who warn the Counselor about the world he has entered, explaining its amoral workings. Reiner warns the Counselor of the consequences he will incur: "You pursue this road you've embarked upon and you will eventually come to moral decisions that will take you completely by surprise. You wont see it coming at all."[99] Westray gives the Counselor a lecture on the facts of life in the narcotic world, emphasizing that this world is *not* all that it appears: "The beheadings and the mutilations? That's just business. You have to keep up appearances. It's not like there's some smoldering rage at the bottom of it."[100] Finally, the Jefe explains to the anxiety-addled Counselor that it is too late. Things can be neither undone nor changed, nor is there a higher authority to whom he can appeal: "I am afraid that there is no one to see."[101] Like the Counselor, he has lost someone dear to him and he urges the Counselor to realize that everything has become different: "At some point you must acknowledge that this new world is at last the world itself. There is not some other world."[102] However, as the Counselor disdained the advice of both Reiner and Westray, so too will he ignore the advice of the Jefe. Intellectual, rational argument is insufficient for the Counselor, as it was for Job, although for very different reasons, and so he is trapped—as Job was—by refusing to see the world as it has been portrayed to him but, unlike Job, receiving no epiphanic encounter that reorients him within that strange new world.

Second, this unfamiliar territory is a world that declares an austere non-anthropocentricity: it is not at the whim of any one individual or even, the work implies, humanity as a whole. Rather, it has its own life and energy. Not even Malkina, who appears most in charge, is totally sovereign here. At the screenplay's end she accepts the inevitability of this, stating that "the slaughter to come is probably beyond our imagining."[103] This suggests that she too is subject to the same unpredictable violence the benefits of which she has momentarily enjoyed. The Counselor's hubristic error lies in his assumption that he can order this uncontrollable world and mold it to his own advantage. He cannot. Neither can he reverse his decision to engage with this Leviathan: "You are at a cross in the road and here you think to choose. But here there is no choosing. There is only accepting. The choosing was done long ago." The Counselor's embroilment in this violence-infused world derives from a single choice and its inexorable consequences. He cannot undo that choice and return to a time before he made it: "the world in which you seek to undo your mistakes is not the world in which they were made."[104] Such irrevocability is a theme throughout the film, whether it refers to the Counselor's choice, the cutting of a diamond,[105] or the incessant tightening of the mechanical *bolito*.[106]

Third, Malkina, embodying the destructive and devouring narcotics trade and representative of chaotic human capitulation to the nothingness of evil, takes her place as string-pulling villain in McCarthy's oeuvre-wide succession of villains.[107] It is she who initiates the scenes of unspeakable horror and savage death, which all involve either decapitation or a wound to the head. Her unusual name may suggest any or all of a cat, a sluttish woman, the female genitals,[108] or even the Hebrew for queen, *malkāh* (מַלְכָּה). It is entirely possible that McCarthy intends all these resonances to be heard and attended to: Malkina's sexual history is unorthodox, conspicuous attention is drawn to her genitals, like ancient royalty she has pet cheetahs, and she rides a "good Arabian horse."[109] The chaos that she represents is so uncontrollable that the Counselor is reduced to "an unsuspecting imbecile who never seizes control of his own narrative."[110]

This issue of control touches on the fourth, almost imperceptible, theme that McCarthy routinely treats: hope. In his works hope is not to be understood as an indication that circumstances will change for the better, or that there will be a happy ending. It is a deeper idea than this sort of cozy wish fulfillment and is more like a possibility for life to be found meaningful when all seems meaningless.[111] By virtue of it being a screenplay and not a novel, *The Counselor* declares a possibility for hope in "a cinematic world in which lurid spectacle is the rule rather than the exception."[112] An Amsterdam Jewish diamond dealer tells the Counselor that "at our noblest we announce to the darkness that we will not be diminished by the brevity of our lives. That we will not thereby be made less."[113] While the Counselor himself fails to make this announcement and so *is* diminished by the darkness that he has willfully entered, the jeweler's challenge remains. The Counselor fails because he refuses to apprehend the nature of the chaotic, non-anthropocentric world into which he has stepped. However, this strange new world *is* the real world and must be accepted as such in order for the hopeful proclamation of which the diamond dealer speaks to be made.[114] The Counselor's refusal to realize this, and his repudiation of the reality of the world he has—at least in part—created in preference for an imagined world that cannot exist, is utterly wrong. As long as he cannot see the reality of the world in which he exists now, he is powerless to live within it. The film adaptation addresses the viewer with the same question. Its opening line, "Are you awake?"[115]—although implicitly addressed to Laura—is actually asked of the audience: "It wants to lead the viewer's eyes beyond the screen's fantasy . . . *The Counselor* does not want to lull us with enjoyable, historically deaf violence. It wants to wake us up to the sobering conditions of our time."[116] Thus *The Counselor*, as is true of all McCarthy's works, has a strong moral sensibility amid the majestic violence and awful carnage. Its offer of hope to the viewer is predicated on the viewer's awakening to the reality of the world around her: acknowledge this world, do not pretend it is otherwise, and do not be diminished by it; rise to the challenge of living well in a world in which there is danger and unpredictability. The Counselor's resistance to living in the world as it is reflects Job's resistance to live in *his* world as it is. However, whereas Job apprehended afresh the world's chaos and could live anew within it, the Counselor did not and remained tragically trapped by his refusal.

These four themes correspond to a journey through the chapters of the book of Job: the dialogues with the comforters in chapters 3–37 reveal the limitations of human theodicy; chapters 38 and 39 posit a non-anthropocentric world; chapters 40 and 41 deal with the presence of chaos in God's good world; and chapter 42 suggests the presence and possibility of hope. It is now time to turn to these.

2

The Fruitlessness of Philosophical Theodicy

AN UNTAMABLE GOD

> A thousand hours or more he's spent in this sad chapel he. Spurious acolyte, dreamer impenitent. Before this tabernacle where the wise high God himself lies sleeping in his golden cup.[1]

> "Why are we counted as cattle?
> Why are we stupid in your sight?" (Job 18:3)

Bildad accuses Job of treating his friends like dumb animals, while in their turn the comforters accuse Job of speaking insubstantial sense (15:2-3; 20:3). Job rejects his comforters' insistence that he has done wrong and that his situation is therefore deserved within the inscrutable justice of the divine mind, Suttree's "wise high God" heavily slumbrous. For Eliphaz, Bildad, and Zophar, there can be no other explanation. But Job will have none of it. It is obvious to him that the reason for his situation lies not with himself and any putative sin he has committed, but with God and God alone. It is so obvious that even creation itself would agree with him:

> But ask the animals, and they will teach you;
> the birds of the air, and they will tell you;
> ask the plants of the earth, and they will teach you;
> and the fish of the sea will declare to you.

> Who among all these does not know
>   that the hand of the Lord has done this? (Job 12:7-9)

Why do people experience misfortune? And how should comfort be given to those who do? Job's comforters failed to do and be what he needed them to do and be for him. This has often led to the assumption that any attempt to bring comfort to someone who is suffering is an enterprise fraught with difficulty and risk, to such an extent that many settle for an easy silence. The attitude is well summarized in Robert Frost's poem "Home Burial":

> The nearest friends can go
> With anyone to death comes so far short
> They might as well try not to go at all.

Is there a way to come alongside a sufferer—is there a way to listen to and speak with a sufferer—that avoids the mistakes of the comforters and the silent avoidance described by Frost?

This is the landscape that McCarthy's writing traverses across several novels, but one scene from *The Crossing* is particularly illuminating in this regard. Reading this McCarthy passage helps the reader to see Job more humanely, as she apprehends afresh the nature of Job's tragedy, his stubborn insistence to cling to the God who he believes has mistreated him so, and why Job's comforters fall so far short.

THE CROSSING

The Crossing is the second book of McCarthy's Border Trilogy, which began in the 1980s with a screenplay entitled *Cities of the Plain*. However, this does not mean that *Cities of the Plain* is the heart of the story, with the preceding volumes—*All the Pretty Horses* and *The Crossing*—relegated to the status of prologues. Many critics consider *Cities of the Plain* an inferior work, but when read as a trilogy the three books complement each other, exploring similar issues from different angles as a loose textual trilogy.[2]

The Crossing comprises four parts, each one describing a journey undertaken by Billy Parham across the border between New Mexico and Mexico. In the first he transports a captured wolf back to its Mexican range; in the second he returns to New Mexico and, having collected his brother Boyd, goes back to Mexico to seek his family's stolen horses; the third details the aftermath of that search; and the fourth follows Billy as he returns once more to New Mexico, attempts to enlist in the army, and then revisits Mexico to seek for Boyd.

Such a straightforward and linear description of the "plot" hides more than it shows, however, for the novel has broader interests than a young man's peregrinations. Billy encounters people on his pilgrimages, many of whom tell their own tales, which might also contain yet further stories.[3] The book is a story that is composed of many different stories while also being about how stories shape people. The interweaving of these stories provides explanations of the storytellers' lives and an account of the world in which the storyteller believes that she lives. Moreover, as Billy hears these different stories and enters into the storyteller's story, he is helped to make sense of his own storied life and enabled to apprehend new perspectives on the nature of the world he inhabits and his place within it. This idea of place is important because Billy frequently encounters people concerned that he is or will be alone in the world:

> He told the boy that although he was huérfano still he must cease his wanderings and make for himself some place in the world because to wander in this way would become for him a passion and by this passion he would become estranged from men and so ultimately from himself.[4]

This is one of McCarthy's strongest echoes of Danish philosopher Søren Kierkegaard's concern for the self: "The greatest danger, that of losing one's self, may pass off as quietly as if it were nothing; every other loss, that of an arm, a leg, five dollars, a wife, etc., is sure to be noticed."[5] This existentialist interest has led some critics to describe the book as a sort of humanist tract about "finding oneself" or the attempt so to do.[6] But *The Crossing* is much more than that; it "wrestles constantly with the nature of a transcendent deity in relation to the world of man."[7] It is this Joban interaction between God and humanity that is of interest, specifically in the story told by the heretical hermit at Huisiachepic, found near the start of the second part.[8]

The aimlessly wandering Billy is returning to New Mexico when he encounters a man in the doorway of a ruined church who offers him scrambled eggs and then tells his tale. This hermit tells Billy of a Caborcan man who took his son to stay with an uncle in nearby Bavispe while he undertook a trading journey. At Bavispe they visited the circus and the next day the Caborcan left his son and continued on his way. The child remained in Bavispe and was killed in an earthquake. Overwhelmed by grief, the Caborcan retrieved his dead son's body, returned to his wife, and then wandered to and fro trying to comprehend what had happened to him. As an old man he returned to Caborca and camped in the broken transept of a church where he berated God. All those who heard his imprecatory prayers and addresses to God were scandalized by his harangues concerning *colindancia*, an unusual Spanish word connoting responsibility, boundary, or appropriate measure. A priest visited and spoke to him of grace, but the Caborcan rejected him as vacuous. The priest grew troubled by the Caborcan's words and tried to accommodate them, referring to creation itself to bolster his natural theology. However, the priest had no investment in what he said, but the Caborcan, whose words were both free and reckless, did. Although a "good," devout, and reverent man, the priest was wrong because he had attempted to corral the divine Being within a humanly constructed doctrine of freedom: "He believed in a boundless God without center or circumference. By this very formlessness he'd sought to make God manageable," and in doing so "had ceded all terrain."[9] The priest pondered much while the Caborcan continued to remonstrate with God before realizing ultimately that God is inescapable, untamable, and able to encompass all. The Caborcan spoke softly to the priest of God's grace, but the priest failed to understand his words. The Caborcan died and the priest—whom the hermit reveals to have been himself—in his reflections realized that the Caborcan had been a truth-carrying messenger to him, to reveal his own questions, without either of them realizing it. The priest concludes at last that "nothing is real save his grace."[10]

The general Joban similarities are easily discerned: the man devastated by the tragic death of his progeny, the suffering man's diatribes against God for this inappropriate treatment, the intellectual quest for meaning, the well-meaning man of religion who is outraged by the sufferer's intemperate tirade and whose arguments present a divine being who accords with human reason, and the suffering man's eventual insights that bring an end to his hot words.

KARL BARTH AND JOB

The twentieth-century Swiss theologian Karl Barth may, at first glance, be an unusual partner to bring into conversation with McCarthy. After all, there is currently no extant evidence to decisively indicate that McCarthy is aware of—let alone has read—Barth.[11] A trivial common interest is that both are devotees of Mozart,[12] but their similar approaches—although from very different angles—to the book of Job may be a more weighty point of intersection between them. One of Barth's major treatments of this is his discussion of Job as a True Witness of Christ in §70 of *Church Dogmatics*. It will be helpful to recapitulate Barth's argument before bringing it into intertextual conversation with McCarthy in order to tease out what the book of Job has to say.

In this paragraph, Barth discusses what it means that Jesus Christ meets humanity as the True Witness to the work of reconciliation that he himself has effected.[13] First, Barth argues that Jesus Christ does this as the Truth that reveals and indicts the man of sin. Second, he unpacks the content of this Truth, which is neither a doctrine nor something gladly and willingly received but a historical, real person, one with whom God has a mutual relationship of unparalleled distinction and equality. Barth explains that God "entrusts" his honor and glory to this man and that this man stakes his all on God in corresponding manner. He wagers on God with the same human boldness as God wagers on him with divine boldness. It is on this relationship that the Witness' Truth rests. Moreover, this human person lives a life devoted to God, which is also a life approved and blessed by God in no uncertain terms. Such a relationship rests on freedom in all respects on both sides. From the human side there is no expectation of reward from God for God is not beholden to humanity.[14] Thus far Barth has been speaking of the relationship between God and Jesus Christ. In an excursus he then adduces Job as a prototype of this True Witness "in distant, faint, fragmentary and even strange yet unmistakeable outline," for in the Joban prologue God "entrusts" his honor to Job, a man approved and blessed by Him. Furthermore, the relation between Job and God is one based in freedom on both sides.[15]

Barth then returns to his main theme: Jesus Christ the True Witness is revealed to humanity not in a pure form, but in a concretely revealed expression that is "hidden, obscure and puzzling."[16] This form is that of the suffering and rejection involved in Jesus Christ's passion. Barth gives a second excursus on Job, who exists for the bulk of his eponymous book in a world of suffering that appears to deny all that had hitherto been said about his relationship with God. It is this perceived disjunction that comprises the heart of Job's complaint, says Barth, for this alien God is the God with whom Job must contend. However, God's alien otherness to Job is not a denial of God's own freedom but a sign of that same freedom, which also calls out of Job a corresponding expression of freedom to give "free if suffering obedience to the One who has become unrecognisable and is concealed in this alien form."[17]

Following this excursus, Barth argues that the truth expressed by Jesus Christ the True Witness is expressed through his suffering, in Jesus Christ's dying sigh, which is therefore the speech of God out of the silence of death. But this speech is one that necessarily entails Jesus Christ's own suffering; although this may be distasteful to human sensibilities, there is no other way than this way of God:

> But let us imagine for a moment that we do not wish to avoid Him as He encounters us in this form. We are ready to receive instruction—this instruction—from Him and therefore from God Himself concerning God. This means that we must be ready to be told by Him that we shall not find God where we think we should look for Him, namely, in a supposed height. It means that we must be ready to be told by Him that we shall find Him precisely where we do not think we should look for Him, namely, in direct confrontation with and at the very heart of our own reality, which, whether we like it or not, reduces itself with the crumbling and tottering of all our previous genuine or illusory possibilities and achievements to the one painful point where each of us is stripped and naked, where each is suffering and perishing, where each is engaged in futile complaint and accusation, where each is alone.[18]

Barth's third excursus on Job begins with a reiteration of Job's complaint, which was "the change in the divine form which found concrete manifestation and expression in the blows of fate which he had suffered."[19] Job faces a dilemma: either he acquiesces to God in this freedom or he claims that God should not be free in this way, thereby suggesting that he knows better than God. The way through this dilemma is revealed by God who justifies Job, showing him to be worthy of having been "entrusted" with God's honor. Job is a True Witness by trusting that God, in God's own time, will set the limit on his distress, and by submitting to God's freedom to do this.[20]

God's answer to Job is neither a doctrine nor a retraction of his freedom, but something conveyed both humorously and tangentially.[21] Moreover, it is an answer given in questions posed *to* Job, and therefore is

> uttered and audible only between the lines in cc. 38–41, not as the declaration and question of the cosmos, but clear and perceptible in this as its echo, and immediately and accurately accepted and understood by Job, the Word of God is spoken. Beyond all the majesty and power which are only lent to creation, but reflected in them, Yahweh Himself is seen directly in it by Job.[22]

God shows Job that he had always known God as free, even when that freedom was expressed in quiet blessing. Barth concludes this excursus, and §70:

> Thus the circle closes as it opened, namely, with man's liberation by and for the free God: by the free God, since it is He who is the Witness speaking against Job yet also for him; and for the free God, since Job, set in the wrong by Him yet also in the right, proves to be the faithful witness of this God.[23]

One may legitimately ask how this relates to McCarthy's tale. A close inspection reveals that what Barth foregrounds through theological argument and idiom, McCarthy does by means of literature, such that in the Huisiachepican hermit's tale-within-a-tale McCarthy covers the same ground as Barth in his analysis of the dialogues of Job, which within the prose framework of Job are also a tale-within-a-tale. There are three aspects to this.

McCarthy and Barth in Conversation about Job

First, Barth describes the book of Job as giving the reader "a seriously disturbing sense of Job's extremity of affliction,"[24] which is also what McCarthy does at the start of the hermit's tale, albeit without the direct link to Job:

> Returning to Bavispe the following day this man met a traveler afoot who told him the news. He could not believe the man's words and he urged the mule on and when he arrived at Bavispe all was in ruin as the traveler had told and death was everywhere in great abundance. He entered the town already in terror of what he should find. He heard gunshots. Dogs ran out that had been at the bodies in the rubble and scampered past him and men with guns ran out and stood in the street shouting. In the alameda the dead lay on mats of river reed and old women dressed in black walked to and fro among the rows with green fronds to keep the flies away. The padrino came to him and wept at the mule's stirrup and could not speak but only took the reins in his own hands and led him sobbing. Through the alameda where lay dead merchants and farmers and the wives of merchants and farmers. Dead schoolgirls. Lying on reeds in the alameda of Bavispe. A dead dog in a carnival costume. A dead clown. Youngest of them all his son crushed and lifeless. He dismounted and there he knelt and clasped the bloody ruin of the child to his breast. The year is eighteen eighty-seven.

In this passage, reminiscent of Lamentations' poetic horror, McCarthy elicits in the reader the same sense of extreme affliction and suffering of which Barth speaks. Like Job's children killed by an unpredictable element in creation (the fire from heaven and the wind from the desert) and the unpredictable consequences of interpersonal evil (the Sabean and Chaldean raiders) the Caborcan is faced with suffering that derives from both the chaos of creation (the earthquake) and human wickedness (gunshots). Faced with this pain, the Caborcan becomes a man for whom "the pin has been pulled from the axis of his universe."[25]

Second, McCarthy makes clear that the Caborcan came to think himself called to such a challenge: "This man saw in himself again what he'd perhaps forgot. That long ago he'd been elected out of the common lot of men." McCarthy's choice of the verb "elect" is suggestive; an author as intelligent as he would not have chosen it were he not intending its theological resonances to be heard and recognized. This is underscored by McCarthy's explicit echo of Job in the Caborcan who "was asked now to reckon . . . that he'd been called forth twice out of the ashes, out of the dust and rubble."[26] The twofold testings, the dust and ashes, the call that is neither easy nor pleasant: all these suggest a divine election in the Joban mold.

Job's election was not by fate but by the God who called him to move beyond dust and ashes. Barth sees election as an important thread in making sense of Job's ordeal. God elected Job, and it is precisely because God elected Job that Job cannot shake off God from his situation:

> It is not in relation to the Subject Yahweh that the problem of Job arises. He would not be Job, the elect of Yahweh, if there could be any problem in this respect. As this Subject God is always known to him. It is in relation to Him that he knows and clings to the fact that in what befalls him he has to do with God. It is on the basis of this knowledge that he disputes with God.[27]

Similarly, the Caborcan cannot rid himself of God: "He knew that the world would forget him but that God could not. And yet that was the very thing he wished for."[28] Here McCarthy takes up the tone of Job 7:16-21, in which Job asks God to "let me alone . . . look away from me," for "you will seek me, but I shall not be." However, just as to Job God now appeared to be a vindictive "watcher of humanity" (Job 7:20), and just as Barth describes Job's God as now being in "the strange and terrifying form of a relentlessly aggressive adversary before whom he is completely defenceless,"[29] so too the Caborcan "came to believe terrible things of Him."[30] McCarthy's echo of C. S. Lewis' *A Grief Observed* is intriguing, but whereas Lewis feared that God would turn out to be different from how he had theretofore conceived him, the Caborcan sees that although this is a different God than he had anticipated he must nevertheless cling to the conviction that it is God and only God to whom he must appeal: "Deep in each man is the knowledge that something knows of his existence. Something knows, and cannot be fled nor hid from. To imagine otherwise is to imagine the unspeakable."[31] This recalls Barth's point that Job knew it was God he had to contend with, not Satan, but that this God was utterly different from that which he had thought he knew: "he encounters Him in a form in which He is absolutely alien."[32]

As in Barth Job contended with this alien God and thereby realized that this was God nevertheless, so too in McCarthy the Caborcan harangues the God from whom he cannot escape and in his tenacious imprecations comes to know God afresh. The Caborcan prays and cajoles God but then begins to dream about a God who ordains and purposes the world to include all,[33] even the inexplicable and unpredictable chaos that has befallen him, but nevertheless appears unreachable:

> In his dreams God was much occupied. Spoken to He did not answer. Called to did not hear. The man could see him bent at his work. As if through a glass. Seated solely in the light of his own presence. Weaving the world. In his hands it flowed out of nothing and in his hands it vanished into nothing once again. Endlessly. Endlessly. So. Here was a God to study. A God who seemed a slave to his own selfordained duties. A God with a fathomless capacity to bend all to an inscrutable purpose. Not chaos itself lay outside of that matrix. And somewhere in that tapestry that was the world in its making and its unmaking was a thread that was he and he woke weeping.[34]

In order to understand this dream, it is necessary to briefly examine the source from which McCarthy has borrowed the imagery: chapter 102 of *Moby Dick*.[35]

In this chapter Ishmael visits a Polynesian temple constructed from the skeleton of a sperm whale, wherein he is overcome by an epiphanic sense of the plenitude of life and its unceasing fecundity and activity. His thoughts turn to the source of such activity, the weaver-god, who "weaves; and by that weaving he is deafened, that he hears no mortal voice; and by that humming, we, too, who look on the loom are deafened; and only when we escape it shall we hear the thousand voices that speak through it."[36] This is a vision of God's focused attention on sustaining and continually creating by the sheer prolixity of God's creative words, which issue forth and entwine in such a dense web of vegetable and animal quiddity as to exclude all human entreaty or petition. Ishmael recognizes that the forceful vitality of the world overpowers the human observer such that its meaning can never be fully comprehended, for so many are the voices that weave and sinuously snake throughout. However, Herman Melville does not suggest that there is no meaning to the world's warp and weft, as Job affirms in Job 7:6—"My days are swifter than a weaver's shuttle, and come to their end without hope"—which is likely the text behind Melville's reference. Job believes his lifespan to be in the hands of a God who relentlessly fabricates regardless of Job's individual situation. Melville and McCarthy both dismantle Job's hopelessness and set the Joban despair against a more hopefully woven backdrop than Job articulates.[37]

Job thinks himself enmeshed in an inscrutable God-operated mechanism, heedless of his own situation, which he can neither stop nor escape from. By contrast, the Caborcan man understands that the sovereignty of God is such that God can "bend all to an inscrutable purpose." Moreover, the world-fabric that is woven includes him: "somewhere in that tapestry . . . was a thread that was he." The Caborcan wakes weeping because he understands what Job could not: that the God against whom he railed, from whom he could not escape, has neither ignored nor forgotten him. The God with whom the Caborcan had remonstrated was none other than the oneiric weaver-god of whom he had dreamed. And this was indeed the good and gracious God into whose tapestry the Caborcan is woven: "It is God's grace alone that we are bound by this thread of life." He is overwhelmed by a hope that remains with him until his death, before which he tells the priest that he has finally apprehended something of God, which was that

> the God of the universe was yet more terrible than men reckoned. He could not be eluded nor yet set aside nor circumscribed

> about and it was true that he contained all else within Him even to the reasoning of the heretic else He were no God at all.[38]

Thus the Caborcan apprehends, as Job did, that the God against whom he railed is "Himself known as the One He was and is even and precisely in this alien form, as the One who has never left the scene but always dominates it," in Barth's words.[39] The Caborcan received no whirlwind theophany yet nevertheless came to a place of peace with the God from whom he knew he could not escape. Previously he had harangued and rejected the priest, but now he implores the priest to recognize their human solidarity and see that their common lot is to deal with this God. Hence the final words that he beseeches the priest to act on: "Save yourself, he hissed. Save yourself. Then he died."[40]

Sure enough, after the Caborcan's death the priest—into whom his words had insinuated themselves with a subtly transformative power—began to realize that his answers were barren "and finally he came to see that they were not the old pensioner's queries at all but his own."[41] The priest-hermit's encounter with the Caborcan had propelled him along a path that led him to see that "nothing is real save his grace."[42] Thus there is a final call not only to the trusting acceptance of God's good grace and the certainty that one's story will be woven up with those of all others, and clarified at the last, but also to the gratuity of that grace and the life-shaping reality of that gratuity. This is fact and is not contingent on man giving God permission:

> He [God] does not ask for his [Job's] understanding, agreement or applause. On the contrary, He simply asks that he should be content not to know why and to what end he exists, and does so in this way and not another. He simply asks that he should admit that it is not he who plans and controls. He simply asks that he should concede that he has nothing to do with his course and direction.[43]

The third point of intersection concerns the rejection of empty answers. The hermit settles in the ruined church at Caborca, a place to which it is obvious to the narrating priest that "he had been brought" and that was "the very thing he sought." The structure is a broken edifice and so perfectly mirrors the Caborcan's theology, both of them shaken and profoundly transformed by natural disaster. Yet it is a place of hope for even as the *golondrinas* (swallows) nest there, so too will the Caborcan, who dwells in God's house, be blessed;[44] thus he "made ready to receive that which had eluded him."[45] He is confident that God *will* speak to him. As in Barth's reading of Job, the Caborcan "suffers from the very faithfulness which means that God will not abandon him nor he God."[46] Like Job, whose origins are unknown, so the Caborcan becomes there a man without history, variously described as a saint or a screwball, who berates God in a way that is scandalous to his spectators. The Caborcan appears to be trying to negotiate a settlement or boundary (*colindancia*) with God, but the narrating priest, and others, are scandalized by this because such decisions are best left to God alone. Their response recalls those of Bildad in Job 8:1-3—"Does God pervert justice?"—or Eliphaz in 15:2-5—"Should the wise . . . argue in unprofitable talk, or in words with which they can do no good?" The priest tries to speak to the Caborcan of God's grace but is rejected for his vacuity: "You know nothing. That is what he shouted. You know nothing."[47] Although the priest recognizes the truth of these words, he continues to visit the Caborcan and entreat with him, answering him according to his "high canonical principles," "liberal sentiments," his "great reverence for the world" and his belief that he could discern "the voice of the Deity in the murmur of the wind in the trees."[48] McCarthy's priest functions as a Joban comforter, wanting to help but not wanting to listen to the "blasphemy" of the Caborcan's outcry, offering an etiological explanation without any pastoral help. Like the comforters, the priest refers to the created world but he reads it wrong. This is indicated by McCarthy's use of the word "Deity" rather than "God": such a deity is the philosophical god and not the God of Christianity. Furthermore, the priest's appeal to natural theology is misguided, as he later reflects: "To see God everywhere is to see Him nowhere."[49] The priest appealed to generalities, principles, and proofs and thereby failed to attend to the specificities of the Caborcan's situation. In the person of the priest McCarthy portrays Job's comforters, who Barth describes as "unquestionably good, earnest and religious," and who "unquestionably speak good, earnest and religious words."[50] Furthermore, Barth points out that their responses to Job are, like the priest's, generalizing words that do not address the specificities of Job's own situation.[51] Their words have the appearance of elegant beauty, but are lifeless and dead.

Although Barth affirms that God's speeches to Job *do* refer to the natural world, he is clear that this is *not* a natural theology, but the deliberate revelatory act of God who chooses in this instance to speak through these things:

> It is not they who do it, but God who enables them to speak in His own self-declaration, summoning in the first address the dry land and the sea, the dawn of day and the night of death, the snow, the hail, the rain, the dew, the clouds and the lightning, the lion, the raven, the coney, the wild ass and ox, the stork, the horse and the falcon, and then in the second address those two formidable monsters. These all speak for Him. God causes them to do so.[52]

McCarthy's priest—like Eliphaz, Bildad, and Zophar in Uz—attempts to give an intellectual explanation of God and God's ways, thereby revealing his interest in the explanatory issue that is secondary both to the Caborcan and to Job before him. They do not seek to know *why* calamity has crushed them, but how to live in a world wherein such calamity is present. The priest's approach is objective and disinterested; he, like Job's comforters, has no investment in what he is saying. McCarthy's description of the priest recalls Barth's words regarding the comforters, who

> speak as those who are totally unaffected by the despairing struggle for the knowledge of God into which Job finds himself plunged by what has befallen him. They speak as those who are totally unaffected by the tension, which stirs Job so profoundly, between his knowledge that in this situation he has to do with Yahweh his God and his ignorance how far he has to do with Him. They obviously fail to see and understand that they have no awareness or categories for what is taking place between God and this man.[53]

Both the priest and the comforters espouse a viewpoint that is "only in their imagination and not in fact the standpoint of God."[54] In contrast, the ground of both Job and the Caborcan is "blessed and fraughtful," and in their words there is "little measure and little of restraint."[55] The priest and the comforters were debating in general terms, as if discussing a philosophical conundrum. Yet both the Caborcan and Job were wrestling with something quite different. The Caborcan "had engaged the living thing," that is, the "God of the universe on ground of that God's own choosing."[56] So likewise did Job. Their words have moved beyond objectivity—neither one insists on drawing up appropriate boundaries or establishing a reasonable *colindancia*—into the boldness that is motivated by personal involvement. Hence it is fraught with danger, for it is the Living God whom they harangue and harass. Yet, as holy ground, this place of their engagement with the God who had elected them to this was also blessed. The priest's vague and formless God reiterates his kinship with Job's comforters, who attempted to reduce God to a manageable entity "by their enclosing of the relationship between God and man in a fixed and orderly structure."[57] The priest turns God's freedom into an objective principle and denies his subjectivity; the comforters deny both God's objective and subjective freedom. However, God as Subject is free and untamable and such a God had no place within either the priest's *colindancia* or the comforters' theology.

JOB WITH FRESH PERSPECTIVE

To draw these points together, in the Huisiachepican hermit's tale of the Caborcan man's suffering and theological searching McCarthy covers similar ground to the book of Job and, in "trying to 'eff the ineffable,'"[58] helps the reader to apprehend truths from Job in four ways.

First, McCarthy's fiction enables the reader to apprehend the dismantling effects of great suffering. The reader can understand—all too easily and shockingly—the tragic depths of the Caborcan's experience, and how he becomes lost and but a shadow of himself, abandoning his wife in his restless roaming and persistent peregrinations. This then feeds into a reading of Job who, although not abandoning his wife as the Caborcan has, seeks to become lost by wishing for his non-presence (chapter 3) and declaring that "The eye that beholds me will see me no more" (7:8).[59] Taken as a biblical text, it is easy for Job's travails to be underplayed and for him to be thought of as a pawn in a theological game. After all, the reader knows the events of the prologue, about which Job is never told. In such a reading Job's suffering is little more than the collateral damage that is sadly needful in order for all those who come after him to understand the mystery of suffering. Such a utilitarian view depersonalizes Job into no more than a theodicean cipher. Rejecting such an approach is not to argue for the literal historicity of a wealthy man from Uz whose life unraveled in tragic circumstances,[60] but it is to argue for the need to reflect seriously on, and grapple with, the terrible losses and suffering that Job underwent. In retelling the Joban experience in a more familiar setting, McCarthy thereby enables the reader to apprehend and be touched by the experience of suffering so that Job can be read in a more humane, compassionate manner.

Second, McCarthy enables the perceptive reader to apprehend how it is that experiences of tragedy intensify the human appeal to God. She apprehends something of why the Caborcan—and Job—do not outright reject and disavow God. McCarthy's skillful literary approach shows her that to do so would be to admit to the meaninglessness of their experiences. Rather, both Job and the Caborcan cling to a conviction that resolution is found only in God. While McCarthy's fiction helps the reader to apprehend this, it should nevertheless be remembered that a conviction that God alone *can* resolve one's confusion does not imply that an answer *will* be forthcoming. The Caborcan received no answer but nevertheless found peace in believing that there was an answer.

Third, McCarthy's approach is a more realistic reading than one in which Job is an everyman whose sufferings are merely an illustrative analogue of those in the real world. This latter approach can often insist that Job's experience is typical for all times such that sufferers today assume that a theophanic experience will be forthcoming, thereby ending their plight. In reality, Job's experience is profoundly unrepresentative, and the biblical book deliberately portrays it as such. Job's suffering is atypical in: (1) his integrity and uprightness, for no one can claim to be "blameless and upright, fearing God and shunning evil" in the way that Job is repeatedly described (Job 1:1, 8; 2:3); (2) the severity and speed of the sufferings that struck him; (3) the satanic circumstances that contributed to his condition;[61] (4) his reception of a direct divine revelation that ended his strife; and (5) the nature of that theophany.[62] None of these things should be assumed to be necessarily true of subsequent sufferers.

McCarthy helps us to apprehend this: the Caborcan does not receive a Joban theophany, but he does come to a quiet place of peace and contentment. Moreover, his determination to live in the fact of this grace in a way that benefited others resulted in the priest himself coming to a similar conclusion to the Caborcan, and being able to accept the world as it is, and move on. Therefore, McCarthy is *more* hopeful than the biblical book of Job. Where Job's dialogues do not bring about any change in the comforters' viewpoints, McCarthy's Caborcan, in his insistent refusal to accept the priest's platitudes, kick-starts the priest himself—his "comforter"—to apprehend anew. Thus McCarthy also helps the reader to apprehend how her life is connected to those of others. And while Job's comforters do not appear to share his newfound insights, the epilogue does speak of them benefiting from Job. Job is tasked with interceding for Eliphaz and the others, and his prayer for them is found acceptable (42:9).

Fourth, in his depiction of the detached priest McCarthy enables the reader to apprehend the illegitimacy of approaching particular questions of suffering with pious but theoretical espousals of dogma and generalized comfort. Therefore he shows the reader the inadequacy of any human explanatory answer that is given from a distance, without pastoral solidarity, and McCarthy also enables the reader to apprehend that an objective construction of God's workings in the world is ultimately insufficient for navigating through life's vicissitudes. This is what Job's comforters had failed to see, despite the fact that certain ideas and themes from their speeches recur in the divine speeches.[63] It is less the content than the tone and direction of their speeches that is problematic. In 15:7 Eliphaz is sarcastic, mocking Job's arrogant pretensions to superior insight,[64] yet God does not wish to trenchantly belittle Job into silence,[65] but to lead him onward into insightful apprehension.[66] Like Job's comforters, the priest wishes the Caborcan to come *back* from his place of imprecation, but the Caborcan will have none of it. Similarly, the comforters' speeches return Job to things they understand, but God's speeches take Job into things he has not yet apprehended, a creation that is "at once moving and inviting and supremely worthwhile, and at the same time baffling and opaque."[67] There is something in the wildness and wonder of creation that, when charged with God's revelatory speech, is able to communicate deeply to a sufferer, a fact borne out by the number of recent memoirs dealing with grief that acknowledge the role of creaturely wildness in moving through and beyond pain.[68] The Joban comforters' error may lie not in what they did or did not say, but to whom they did or did not say it: they did not talk *to* God about Job, only *to* Job about God.[69] Thus they failed to be the advocates for whom Job had expressed such longing throughout the book.

CONCLUDING REFLECTIONS

Thanks to McCarthy Job can be read more humanely, just as thanks to Barth Job can be read more theologically. The "traveler afoot" who tells the Caborcan of the tragedy that has befallen Bavispe echoes the Joban descriptive refrain of chapter 1's messengers of doom ("While he was still speaking another came and said . . ." [1:16-18]) and opens up an imaginative space within which the reader of Job is reminded that Job is portrayed as a person, with hopes, dreams, and feelings, many of which have been dashed by what he has experienced. McCarthy helps the reader to see how it is that the situation of both the Caborcan and Job is complicated by their sense of having been elected to their fates. It is the entanglement of believing himself elected to this fate that makes the situation of both of them so intolerable. This is why both of them cleave to God rather than being cleft from Him. Both the Caborcan and Job intuit that God is the one who is ultimately responsible for their situations and so must be held to account for His treatment of them. McCarthy also shows up for what it is the easy and trite theologizing and facile posturing that so often characterize our attempts to engage with those who are suffering. When we read Job, none of us like to think that we are Eliphaz, Bildad, and Zophar. We would do things differently, we reassure ourselves. We would not speak so easily and confidently about why these things have happened to our friend. We would not dare presume such an authoritative diagnosis. But McCarthy helps us to see how easily we take on the mantle of comforter, scandalized by the sheer rawness of the emotions on display. As Barth saw, so McCarthy fleshes out: it is easier to respond with a general answer about why tragedy befalls human beings than to attempt to enter into the specificities of why *this* man is being treated in *this* way. Such a stance is always only ever inadequate. In enabling the reader to perceive Job and the comforters in this way, McCarthy implicitly points to a possible way of coming alongside a suffering friend without falling into the silencing speech of the comforters.[70]

How this can be done is illuminated by an encounter later on in the book. In the novel's third part Billy meets a woman and her husband, a blind man or *ciego*, who "had given his eyes for the revolution."[71] They invite Billy in and give him milk to drink and food to eat.[72] The *ciego*'s wife tells Billy how the blind man lost his sight to a sadistic German officer, Wirtz, in 1913. In her telling of her husband's life there is a recurrent Joban motif. In the days following the loss of his eyes her husband had lived in a "disassembled world" that "could never be put right again,"[73] which recalls Job's words that "my eye will never again see good" (Job 7:7). The blind man "could not see the face of his enemy. The architect of his darkness. The thief of his light,"[74] which echoes Job's powerlessness in the face of God's invisible hiddenness: "Why do you hide your face, and count me as your enemy?" (Job 13:24).[75] Like Job, whose friends cannot see beyond his parlous state to give him the comfort he so desires—"Have pity on me, have pity on me, O you my friends, for the hand of God has touched me" (Job 19:21)—the blind man ceased to be treated as an individual by those around him and instead became a mere object of discussion and debate: "Some said of course that this man Wirtz had saved his life for had he not been blinded he'd have surely gone to the wall. Some others said that would have been the better course. None asked the blind man for his views."[76] In addition to these Joban echoes the blind man's wife tells Billy of three important encounters that the man had in the twenty-eight years of his post-tragedy travels. The individuals described in each of these encounters recall Job's three friends but, unlike Eliphaz, Bildad, and Zophar, and unlike the priest who harangued the Caborcan, these three do provide some measure of help to *el ciego*.

Their help consists precisely in the fact that they do not try to explicate his experiences. Rather they help him to plumb the depths of his experiences honestly and apprehend how they might illuminate his former life, and his life to come. First, he meets a woman who "asked him if he had always been blind." Even though he had not, he "weighed the question and after a while he said that yes he had."[77] Even when he had been able to see, he had been blind, indicating that there was something about his actual blindness that—paradoxically—enabled him to see more clearly. Second, having sunk into despondency through a belief that his blindness had estranged both him from the world and the world from him, he attempts to kill himself, but fails.[78] A man "who was on the point of coming to his rescue"[79] calls to him, signaling that the blind man is not in fact estranged from the world, and in their subsequent conversation the blind man tells the stranger that he believes he has "outlived his estate." The stranger tells the *ciego* that it is "a sin to lose heart."[80] Although to the blind man the world seems to move "in eternal darkness and darkness is its true nature and true condition,"[81] the stranger corrects him as they take their leave from one another, heading in opposite directions that mirror their opposing viewpoints: "Hay luz en el mundo, ciego . . . Como antes, asi ahora."[82] Having been given wisdom through his first encounter, in this second he is given hope. This hope is not the hope that things will necessarily improve, or that his sightlessness will be undone. Rather, it is a hope for possibility, a hope that in a world of such unimaginable inscrutability life is worth living and embracing in however constrained and thin a fashion.[83] The third encounter is with a child, a young girl whose father and brothers had been killed by Huertistas and who has no living family. In one of the novel's characteristic tales-within-a-tale, there then follows an account of the girl's conversation with a gravedigger (*sepulturero*), who tells her that "while one would like to say that God will punish those who do such things and that people often speak in just this way it was his experience that God could not be spoken for and that men with wicked histories often enjoyed lives of comfort and that they died in peace and were buried in honour."[84] She relates this to the blind man, along with the gravedigger's exhortation to remember the dead: "Faces fade, voices dim. Seize them back, whispered the sepulturero. Speak with them. Call their names. Do this and do not let sorrow die for it is the sweetening of every gift."[85] She then leads the *ciego* to her house and dresses him in some of her father's clothes before setting out on the road with him. In this third encounter the blind man receives the gift of company from the girl, who, it transpires, is the woman telling Billy the story.[86] The *ciego* is helped by the girl to realize that what befell him, terrible and tragic as it was, was neither unique, unusual, nor unprecedented.

If Eliphaz, Bildad, and Zophar are "comforters" who give no comfort, then these three individuals can be thought of as anti-comforters, who nevertheless do provide some genuine "comfort." They do this not by explaining why but by listening to the blind man, treating him as an individual, and attending kindly to him. Such things are profoundly sustaining.

3
The Decentering of the Human Subject

ANTHROPOCENTRIC IMPOTENCE

> We are come to a world within the world. In these alien reaches, these maugre sinks and interstitial wastes that the righteous see from carriage and car another life dreams. Illshapen or black or deranged, fugitive of all order, strangers in everyland.[1]

> "What are human beings, that you make so much
> of them,
> that you set your mind on them,
> visit them every morning,
> test them every moment?
> Will you not look away from me for a while,
> let me alone until I swallow my spittle?" (Job 7:17-19)

The sentiment that in Psalm 8 is a dignifying source of comfort and joy for humanity is transformed by Job's suffering into sardonic resignation. Why can humanity not cease to be the center of God's unflinching and—to Job—baleful gaze? However, the ash-dusty Job must wait another thirty-one chapters before God speaks to him, and when this address comes, Job's plea is answered. When God thunders from the whirlwind, God speaks neither of humanity nor of its accomplishments, its dignifying status as carrier of the image of God, or its place in the created order. God's gaze sweeps across different territories, to the firmament and the foundation, the axial spin that brings morning and evening, hailstorms, lions, and ravenous ravens. God draws Job's attention to this "world within the world," whose personified denizens quietly go about their business, only strangers because perpetually unseen and overlooked.

The above quotation from *Suttree* is just one incidence of many from that book—and throughout McCarthy's oeuvre—that exemplify how it is that McCarthy consistently directs the reader's attention beyond the human to the world as it exists on its own terms. That the world has a quiddity independent of any human imposition of meaning onto it is a truth that is also highlighted in the book of Job. In both McCarthy and Job this truth is of first importance for navigating encounters with chaos and inexplicable confusion, for to realize that the world exists on its own divinely ordered and appointed terms, as McCarthy's prose suggests, and is independent of human enterprise on it or definition of it, as the book of Job agrees, is to realize that the game has changed and all prior assumptions are open to rethinking.

BLOOD MERIDIAN AND OPTICAL DEMOCRACY

Blood Meridian is "a work of great intellectual power, erudition and linguistic virtuosity."[2] It is a historically rooted novel that follows an unnamed protagonist (the kid) who falls in with a roving gang of scalp-hunters led by Joel Glanton, and marauds with them through the savagely violent and blood-spattered United States–Mexican borderlands of the late 1840s. The descriptions of the Western setting through which McCarthy drags these bloodthirsty brigands are literary constructions of such poetic exuberance that the wildness of landscape reflects the wildness of the Glanton gang's own hearts.[3] The particular literary techniques that McCarthy employs to describe this landscape serve to deconstruct an anthropocentric viewpoint and enable the reader to apprehend a sense of the smallness of humanity's place in the vastness of creation, something to which the divine speeches in Job 38–39 also attest.

The novel's beginning sets the tone for the interplay between specific character and general landscape: "See the child. He is pale and thin, he wears a thin and ragged linen shirt. He stokes the scullery fire. Outside lie dark turned fields with rags of snow and darker woods beyond that harbor yet a few last wolves."[4] The first three sentences are short and staccato in their descriptions of the human agent but are dwarfed by the splendor of the fourth sentence's scope that contains not only the serried landscape of human cultivation but also the wider wolf-ridden world from which its fields have been cut. While the rest of the opening chapter follows the kid's mindless peregrinations across eastern Texas and his induction into the violence that will accompany him all his life, the haunting image of the wilderness lingers in the imagination. It is reiterated at the start of chapter 2:

> Now come days of begging, days of theft. Days of riding where there rode no soul save he. He's left behind the pinewood country and the evening sun declines before him beyond an endless swale and dark falls here like a thunderclap and a cold wind sets the weeds to gnashing. The night sky lies so sprent with stars that there is scarcely space of black at all and they fall all night in bitter arcs and it is so that their numbers are no less.[5]

The contrast between the sparse prose describing the kid's empty wandering and the richness of the descriptions of the natural world is striking, made all the starker by the long unpunctuated sentence's repetitive use of the noncausal "and" as a connective (rather than the more usual "by" or "then"), which joins the short pictorial phrases into a long sentence that fills the reader's imaginative space with image upon image so as to render all subjects to the reader equal in valence. This exemplifies the book's relentless drive to describe nature in its essential truthfulness, independent of any connection to humanity.[6]

McCarthy's deliberately deconstructive effect recurs repeatedly through *Blood Meridian*, a paradigmatic example being the 234-word sentence that depicts the massacre of Captain White's company at the close of chapter 4, in which the Apaches are depicted in terrifying aspect:

> Now driving in a wild frieze of headlong horses with eyes walled and teeth cropped and naked riders with clusters of arrows clenched in their jaws and their shields winking in the dust and up the far side of the ruined ranks in a piping of bone flutes

> and dropping down off the sides of their mounts with one heel hung in the withers strap and their short bows flexing beneath the outstretched necks of the ponies until they had circled the company and cut their ranks in two and then rising up again like funhouse figures, some with nightmare faces painted on their breasts, riding down the unhorsed Saxons and spearing and clubbing them and leaping from their mounts with knives and running about on the ground with a peculiar bandy-legged trot like creatures driven to alien forms of locomotion and stripping the clothes from the dead and seizing them up by the hair and passing their blades about the skulls of the living and the dead alike and snatching aloft the bloody wigs and hacking and chopping at the naked bodies, ripping off limbs, heads, gutting the strange white torsos and holding up great handfuls of viscera, genitals, some of the savages so slathered up with gore they might have rolled in it like dogs and some who fell upon the dying and sodomized them with loud cries to their fellows.[7]

Like the compressing of visual perspective rendered by a telephoto lens, McCarthy's technique flattens the images onto an equal backdrop, neither preferring any one subject nor allowing the reader to impress any subjective partiality onto any point of the tableau rendered in such astonishing prose. This stylistic effect, first identified by Steven Shaviro, is known among McCarthy critics as optical democracy, which term derives from the text of *Blood Meridian* itself:

> In the neuter austerity of that terrain all phenomena were bequeathed a strange equality and no one thing nor spider nor stone nor blade of grass could put forth claim to precedence. The very clarity of these articles belied their familiarity, for the eye predicates the whole on some feature or part and here was nothing more luminous than another and nothing more unshadowed and in the optical democracy of such landscapes all preference is made whimsical and a man and a rock become endowed with unguessed kinships.[8]

In this passage, what is communicated to the reader is not the murderous brutality and incoherent violence of the book's protagonists but the very fabric of creation itself such that humans are rendered as no more important than anything else. Furthermore, throughout *Blood Meridian*, McCarthy's description of the landscape through which the Glanton gang passes is characterized by his optically democratic viewpoint.[9] Whether the referent is the natural world or the inhabitants thereof, this particular literary technique serves to distance the reader from the world so depicted by a driving syntax that carries her helplessly with no pause for lexical breath or gifting of interpretative space to sort or process this barrage of images that flash past with such force and rhythmic relentlessness that "the images flood the pages intellectually unprocessed."[10]

OPTICAL DEMOCRACY IN THE BORDER TRILOGY

This technique is not solely the preserve of *Blood Meridian*. It recurs in both *All the Pretty Horses* and *The Crossing*, although less frequently. In both texts it serves the same anthropological function as in *Blood Meridian*, that of minimizing the human inhabitants within the landscape:

> Days to come they rode through the mountains and they crossed at a barren windgap and sat the horses among the rocks and looked out over the country to the south where the last shadows were running over the land before the wind and the sun to the west lay blood red and among the shelving clouds and the distant cordilleras ranged down the terminals of the sky to fade from pale to pale of blue and then to nothing at all.[11]

The first four verbs in this sentence ("rode," "crossed," "sat," and "looked") have John Grady Cole and his companion as their subject, but this shifts to, first, the evening shadows and, second, the waning sun. By the end of the sentence the human subjects that began it have receded into the background and are no more important than any other part of the crepuscular Mexican landscape.

A similar shift of subject occurs in *The Crossing*:

> They rode up off the plain in the final dying light man and wolf and horse over a terraceland of low hills much eroded by the wind and they crossed through a fenceline or crossed where

> a fenceline once had been, the wires long down and rolled and carried off and the little naked mesquite posts wandering single-file away into the night like an enfilade of bent and twisted pensioners.[12]

Here, the initial "they" encompasses Billy, the she-wolf he is transporting, and his horse, thus minimizing any emphasis on the human subject over the animal, but the subject matter then shifts to inanimate fencing material in the second half of the sentence. Once again, the prose gives a wide-angle feel to the text, albeit one that highlights small details of the nonhuman landscape.

As in *Blood Meridian*, so too in these works there is an anti-anthropocentric vision, although not as forceful as in that novel's apogee. *All the Pretty Horses* highlights this relativization of the place of humanity when John Grady visits Abuela's grave. He holds out his hands, perhaps in benediction or perhaps just in recognition that "the world was rushing away and seemed to care nothing for the old or the young or rich or poor or dark or pale or he or she. Nothing for their struggles, nothing for their names. Nothing for the living or the dead."[13] This is an explicit affirmation of the world's existence and sufficiency independent of any meaning that humans confer on it, and it subverts any outlook that sees the world as existing for humanity's benefit. Similarly, the wolf-trapper Don Arnulfo in *The Crossing* tells Billy that men "see the acts of their own hands or they see that which they name and call out to one another but the world between is invisible to them."[14] This underscores the failure of humans to see the world as existing other than for their own ends. It is unrecognizable to them as a thing in itself. Yet it is its own entity, existing for nobody's privileged purposes.

From *The Orchard Keeper*'s two pages written with a mountain lion as the main subject, to the last paragraph of *The Road*, which eschews any human subject in favor of the mystery-humming glens in which the brook trout once lived, an anti-anthropocentric vision is a consistent feature in McCarthy's fiction.[15] Just as *The Crossing*'s embedded tale of the Caborcan enables the reader to apprehend that a rational explanation of the ways in which God interacts with His creation is inadequate for addressing the pastoral questions generated from the aftermath of those interactions, so the relentlessly equalizing tone of *Blood Meridian*'s descriptive prose enables the reader to apprehend that creation is not centered solely on humanity. When Judge Holden tells his fellow scalp-hunters that "even in this world more things exist without our knowledge than with it and the order in creation which you see is that which you have put there, like a string in a maze, so that you shall not lose your way," he is voicing a denial of this presumption of anthropocentric dominance.[16]

THE MARGINALIZATION OF THE HUMAN IN JOB

This marginalization of the human is something that the Joban divine speeches also accomplish, in a similar—but not identical—manner. They begin with an overwhelming avalanche of deliberately unanswerable questions—thirty-nine in the NRSV[17]—that arrest both Job, to whom the speeches are addressed, and the reader: Who shut in the sea? Have you comprehended the expanse of the earth? What is the way to the place where light is distributed? Can you bind the chains of Pleiades or loose the cords of Orion? There is neither time nor space for Job to answer, and the relentless insistence that Job listen—and listen well—to these questions shifts the perspective away from Job himself and his complaint, away from the comforters and their mistaken explanations and away from the human to a consideration of the magnificent grandeur of God who alone can do these things.[18] The tone is therefore not one of divine bullying that puts Job in his place, for nowhere does God dismiss or attack Job.[19] Rather, it is like that of a parent to a child, or a teacher to a pupil, in which there is no belittling or mockery, but an attempt to move from incomprehension to apprehension. In doing this, the speeches serve an implicit corrective function of censuring some attitudes—such as an anthropocentric perspective—and encouraging others. The speeches' tone and function are therefore inextricably connected.

One of the corrective functions of the speeches is to resituate Job in creation, because "how the subject perceives the world is critical to how he or she lives and acts in the world."[20] This is done in chapter 38 by an extended lyrical poem that focuses on the cosmological and meteorological backdrop to creation as well as on the inner workings by which God maintains that creation as itself. These beautiful descriptions emphasize the nonfunctional and essential quiddity of each creature.[21] Everything that exists does so for a reason independent of human benefit as the rain-drenched grasslands "empty of human life" (38:25-27) demonstrate.[22] This subversion of an anthropocentric imposition of meaning onto creation is shown by the absence of humans from these chapters until the brief allusion to "the horse and its rider" in 39:18.

This holding of Job's—and the reader's—attention on the nonhuman introduces a sense of liminality that continues in chapter 39's litany of beasts.[23] Humans were ignorant of these morally ambiguous creatures, which lived in the uncivilized salt flats or mountain areas, and they tended to identify them as malevolent forces both independent of and useless for human service.[24] However, the divine speeches show Job that these category-defying beasts enjoy a boundless freedom, thus "the divine speeches are structured to take Job, imaginatively, from places of secure boundaries to places where boundaries are put at risk."[25] Furthermore, chapter 39's focus on these liminal beasts disorients Job by exploding his moral horizons and subverting his previously cherished assumptions.[26] It does not merely offer a zoological procession of unusual fauna; it underscores that these creatures are under God's providential care. This is important for Job's understanding of himself in creation because he had imagined himself among the beasts in isolation, "a brother of jackals, and a companion of ostriches" (30:29) in disgrace and exclusion amid a barren landscape, but no: God has shown him that this *terra damnata* contains life and liberty in creatures with whom, if he wishes, he can align himself.[27] Job had imagined himself godforsaken, but no: there is neither barren desert nor haunt of jackal that is beyond God's concern.[28] Job had imagined that the wicked were like the wild ass of the salt flats, far from the purview of God (24:5; cf. 30:7), but no: it was God who gave the onager such a habitat (39:6). Job had been ill-equipped to see creation from anything other than a human viewpoint. The idea that God could sovereignly be at work, directing, guiding, and providing for God's own creation in the way that God sees fit, was alien to him. The divine speeches helpfully problematize Job's insistence on a straight justice-injustice polarity to a more complex picture of order and disorder.[29] This movement from "justice-injustice" issues to "how the universe is run," which culminates in the descriptions of Behemoth and Leviathan, is a relativization of the human claims to justice, and a corresponding marginalization of humanity itself, as Job attests when he states "I am of small account" (40:4).[30]

THE FUNCTION OF FIGURATIVE LANGUAGE

To leave Job for a moment, McCarthy's recurrent use of this "Optically Democratic" viewpoint both stylistically and syntactically emphasizes a horizontality in the text, a physical factuality to the thing described. This is achieved in part by McCarthy's masterful use of figuration. The reader is alerted to the presence of a simile by McCarthy's use of "like" or "as," but the same reader is then confounded by McCarthy's apparent failure to punctuate in such a way that the resemblance is clearly denoted.[31] This can be seen in the aforementioned passage describing the Apache attack on Captain White's men, in which the Apaches are "running about on the ground with a peculiar bandy-legged trot like creatures driven to alien forms of locomotion and stripping the clothes from the dead . . ."[32] However, what superficially might be thought to be poor and confusing punctuation is far from it. McCarthy presses punctuation into his own service, as Faulkner also did before him. McCarthy's innovative use of metaphor and simile is perfectly suited to the purpose of his communication, which is to enable the reader to apprehend that the world exists independently of human attempts to impress meaning onto it. His peculiar literary style, with its deliberately obtuse similitude and its high-definition descriptive precision, dismantles the mental apparatus of anthropocentric assumption so that "we are given instead a kind of perception before or beyond the human."[33]

The egalitarian horizontality generated by McCarthy's paratactic style underscores *Blood Meridian*'s anti-anthropocentric vision. By using a style that enables him to look at and write about landscape in a way that rejects any assumption of anthropocentric dominance or superiority, McCarthy questions and critiques the reader's preconceptions about the place of the human in denoting meaning to the world.[34] He does this by simultaneously foregrounding the materiality of the created world while causing the human figures to recede into the background. This is one aspect of what the Joban divine speeches also do: the assumed answer to chapter 38's barrage of questions is "No, neither Job nor humanity can do these things," thereby underscoring human impotence. Chapter 39 underscores this impotence by explicitly stating the untamability of the onager (39:7) and the wild ox (39:9), as do the second speech's references to Behemoth (40:19, 24) and Leviathan (41:1-2, 7-9).

McCarthy's anti-anthropocentric perception is due to the way his prose's descriptive arcs permit "the recollection and preservation of the thing as it was prior to inscription by the subject."[35] That is, it allows the thing's quiddity to be revealed without reference to its usefulness or function from a human viewpoint. Objects are not rendered meaningful by a rational subject, but are things with their own essence, untranslated.[36] McCarthy's epistemology—seen most clearly in *Blood Meridian*—therefore rejects any subject-object dualism, instead asserting that despite human imposition of importance there is simply no difference between the wildness of human and animal and wilderness that encompasses each and all of them.[37] All are equalized by such a gaze that connects wildness and wilderness to all strata of life.[38]

METAPHOR AND MEANING

McCarthy's use of figuration is therefore an inescapable ingredient in *how* his novels communicate to the reader. Metaphor is not reducible to mere literary ornamentation, a sort of rhetorical flourish that shows off what the author can do. Although it can seem to be like a grammatical eel that twists out of the hand of the linguist the more tightly she attempts to definitively grasp it, one of the most helpful explanations is that offered by Janet Soskice, who, while recognizing that a satisfactory definition may be unattainable, suggests that "*metaphor is that figure of speech whereby we speak about one thing in terms which are seen to be suggestive of another*."[39] Metaphor is fundamentally communicative, and powerfully so, for the metaphor constitutes its own unique unit of meaning, which cannot be articulated by dismantling the metaphor and reconfiguring it in an alternative manner. The metaphor and its meaning are inseparable.[40]

Therefore metaphor cannot be expurgated and replaced by a putative literal equivalent without changing the meaning of what is being said. Similarly, to ask "What is *this* a metaphor for?" is to ask a misguided question that assumes that the true meaning is something hidden by the metaphor, rather than something accessed through it. It must be understood that metaphorical and figurative language provide a new way of conceiving reality and thereby can create something new because through the metaphor the reader is able to experience the world in a new and different way.[41]

Metaphor should be neither denigrated as inferior nor approached with the assumption that one can circumvent it to locate some unadorned objectivity that is assumed to be superior.[42] Metaphor should be embraced and allowed to communicate its conceptually transformative insights as they are, without translation, precisely because it can generate new meaning and understanding. The meaning and understanding that derives from using metaphorically rich language ought never to be assumed to be inferior to a linguistic style in which metaphor is avoided.[43]

The communicative potential of McCarthy's optically democratic similes and metaphors is suggestive for the reader of Job, for the divine speeches are poetic and so their meaning is not superficially comprehended.[44] Yet their form is not merely poetry; it is highly metaphorical poetry, and the speeches communicate to Job in part by virtue of these inventive and original metaphors. This is important because God's speeches instruct Job by bombarding him with images, pictures, models, and metaphors that constitute their own meaning. Such metaphorical plenitude can communicate truth in a profound and insightful way, sometimes more insightfully than precise propositional language.[45] If it is the case that to understand an utterance is to know how to respond to it, not to get "behind" it to an objective content,[46] then the book of Job's epilogic description of Job's deliberate reengagement with life indicates that he has understood something from the divine speeches' metaphors. At the end of the divine speeches, Job knows about God's righteousness "not in the form of a theory of the matter, but much better, much more fundamentally."[47] Something profound has been communicated to Job through the metaphorical plenitude of the divine speeches, and Job has apprehended it, as evidenced by his late fatherhood, his inheritance plans, and his reordered property portfolio.

THE DIVINE SPEECHES' METAPHORS

A brief survey of Job 38–41 reveals that the richest metaphorical treasures are found in chapters 38 and 41, with further occasional gleams in chapter 40's description of Behemoth. Although metaphors flower in virtually all the stanzas of chapter 38, space precludes an in-depth discussion of them all, so attention will be given to those of 38:8-11 before considering those in 40:15–41:26.

The metaphors of 38:4-7 combine to suggest the model of creation as a building.[48] This ordered house of creation is juxtaposed with 38:8-11's broiling sea, the metaphors for which suggest two models: the Sea as a newborn infant, and the Sea as a proud invader, both requiring restraint.[49] The unified poetic picture is of the Sea as the object of God's concern, clothed with mist but energetically unruly, encompassed with bars and doors. It is a raging creature that must be, and is, successfully enclosed.[50]

The description of Behemoth in 40:15-23 is notable for its concentrated use of illustrative similes (40:15, 17-18), which aid comparison, as well as the metaphorical suggestion of Behemoth as a torpid ruler, for whom the mountains produce food (40:20). The picture is of a creature whose great size, indolent imperturbability, and massive strength combine to awesome effect, yet Behemoth carries no necessary connotation of threat to humans.[51]

Chapter 41's description of Leviathan likewise abounds in illustrative (41:5, 20, 24, 29, 31) and modeling similes (41:18, 30). These latter descriptions are closer to metaphor and aid a more expansive exploration.[52] Together they depict an incomparably impregnable beast (41:13, 15, 29) who bristles with weapon-like danger (41:30). In contrast to Behemoth, Leviathan suggests a latent danger easily awoken into terrifying violence against humans (41:8-11).[53] Leviathan and Behemoth are qualitatively different, for compared to Leviathan the massively solid frame of Behemoth is fragility (41:27; cf. 40:18). Leviathan will not beg for mercy, for none can master his fearsome thrashings.

METAPHORICAL SUGGESTIVENESS

To enquire what these metaphors are communicating is to ask a question that cannot be completely answered, for metaphor pushes us beyond equivalence into yet further metaphor such that categorical meaning cannot be imposed once and for all.[54] Biblical metaphor should not be reduced because "part of the point may be that there is no single point, but a range of possibilities now allowed to be brought into play."[55] Yet an answer must be essayed in order to explore what the metaphors are suggesting.

First, the metaphors suggest an awesome power in the world, albeit within bounded limits. The Sea's energetic unruliness suggests a destructive threat, despite being demarcated (38:11). God sets bounds so that godforsaken inundation becomes impossible. Inevitably, then, these metaphors suggest the omnipotence of God who not only creates such awesome and terrifying power but also contains it. Behemoth and Leviathan do not constitute examples for Job to emulate, for "the point does not seem to be any identity between Job and Behemoth but the fact that Behemoth, for all its fearsomeness, is a deliberate creation of God," like Job. Behemoth and Leviathan—like the Sea—suggest a curtailing of threat within creation.[56] Taken together, the metaphors evoke a structured order to creation within which such terrifying entities as the Sea, Behemoth, and Leviathan are approved.

Second, the metaphorical language suggests unconventionality and the upending of assumed patterns. God cares for humanity but he does not care *solely* for humanity. In 7:12 Job had complained about being treated like the Sea, under God's guard, but in chapter 38 God reveals to him that the Sea is the recipient of both divine containment and nurturing maintenance.[57] God graciously gives food (40:20), habitat (40:21-22), and a serene self-confidence (40:23) to the mightily intimidating and imperturbable Behemoth. God's bounteous care for Behemoth and his exuberant description of the fearsome Leviathan indicate God's freedom from the conventions within which Job and his friends attempted to corral God. Just as chapter 39 enabled Job to see the liminal creatures anew, so too chapter 38 conveys to Job a new apprehension of the Sea as the object of God's care, and chapters 40–41 impart to him an apprehension of Behemoth as the recipient of God's provision, and Leviathan's place in creation.

CONCLUDING REFLECTIONS

McCarthy's novels articulate an anthropology that is at stark odds with that which is assumed to be normal. His insistence on the relativization of the human "ownership" of the world—whether this is through describing the world solely in terms of human utility or by only seeing it as something with an anthropocentric meaning inscribed onto it—opens the way for his reader to apprehend a different way of being in the world: there is no reason to assume that the world exists for the reader's benefit.

This then permits a reading of Job in which to be properly human is to recognize that the world exists on its own terms. This does not deny the human calling in creation, but relativizes it. The Joban author's literary style means that the divine speeches display an immense indifference to the human world and its concerns, but this is no negligent oversight. Rather, it is a deliberate rhetorical strategy in order to communicate to Job that creation is not governed *solely* for human benefit. Part of what the book of Job does is to explore the tension between the human as dust and the human as *imago Dei*, and to investigate whether human experience prioritizes one metaphor over the other.[58] Humans tend to recoil from frailty and transience and assume that, as they are bearers of the *imago Dei*, God is bound to uphold their happiness. This is, in part, what Job himself did and what the comforters also assumed. However, through the divine speeches God challenges Job to recapture, or reimagine, his vocation as *imago Dei* and therefore overlord of creation.[59] Within this challenge, though, the task of imposing order on creation is relativized: to be truly human—truly the *imago Dei*—is not to seek to impose order on creation by subjective fiat, insisting that "this is how the world ought to be." Rather it is to live humbly and thankfully within creation, trusting in God's good sovereignty.[60] Furthermore, in order to be truly human Job must be situated against the backdrop of creation as a whole, not merely human institutions such as family and village. These latter institutions should be seen in the light of creation, not the other way round.[61] Part of Job's error lay in seeking to create a world of value and meaning, seen especially in chapters 29–31, that would explicate his own experience. But such a quest is ultimately fruitless, because the bigger picture is one in which the ordered and structured cosmos is not ordered and structured around the human enterprise, let alone Job's own life. There is at work here a more magnificent mind than the merely human.

4
The Looming Threat of Chaos
AN UNPREDICTABLE CREATION

> Suttree took his bedding off down to the river and lay there with his hands composed upon his chest. Watching up at the starless dark. The shapes of the trees rearing dimly in the lightning. A distant toll of thunder. The sound of the river. Each drift of wind brought rainwater from the trees and it spattered lightly in the leaves and on his face. He'd had enough of rain. The fire had died, he eased toward sleep. The next moment all this was changed forever.[1]

> "I am not at ease, nor am I quiet;
> I have no rest; but trouble comes." (Job 3:26)

"Trouble comes," states Job at the close of his first speech in the dialogues, in what must be one of Scripture's most understated reflections on the upheaval of personal circumstance. Self-evident though this observation may be, it is nevertheless one that goes frequently unheeded. Too often life is lived as if trouble is *not* going to come, and when it does we are more often than not utterly unprepared for all the emotional flotsam that washes up in its wake. The troubles of Job's life were unexpected irruptions of chaos that spun his ordered life—and his theology—into turbulent free fall. Sabean raiders, fire from heaven, Chaldean militias, and a wind from the desert descend with equal suddenness. Truly, in a moment all can be changed forever, as Suttree found in such tragic fashion.

McCarthy helps the reader to apprehend the existence of a world in which there is a chaotic unpredictability that disturbs life. This chaotic unpredictability is a recurring theme in his novels, and it is often embodied in a specific character or group of characters. These characters—whether deliberately or not—have been written in such a way that they inflect the richly metaphorical Joban descriptions of Behemoth, Leviathan, and the Sea, chaotic entities that disrupt human experience and endeavor.

In *Blood Meridian*'s reflection on the Delaware Indians' congruence with the wilderness through which they track a bear, the narrator ruminates that

> If much in the world were mystery the limits of that world were not, for it was without measure or bound and *there were contained within it creatures more horrible yet* and men of other colors *and beings which no man has looked upon* and yet not alien none of it more than were their own hearts alien in them, whatever wilderness contained there and whatever beasts.[2]

Later on in the novel, the grotesque Judge Holden lectures the gang: "Even *in this world more things exist without our knowledge than with it* and the order in creation which you see is that which you have put there, like a string in a maze, so that you shall not lose your way."[3]

Both these passages explicitly state the unknowable strangeness of creation's denizens. The world's incomprehensible plenitude is a recurring idea throughout McCarthy's novels, whose interest lies not in zoological alterity but in the presence within the created world of agents of chaos that present to the reader a picture of the world in which chaos exists, yet is bounded. This chaos is expressed most clearly by McCarthy in *Outer Dark*, *Blood Meridian*, and *No Country for Old Men* in the form of the grim triune, Judge Holden, and Anton Chigurh, respectively.[4]

OUTER DARK AND THE GRIM TRIUNE

Outer Dark is a novel about journeys. The narrative follows siblings Culla and Rinthy Holme through an unnamed landscape. Rinthy seeks her child, infanticidally exposed by her brother but found by an itinerant tinker. Culla seeks Rinthy, yet is also in flight from his home and his guilt, for he is the child's father. On their journeys they encounter a grotesque panoply of types but are received in different ways. Culla is met with suspicion, ill-feeling, and mistrust—and twice narrowly avoids being lynched. Rinthy is met with kindness, compassion, and generosity, receiving unsolicited invitations to eat with strangers and escaping unscathed from those few situations she encounters in which there is threat or violence. Their journeys run mostly in parallel but occasionally intersect, although they fail to meet. Rinthy is graceful, light, "humming softly to herself . . . turning her face up to the sky and bestowing upon it a smile all bland and burdenless as a child's," and as she travels "butterflies attended her and birds dusting in the road did not fly up when she passed."[5] But Culla travels "hands pocketed and head cupped between his shoulder blades," suspiciously and mistrustfully: "He carried a stick with him and prodded each small prone shadow through which he passed but this road held only shapes of things."[6]

Rinthy, Culla, and the tinker are not the only characters in the novel. There is a mysterious triune of wanderers, introduced in italicized interludes but then moving into the main body of the narrative: one is bearded, one is named Harmon, and one is a nameless "mute," whether by choice or circumstance it is unclear. They are dangerous and lawless and appear to be the cause of much violence in the novel, culminating in one of the most shocking incidents in McCarthy's books as they garrotte Culla's incestuously begotten son before his eyes, feed on his arterial blood, and, it is implied, cook and consume the infant.[7]

Gnostic or Not?

The novel is, admittedly, bleak and hard, and it depicts a world in which "the sense of evil remains vague and endemic," seeming to inhabit the landscape's very essence:[8]

> The air was dank and stormy. Night fell long and cool through the woods about him and a spectral quietude set in. As if something were about that crickets and nightbirds held in dread. He went on faster. With full dark he was confused in a swampy forest, floundering through sucking quagmires and half running. He did not come upon the river but upon the creek again. Or another creek. He followed it down, in full flight now, the trees beginning to close him in, malign and baleful shapes that reared like enormous androids provoked at the alien insubstantiality of this flesh colliding among them.[9]

It is through this world that Culla and Rinthy wander helplessly and apparently hopelessly, blind and maze-held, with no exit possible.[10] Many critics have described the book in gnostic terms, but it does not require that reading.

Indeed, the book's descriptions of Culla's and Rinthy's peregrinations are markedly different: Culla, tormented and forgiveness-seeking but ultimately self-isolating, is associated with darkness and shadow,[11] but Rinthy, pure, tranquil, and harmonious with her natural surroundings,[12] is associated with light and grace.[13] A further counter to the gnostic reading is the inconvenient fact that there are notes of kindness in the book. These tend to be performed to Rinthy,[14] and the characters who show this kindness are set apart by it such that they do not meet the same violent end as others.[15] Culla is in flight, whether or not he knows it, through a landscape of barren desolation that reflects his own consciousness, tormenting and confounding him inescapably.[16] He will not admit to his responsibilities and so, despite both wanting and direly needing grace, he cannot receive it.[17] Although there is no explicit authorial ingress to the interior world of either Rinthy or Culla, each character's psychology is nevertheless manifested on their journey through the temporally and geographically ambiguous landscape such that they both somehow contribute to the construction of the worlds they inhabit.[18] Their experience of the external world both reflects and is predicated upon their internal experience of it: for Culla, a distrustful disdain, and for Rinthy, a tranquil tenderness.

The Grim Triune

It is against this metaphysical backdrop that the grim triune should be investigated. Critics have explained them in various ways without reaching a consensus.[19] They are certainly a part of McCarthy's oeuvre-wide investigation into chaotic unpredictability, but to describe them—as some have done—as incarnations of evil is unhelpful, as this judgment is too readily taken to imply that evil is a personal force to be opposed and resisted rather than something with which the reality of must be reckoned.[20] That this is McCarthy's intention is suggested by the fact that the triune's presence in the world of the novel is assumed, although unexplained. McCarthy does not indulge the reader's curiosity by giving the grim triune a backstory: they are a baleful presence in the world of the novel, indicated thus from the outset. The novel's first sentence shows them already engaged in a journey from who knows where.

> They crested out on the bluff in the late afternoon sun with their shadows long on the sawgrass and burnt sedge, moving single file and slowly high above the river and with something of its own implacability, pausing and grouping for a moment and going on again strung out in silhouette against the sun and then dropping under the crest of the hill into a fold of blue shadow with light touching them about the head in spurious sanctity until they had gone on for such a time as saw the sun down altogether and they moved in shadow altogether which suited them very well.[21]

The triune are shadowy beings, restless and hungry, implacable as a river and incessant in their movement. They have a destructive dyna mism that drags almost all whom they encounter into its murderous wake: after killing Salter, they disinter and grave-rob the clothes from three corpses at Cheatham; their dark-suited, bearded, ill-shod leader galvanizes a mob and instigates a hypocritical manhunt for his putative killers, resulting in two dawn lynchings; together they spatchcock a snake hunter who had watered Culla; their predilection for mindless killing makes them the likeliest culprits for the murder of the white-suited Clark, upon whose buzzard-harried makeshift gibbet

Culla chances, soon after sensing that "there was something fearful about."[22] Finally, they murder Culla and Rinthy's son and drink his carotid blood.

Further descriptions of them underscore their strange and almost supernatural otherness: they move with alarming rapidity and one of them grins with a "mindless smile," but they are not mindless—for they deliberately alter course to intercept Squire Salter's wagon.[23] The bearded one's size alone is the source of his lynch-inducing authority; the three of them together are a "consubstantial monstrosity."[24] This ontological strangeness is intensified as the novel progresses and is suggestive of their figuration as chaotic elements:

> Holme looked at the man. The fire had died some and he could see him better, sitting beyond it and the scene compressed into a kind of depthlessness so that the black woods beyond them hung across his eyes oppressively and the man seemed to be seated in the fire itself, cradling the flames to his body as if there were something there beyond all warming.[25]

In the final italicized section they are described in almost wraith-like manner: "The three men when they came might have risen from the ground. The tinker could not account for them."[26] The triune's nature could be summarized as an almost supernatural, dynamic, dangerous presence that is an assumed given in the world of the novel, damaging all those who brush up against it.

JOB

One might reasonably ask what such horrific entities have to do with the book of Job. Yet in the second divine speech (chapters 40 and 41) God specifically directs Job's attention to Behemoth (40:15), which is an instruction not merely to identify the creature, but to contemplate it, meditate on it, and reflect on it.[27] This suggests that there is something about Behemoth that yields wisdom for Job in his struggle to understand God's design.[28] Furthermore, just as the speeches are the climax of the book, so the description of Leviathan, being the final element in the divine speeches, has particular importance to Job, before whom it is "paraded by Yahweh as in some sense the key to the meaning of the universe."[29]

Exactly how these beasts should be understood has occasioned much discussion among biblical scholars. Thomas Aquinas understood Behemoth to be the elephant and, foreshadowing *Moby Dick* by several hundred years, Leviathan to be the whale. Most scholars today, if pressed to a naturalistic identification, would see Behemoth as the hippopotamus and Leviathan as the crocodile,[30] although there is a minority view that Leviathan is a bovine.[31] But if that's all they are, then why did the author of Job not name them as such? Others connect them to the *Chaoskampf* motif of ancient Near Eastern mythology, and read them as chaotic monsters in conflict with God.[32] But the presence of Babylonian and Canaanite mythological features in the Old Testament is not unanimously accepted, which fact should encourage caution regarding an overly strong identification of *Chaoskampf* motifs in Job also.[33] It may well be that the Joban author, by calling the crocodile Leviathan, is deliberately alluding to God's vanquishing of the chaos monster, but this would mean no more than that Leviathan has a multivalent meaning in Job as elsewhere in the Old Testament.[34] Still others read these beasts as loosely symbolic, and it is likely that their exact identification is irrelevant, for the point seems to be that they surpass in wonder and awe those creatures already mentioned.[35] The sense of liminality introduced in chapter 38, and underscored by the desert- and salt-flat-dwelling creatures of chapter 39, may be extrapolated into the descriptions of Behemoth and Leviathan: they are liminal creatures who embody an alien and other chaos that is not adversarial to God but extolled by Him. The presence of this chaos in creation is what God is trying to help Job to apprehend.[36] That this is the case may be deduced from a close reading of their descriptions.

Behemoth is portrayed as indolent, lying "under the lotus plants . . . in the covert of the reeds and in the marsh" (40:21), utterly nonplussed by the force of the created world around it: "Even if the river is turbulent, it is not frightened" (40:23). "Can one take it with hooks or pierce its nose with a snare?" asks the Lord in a rhetorical aside (40:24). The obvious answer is no for Behemoth, whose strength and power are explicitly mentioned; with its bones like bronze and limbs like "bars of iron," it is massive and strong (40:16-18). Yet for all the enormity of the creature's potential dynamism there is no suggestion of malevolence or aggression in this creature that Job is told was "made just as I made you" (40:15) as "first of the great acts of God" (40:19).

The metaphorical language used in the divine speeches repeatedly evokes boundaries, constraints, containment, and the curtailing of a terrifying unpredictability. In considering Behemoth, Job is to understand that he inhabits a creation that necessarily includes an element of unpredictability. Such created unpredictability—powerful and untamable (40:24) as it is—is nevertheless an inherent element in creation and can be no more tamed than the rain, but it is not maliciously hostile to humanity. Behemoth—manifest to Job in the whirlwind and the fire from heaven that contributed to his suffering—is a legitimate inhabitant of creation, fulfilling its created function regardless of any impingement on human activity, even though utterly uncontrollable from a human perspective.

Leviathan is different, however, altogether more fearsome than Behemoth. Behemoth's strength was likened to bronze and iron (40:18), but to Leviathan such lustrous hardness is mere rotten wood and straw (41:27). Leviathan is both fierce and fearsome, able to be neither controlled nor tamed (41:1-9), and will not deign to serve anybody (41:4). Leviathan cannot be toyed with as a pet (41:5) or traded (41:6). So great is the potential violence unleashed by this creature that "no one is so fierce as to dare to stir it up" (41:10). Leviathan is unequaled in creation and utterly fearless (41:33), and will shrug off every weapon fashioned against it as straw (41:26-29). Even its underparts bristle with danger (41:30).

As the consideration of Behemoth yielded important information about creation to Job, so too does Leviathan. This creature is the climactic apogee of the divine speeches, after which Job answers the Lord and turns to a different course of action (42:1-6). What does this creature mean to Job? The chaotic events that launched Job on his voyage of complaint were not just the Behemothic consequences of created unpredictability, or "natural" evils. They also included the unforeseen depredations of the Sabean and Chaldean raiders, and it is this moral evil unleashed into creation by human sin that the terrifying and uncontrollable presence of Leviathan represents. Leviathan is untamable and uncontrollable, just as the consequences of moral evil performed by others cannot be controlled or manipulated. Such was the error of *The Counselor*'s titular protagonist, for he failed to appreciate that Leviathan cannot be exploited, for moral evil is too great a power to ultimately serve any one person's interests. Leviathan is too dangerous for tomfoolery, just as moral evil is ruthlessly rapacious. Leviathan should be undisturbed lest his violent raging is unleashed, and likewise there is a latent and insatiable ferocity to moral evil. Leviathan's moral evil is terrifyingly malevolent, in every way indicative of its own essence (41:12ff.), and Leviathan—like moral evil—is utterly unique in creation (41:33). However, the divine speeches are clear that, like Behemoth, Leviathan, terrifying in his latent violence, is part of that "everything under heaven" which belongs to God (41:11, NIV), and is no antagonistic trespasser into creation that would threaten its God-governed and God-ordered structure.[37]

Part of the point of God directing Job to consider these creatures is to help him to see that the good world God made is *this* type of world, with *these* possibilities—both positive and negative, anthropocentrically speaking—built into it. Thus those things that cause chaos and unpredictable disorder—earthquakes, great winds, raiders, and bandits—are a part of life, and neither something that God will excise for human benefit nor adversaries to be defeated.[38] This is a further example of how the book of Job relativizes anthropocentrism: those chaotic disturbances into life appear to humans as ugly and invasive, but this gross unloveliness serves merely to challenge the self-focused assumptions that shape human thinking.

To recapitulate, the grim triune are portrayed in *Outer Dark* as an assumed presence in the novel's landscape, and are given no explanation. They are portrayed as larger-than-life, almost supernatural beings, with a dangerous energy all of their own and a tendency to harm anyone unfortunate enough to encounter them. Their ontological peculiarity suggests a correspondence with Leviathan and Behemoth, which are similarly confounding, created by God and bewilderingly—to Job and to the book's subsequent readers—granted a place in the world. Furthermore, as Behemoth is overwhelmingly powerful and Leviathan is threatening in his potential for violence, so too the grim triune have a powerful and minatory violence that is manifest seemingly without cause from any but themselves. Although their callous cruelty can appear random, they are described as "blind with purpose," and emerge from a barn "marvelously armed with crude agrarian weapons," which recall the spiky potsherds of Leviathan's belly (Job 41:30);[39] such single-mindedness is also suggested in the attack on Squire Salter.[40] As God asked Job of Leviathan, "Who can stand before it? Who can confront it and be safe?" (41:10-11) so too could it be asked of the triune, who—like Leviathan—appear to be fearless creatures without equal. In describing this terrifying Tennessean triune in such a way as to evoke Behemoth and Leviathan, McCarthy allows that the world that Culla and Rinthy inhabit is a world in which unpredictability and chaos have a permitted place. His literary interest in how individuals navigate such a world and respond to this chaos when it erupts into their ordered existence, whether or not through their own fault, is not limited to *Outer Dark* but recurs through several other works. That this is so is strengthened by the clear connection between this maleficent threesome and *Blood Meridian*'s Judge Holden.[41]

BLOOD MERIDIAN AND JUDGE HOLDEN

Judge Holden is one of McCarthy's most enduring and opaque creations. Putatively based on an apparently historical person, at least in name, but perhaps also in his pederastic deviancy, he is the story's dominant character.[42] Although the book's narrative follows the kid from his birth on the novel's first page, it is the judge who drives the story forward.

The novel's narrative is relentless in its onward momentum through the godforsaken wildlands of the Southwest border regions and also in its descent to an almost benthic savagery in the human person, unflinchingly portraying the horrors of both desert heartland and the deserted hearts of depraved humans. Reminiscent of T. S. Eliot's *The Waste Land*, *Blood Meridian* is a physical and moral landscape of godlessness in which McCarthy presents a declined Western spirituality through the story's frequent ruined churches and icons and its repeated comparisons between vultures and clerics.[43] Thus it is unsurprising that critics have seen in it an exploration of meaning and divinity.[44] Literature's primary appeal to the imagination enables theological truths to be expressed in embodied characters and worlds and thereby explored to see where such ideas lead.[45] Therefore, it may be that the namelessness of the protagonists in *Blood Meridian* suggests a symbolic reading,[46] such that the text functions as a literary investigation into divine sovereignty.[47] However, such readings can tend to flatten the rich contradictoriness that the judge embodies.

The judge is a physical anomaly, whose preternatural strength, massive size, unnatural pallor, and hairlessness are often concatenated to create an unforgettable image.[48] McCarthy draws attention to "the immense and gleaming dome of his naked skull" as he enters the public baths.[49] Despite his monstrous size, he is an adept dancer, whose "feet are light and nimble."[50] This mercurial aspect is also reflected in his numinous quality: "The judge like a great ponderous djinn stepped through the fire and the flames delivered him up as if he were in some way native to their element."[51] Thus from a merely physical and visual viewpoint, he is a confoundingly ambiguous character.

This ambiguity is seen in his social behavior. He is comfortable in all company, able to deal diplomatically with tense encounters, and seemingly accustomed to influential circles.[52] He is a polyglot polymath, but uses his intellect to mock others.[53] He is omnicompetent, as shown by his redemptive action on first encountering the Glanton gang who, spent of their gunpowder, are harried by persistent Apaches.[54] The judge leads the hapless gang into the hills to manufacture charcoal, extract potassium nitrate from bat dung, and gather sulfur flakes from a natural deposit. He then concocts this charcoal, saltpeter, and sulfur with the men's urine to make a paste that desiccates to a primitive gunpowder.[55] In contrast to such skillfulness and intellectual refinement, he is repeatedly implied to be a violent pedophile, as well as explicitly identified as a child-murderer.[56] However, he is also capable of tender kindness, such as nursing a drink-crazed Glanton at Jesús María, or rescuing the "idiot" James Robert from drowning at a ferry crossing.[57]

There is further ambiguity in his metaphysical and ontological status. He is human but described in ways that transcend human embodiment. The ex-priest comments, "It was like . . . You couldn't tell where he'd come from."[58] His first meeting with the gang in the desert is "a manifestation rather than an appearance," which "deliberately precludes rational explanation."[59] His metaphysical complexity is evidenced in his relationship with the created order, over which he claims authority as a suzerain, whose role is to know all of his remit: "Whatever in creation exists without my knowledge exists without my consent."[60] This is shown in his meticulous keeping of records, sketching, and note-taking of all that he encounters, which often leads to the eradication of whatever physical artifact he was studying.[61] He does this because "in order for it to be mine nothing must be permitted to occur upon it save by my dispensation."[62] After one sketching and note-taking exercise, the narrator describes him as "much satisfied with the world."[63] He has an unnatural relation to time, appearing and disappearing with alarming suddenness, being unaffected by the aging process, and claiming immortality.[64]

Moreover, the novel portrays him as able to control the lives of those he meets: he purposefully engineers confused discord, he specifically insists that itinerant fortune-tellers read first the kid's then Glanton's tarots, and all the members of Glanton's gang claim to have met him prior to his joining them in the desert.[65] Tobin recalls that once the judge had infiltrated the gang he "looked about him with the greatest satisfaction in the world, as if everything had turned out just as he planned and the day could not have been finer."[66]

Thus the judge is hinted at being an eternal figure, sovereign over not only his own fate—he appears conspicuously nonchalant when faced with threat—but also over those whom he encounters.[67] His omniscience is implied by the ex-priest recounting how he led the disheveled and hopeless band into the hills to manufacture gunpowder: "And how did he come to know of it? How to find it? How to put it to use?"[68]

As the novel progresses, the judge's ambiguity develops. Toward its climax he becomes expositor and explains to the kid that there is a bigger backdrop—the Dance—against which individuals live and act, unknown to them but nevertheless real. In the Dance the judge sees a predestinate determinism from which none can escape. Moreover, for the judge it is inconceivable that any would want to. While some might deny the Dance's reality, he avers, that does not negate its existence: "order is not set aside because of their indifference."[69] He implies that it is he—the judge—who is controlling the Dance and all the dancers within it, and it is futile to fight against the Dancemaster's call, for in the end all will join in:

> Any man who could discover his own fate and elect therefore some opposite course could only come at last to that selfsame reckoning at the same appointed time, for each man's destiny is as large as the world he inhabits and contains within it all opposites as well. This desert upon which so many have been broken is vast and calls for largeness of heart but it is also ultimately empty. It is hard, it is barren. Its very nature is stone.[70]

The empty desert is the meaninglessness of life, which is so abhorrent that there arises a deep drive to find meaning, but there is no precedent, no ordering principle to life other than that which we impose on it: "For existence has its own order and that no man's mind can compass, that mind itself being but a fact among others."[71] Thus the hard, stony truth remains.

The judge continues by likening the Dance to a ceremony or a ritual, which necessarily involves savage violence lest it be false.[72] This idea of falsity is developed at the close of his speech to the kid:

> I tell you this. As war becomes dishonored and its nobility called into question those honorable men who recognize the sanctity of blood will become excluded from the dance, which is the warrior's right, and thereby will the dance become a false dance and the dancers false dancers. And yet there will be one there always who is a true dancer and can you guess who that might be?[73]

As the violent and amoral savagery that comprises the judge's worldview is denied and repudiated, the judge is saying, so will those who propound it be marginalized by others who wish to reconfigure the Dance in a more humane and civilized way. Nevertheless, at its heart will lurk evermore the judge, and what he represents. Thus it is only the one who has offered himself wholly to violence who can be the true dancer. Savagery and violence are an inescapable part of life, no matter how many rail against it or try to delimit it.

McCarthy scholars have interpreted the judge's metaphorical multiplicity in many different ways: he is Shiva, whose multiple arms manipulate many destinies;[74] or he is Melville's Moby Dick, or Ahab.[75] As Tarot's Fool he is simultaneously "creator, destroyer, ruler and trickster;"[76] but in a quasi-Marcionite reading he is wrathful Old Testament Yahweh.[77] Alternatively, he is Satan,[78] or a devil, or a gnostic archon—a lord of the lower realm—seeking full dominion of his planetary fiefdom.[79] Perhaps he is an eternal force connected to the Platonic demiurge;[80] he is culture;[81] he embodies "the epistemological dream of Enlightenment rationalism,"[82] as a "totalitarian scientist" and "fascist intellectual,"[83] embodying "reason's struggle for supreme knowledge of and authority over nature."[84] He is the epitome of antebellum illusionist and trickster confidence man,[85] a "playful agent of chaos, self-indulgent and satisfying his own needs";[86] he "represents the human capacity to exploit the imprecision of language and forge insidious ideologies";[87] he is Jungian *Senex* to the kid's *Puer*, and "Thanatos incarnate";[88] he is an "imaginative picturing of a world defined by divine omni-causal determinism. He also shows how absurd such an idea is and why it should be rejected."[89] There is no consensus: "Holden transcends any one image or set of images."[90] As Emily Stinson notes, he is "leader of the Glanton gang, an artist, an historian, a scientist, an anthropologist, a conjurer, a magician, a storyteller, a dancer, a fiddler, a pedophile, a wanderer, and, of course, a judge," who has been interpreted as "God, the devil, the ruler of the Earth, a trickster figure, an ethnographer, and Adam, to name a few."[91] Edwin Arnold cryptically suggests that whatever and whoever the judge is, he cannot be explained by reason.[92] There is a tendency and a temptation to propose an interpretation of the judge so strongly that it denies any polyvalence to the character that McCarthy has created. The multiplicity of interpretations listed above need not be mutually exclusive. Yes, there is of course a Nietzschean dimension to Holden (as there is also for Anton Chigurh too in *No Country for Old Men*) that recalls Zarathustra, as seen in his dancing playfulness and his meridian meeting with the Glanton gang,[93] but that reading—or any other—cannot be allowed to foreclose further investigations into, and alternative explanations of, these grotesque types.

A recent iconoclastic approach argues that the text acts to deliberately bamboozle the reader into interpreting Holden as more than merely mortal when really he is no more than a trickster prestidigitator befuddling the gullible:[94]

> The truth about the world, he said, is that anything is possible. Had you not seen it all from birth and thereby bled it of its strangeness it would appear to you for what it is, a hat trick in a medicine show, a fevered dream, a trance bepopulate with chimeras having neither analogue nor precedent, an itinerant carnival, a migratory tentshow whose ultimate destination after many a pitch in many a mudded field is unspeakable and calamitous beyond reckoning.[95]

We *want* to understand the judge as a transrational, otherworldly being rather than a tall, bald, brutal pederast. In this reading, the epilogue of the judge's paleological lecture to the dumbfounded gang members aptly summarizes this approach's own admonition to *Blood Meridian*'s readers: "Your heart's desire is to be told some mystery. The mystery is that there is no mystery."[96]

This thesis is attractive, but it fails to do justice to the confounding complexity of McCarthy's portrayal of the judge: "The mystery McCarthy propounds is that we are blind to the mystery that is the very stuff of our existence."[97] This mystery that lies at the heart of our existence is clarified by McCarthy's deliberate but cryptic suggestion to the reader of a way of understanding the judge, one hitherto unexplored by critics: the judge embodies Leviathan and Behemoth as Joban chaos. McCarthy suggests this by deliberately inflecting God's whirlwind answer to Job from Job 38:1 ("Then the LORD answered Job out of the whirlwind"):

> Far out on the desert to the north dustspouts rose wobbling and augured the earth and some said they'd heard of pilgrims borne aloft like dervishes in those mindless coils to be dropped broken and bleeding upon the desert again and there perhaps to watch the thing that had destroyed them lurch onward like some drunken djinn and resolve itself once more into the elements from which it sprang. *Out of that whirlwind no voice spoke* and the pilgrim lying in his broken bones may cry out and in his anguish he may rage, but rage at what? And if the dried and blackened shell of him is found among the sands by travelers to come yet who can discover the engine of his ruin?[98]

This passage describes the mindlessly chaotic dustspouts as djinn-like, comprising some yet indefinable elements that appear to have their own ontology. The novel's perceptive reader may remember a similar description from a few pages earlier, already quoted.[99] The judge himself is djinn-like, apparently likewise comprising some peculiarly nonhuman elements that belie his apparent physicality, and yet the judge is a murderous figure whose encounter with any unlucky traveler is likely to end with that wayfarer's reduction to a blackened corpse. Given that these passages are the novel's only two occurrences of the word "djinn," they suggest a Joban connection that is steadily unpacked throughout the novel.

The chaotic elements within creation are represented in Job by the Sea, Behemoth, and Leviathan. The Sea is described as an infant (38:8-11), and in *Blood Meridian* the judge is depicted infrequently, but importantly, in childlike terms. In the first chapter his face is "strangely childlike," and later on he is described as "a pale pink beneath his talc of dust like something newly born," while at the novel's close he dances naked among the ladies "huge and pale and hairless, like an enormous infant."[100] Thus the reader's first and last glimpses of him underscore this resemblance. The judge's immense physical size, savage violence and lawlessness, and metaphysical and ontological ambiguity all recall the descriptions of Behemoth and Leviathan. The judge is utterly different from every other character in the book, and, the novel implies, to all humanity:

> he was among every kind of man, herder and bullwhacker and drover and freighter and miner and hunter and soldier and pedlar and gambler and drifter and drunkard and thief and he was among the dregs of the earth in beggary a thousand years and he was among the scapegrace scions of eastern dynasties and in all that motley assemblage he sat by them and yet alone as if he were some other sort of man entire.[101]

There is, then, an alien otherness to him, an alterity that corresponds to the way in which Behemoth and Leviathan embody the concept of the unwanted, chaotic "other" that exists within creation. The narrator describes the judge's entry to the baths:

> As that great bulk lowered itself into the bath the waters rose perceptibly and when he had submerged himself to the eyes he looked about with considerable pleasure, the eyes slightly crinkled, as if he were smiling under the water like some pale and bloated manatee surfaced in a bog, while behind his small and close-set ear the wedged cigar smoked gently just above the waterline.[102]

The description of the judge being like a "manatee in a bog" evokes both Behemoth, who lies "under the lotus plants . . . in the covert of the reeds and in the marsh" (Job 40:21), as well as—through the judge's gently smoking cigar—Leviathan, from whose "mouth go flaming torches; sparks of fire leap out. Out of its nostrils come smoke, as from a boiling pot and burning rushes. Its breath kindles coals, and a flame comes out of its mouth" (41:19-21).

Leviathan is "king over all that are proud" (41:34) in much the same way as the judge claims suzerainty over the earth "as if his counsel had been sought at its creation."[103] This echoes Job 40:19, in which Behemoth is ranked as first among God's works. The judge's pride is also seen in his amassing of knowledge in his notebooks. As stated above, the judge is bewilderingly unafraid when faced with threat, like Behemoth (Job 40:23), and he alone emerges from the book's tortuous wanderings unscathed, much as Leviathan is impervious to attack (41:26-29). When the Yumas attack the ferry crossing and encounter the erect judge in defiant opposition, they "fell over one another backward"—much as when Leviathan rises up, "the gods are afraid; at the crashing they are beside themselves."[104] Twice the judge engineers chaotic confusion for no seeming purpose other than his own pleasure. In the first chapter he slanders the Reverend Green as a sexually deviant fugitive from justice. This leads to someone unnamed drawing and discharging a pistol, presumably at the hapless minister. On escaping from the consequent violent uproar the kid encounters the judge standing at a bar, who admits, "I never laid eyes on the man before. Never even heard of him."[105] In the final chapter the judge's generation of violent and savage chaos is less explicit, but nevertheless he is clearly its cause. The paragraph that begins "When he [the kid] turned the judge had risen and was speaking with other men" ends with another drawing of a pistol. This time it is a dancing bear that is shot, and after the melee the kid once more finds himself by the judge, standing at a bar.[106]

It is in this embodiment of chaos that the judge's ambiguity is sharpened. Is he friend or foe? The judge enacted a soteriological role by redeeming the lives of the band from death and transforming them through brutal violence, alchemically transmuting their waste into the means of their salvation. Thereby he bound them to himself in a debt of gratitude, albeit one that is not explicitly acknowledged, yet the ex-priest assumed that the judge had been sent to them as a curse: "And yet he proved me wrong. At the time he did. I'm of two minds again now."[107]

On whose side is he? As chaos, there is no comprehensibility to the judge's actions. He rescues an Apache boy from a massacre and rides with the child for three days before killing and scalping him. Toadvine is appalled, incognizant of the essential equivalence between his own murderous violence in the attack on the Apache camp and the judge's slaying of someone whose trust he had fostered. The judge deliberately steps out of all boundaries. He serves war, and in some respects he embodies war, and in serving savage violence, all natural, moral, and spiritual laws are subordinate.[108] In recognizing this unpredictability in him, the gang "grew cautious and spoke with circumspection among themselves as if they would not waken something that had better been left sleeping."[109] As God speaks of Leviathan: "No one is so fierce as to dare to stir it up" (Job 41:10).

McCarthy's depiction of the judge repeatedly evokes the chaotic element in Job, embodied in the Sea, Behemoth, and Leviathan. Judge Holden—like the grim triune of *Outer Dark*—is suggestive of the presence in the world of a seemingly lawless chaotic element that encompasses both created unpredictability and the moral evil unleashed into creation by human sin. The question is not "how and why did he get there?" but "how to live in the light of such a being's existence?" Many have noted a similarity between *Blood Meridian* and *No Country for Old Men*, and more specifically between Judge Holden and Chigurh.[110] Chigurh has also been connected to the grim triune from *Outer Dark*, and so he too must be now considered.[111]

NO COUNTRY FOR OLD MEN AND ANTON CHIGURH

No Country for Old Men is the story of Llewellyn Moss, a welder who stumbles across a case of money from a drug deal turned violent. Taking this initiates a chain of events from which he cannot extricate either himself or his young wife, Carla Jean. Anton Chigurh is the tireless antagonist who hounds Moss in order to retrieve the money, and who is doggedly pursued in turn by the tired local sheriff, Ed Tom Bell, whose thirteen italicized ruminations on the world and his understanding of it pepper the book.[112] The novel is unusual in McCarthy's oeuvre because it reveals so much of the inner thoughts of its protagonist, Bell (and possibly, McCarthy's own sentiments).[113]

Chigurh has been described as the epitome of danger in McCarthy's literature,[114] which raises the question of how he should be understood. Some read him as an angel of death, but there is much death in the novel of which he is not a part.[115] Neither should Chigurh be interpreted purely semiotically as a "signifier of metaphysical evil," or as the Joban Satan "going to and fro" (Job 1:7) but unconfined by the divine.[116] Chigurh is not outside the world's constraints, even if he wishes he were.

Just as *Blood Meridian*'s Judge Holden represents "the other," so too does Chigurh: no one in the book can articulate or comprehend who or what he is.[117] His way of speaking is unusual and seems out of place,[118] as is his "oddly erect" bearing.[119] He has an "odd smell," which is "faintly exotic. Beyond Moss' experience."[120] He is described as a ghost, calling into question his physical reality: "As indeterminate as his origin is, nevertheless, he lives in a precise existence, though one seemingly outside of the text itself, as he moves in and out to execute with terrible purpose the end of its characters."[121] This ambiguity is further heightened by his sudden appearance at the book's start, and his equally sudden exit as he staggers away from a car crash, never to be seen again by the book's characters, although they remain haunted by his presence.[122] He is emotionally cold and unfeeling, and appears impervious to usually debilitating sensations such as cold or pain.[123] There is something about Chigurh that engenders a sense of palpable unease and fear in others, as evidenced by the filling-station proprietor's responses to his questions.[124] Throughout the book, various lawmen speak of the savage violence that Chigurh causes as being unprecedented in their experience.[125] All of this creates a sense that Chigurh is an alien "other," not just to the West Texas landscape and its inhabitants but to all those he encounters. The one person with whom he might be expected to share a kinship, the "fixer" or bounty hunter Carson Wells, is clear that Chigurh has an alterity that marks him out, describing him as crazy, a psychopath.[126] His attempt to buy Chigurh off fails, further underscoring the difference between them: for Wells, money is the bottom line; for Chigurh, it is twisted principle.[127] Even the novel's narrator cannot fully comprehend all that Chigurh is and does: "He paid and went out and got in the ram charger and started the engine and then sat watching the building in the rearview mirror. As if he might be thinking of something else he needed, but that wasn't it."[128] What was he thinking? We are not told; Chigurh's obscure otherness permits no insight into his psychology.

Furthermore, Chigurh—like Judge Holden before him—is portrayed as being somehow transhuman. Chigurh is "not to be read as a human being," and the judge appears to have a metaphysical complexity that questions his ontological status as human, and for both characters the issue of control of events is key.[129] The judge is perceived, at least by his fellow companions, to be in control of the lives of others, engineering their fates according to his whims. Chigurh likewise implies that he is in control of events, and he wants his victims to acknowledge that their lives hang from a thread that Chigurh himself holds.[130] When Carla Jean pleads with Chigurh to spare her, he replies:

> You're asking that I make myself vulnerable and that I can never do. I have only one way to live. It doesn't allow for special cases. A coin toss perhaps. In this case to small purpose. Most people don't believe that there can be such a person. You can see what a problem that must be for them. How to prevail over that which you refuse to acknowledge the existence of. Do you understand? When I came into your life your life was over. It had a beginning, a middle, and an end. This is the end. You can say that things could have turned out differently. That they

> could have been some other way. But what does that mean? They are not some other way. They are this way. You're asking that I second say the world. Do you see?[131]

In this short speech Chigurh not only shows his desire to exert control over life and death, but also his adherence to a strict code. The reference to a coin toss recalls the encounter with the filling-station proprietor earlier in the book.[132] In that earlier encounter it appeared that the toss of the coin could genuinely alter Chigurh's behavior, but here it cannot. Chigurh admits that the coin toss is of little consequence with Carla Jean. So is Chigurh someone who lives by a strict code of adherence to fate, as the earlier encounter would suggest, or someone who freely determines how to act regardless of the appeal to chance that a coin toss implies? The book does not explicitly resolve this contradiction. This speech also shows how Chigurh routinely engages in explanatory dialogue with his victims prior to executing them, which may be read as an attempt to help his victims jettison an anthropocentric view of life in which notions of fairness and unfairness play an important role and accept that there is no true justice or fairness, only choice, consequence, and chance.[133]

The role of a randomness in life, whether understood as luck, chance, or fate, is a consistent interest of the book. Bell recalls his sheer good fortune in meeting Loretta, his wife, and then refers to Moss and Carla Jean as lucky people for not having the sort of marital problems that most couples do.[134] This is ironic, for Moss has already realized that he is surviving out of luck and that this luck will inevitably dissipate. A similar sentiment is voiced by Wells, who tells Moss that although he might "get lucky" and evade capture for a while, his end is inevitable.[135] Carla Jean reflects that she is lucky to have had such a mother as she has. The night clerk's accidental death by virtue of being in the wrong place at the wrong time is put down to sheer bad luck. In these examples luck is something that happens to other people, and the characters' reflections on it suggest that it is an impersonal agent over which they have no influence.[136]

However, other examples suggest that luck is something that can be made or influenced: Bell noting that defaming the dead will certainly not bring good luck; Carla Jean's story of working ninety-nine days at Walmart before meeting Moss; Wells' refutation of the idea that he has led a "charmed life," arguing that charm is not the issue, implying that he too makes his own luck by being careful.[137] Finally, there is the redheaded hitchhiker's declaration that "I was always lucky," which is soon proven tragically hollow.[138]

Chigurh is the bridge between these two ideas: some things happen by chance, and some are determined by our actions, and the two are more closely connected than is realized. As Uncle Ellis tells Bell, "you never know what worse luck your bad luck has saved you from."[139] Although Chigurh is the bringer of "good luck" or "bad luck" to characters in the book and thereby represents a chaotic randomness, untamable and unstoppable but nevertheless present, he denies that luck even exists. For him there is only the unstoppable momentum of consequence: "For things at a common destination there is a common path. Not always easy to see. But there." Furthermore: "Every moment in your life is a turning and every one a choosing. Somewhere you made a choice. All followed to this."[140] These twin ideas of, first, one's place in a larger complex of the web of life in which all choices occur and impinge on all others, and second, the consequences of choice are closely connected and are of sustaining interest to McCarthy, who introduced them in the Border Trilogy.[141]

In *All the Pretty Horses*, John Grady Cole travels to Mexico and finds work on a ranch where he courts Alejandra, the owner's daughter. Alejandra's great-aunt, the Dueña Alfonsa, tells Cole of her father who

> claimed that the responsibility for a decision could never be abandoned to a blind agency but could only be relegated to human decisions more and more remote from their consequences. The example he gave was of a tossed coin that was at one time a slug in a mint and of the coiner who took that slug from the tray and placed it in the die in one of two ways and from whose act all else followed, cara y cruz. No matter through whatever turnings nor how many of them. Till our turn comes at last and our turn passes.

The foreshadowing of Chigurh's numismatism is particularly clear.[142] Alfonsa continues: "I think if it were fate that ruled our houses it could perhaps be flattered or reasoned with. But the coiner cannot." Thus there is no fate-setting agent to be beseeched and entreated with, only an impassive "coiner" who represents the consequence of choice:

> For me the world has always been more of a puppet show. But when one looks behind the curtain and traces the strings upward he finds they terminate in the hands of yet other puppets, themselves with their own strings which trace upward in turn, and so on.

The Dueña is ambivalent about whether we choose our own way through the web of life, or whether we read back into our histories the pattern that we wish to see there.[143]

In *The Crossing* Billy and Boyd are given a map by an old man whose companion cautions them that it is a fantasy, belying his knowledge of the landscape, which can change so suddenly and utterly. The old man's map is no more than the drawing of an old journey, which the old man wants to be true but is not.[144] Later in the book Billy hears a *corrido* and believes it to be about Boyd, but it is not: Billy was looking for meaning in it and he found what he sought but it was not truly there.[145]

This tendency to attribute meaning to life's vicissitudes and tortuous wanderings is an attempt to protect oneself from the unexpected. However, life is always unexpected, with unforeseen consequences: "You do not know what things you set in motion, he said. No man can know. No prophet foresee. The consequences of an act are often quite different from what one would expect."[146] It is only at the end of things that we can trace a route—"This is a story of misfortune. Or so it would seem. The end is not yet told"[147]—but even that hindsight is unreliable, for people tend to "attribute great consequence to trivial things."[148] All that remains is the challenge of living the life that is, setting aside as moot the argument concerning how a life is determined: "whether a man's life was writ in a book someplace or whether it took its form day by day was one and the same for it had but one reality and that was the living of it."[149]

Finally, *Cities of the Plain* reinforces this:

> Each act in this world from which there can be no turning back has before it another, and it another yet. In a vast and endless net. Men imagine that the choices before them are theirs to make. But we are free to act only on what is given. Choice is lost in the maze of generations and each act in that maze is itself an enslavement for it voids every alternative and binds one ever more tightly into the constraints that make a life.[150]

The net—or web of strings—comprises our choices and the choices of all others, yet these choices are not really a free choosing at all: "he thought about his life and how little of it he could ever have foreseen and he wondered for all his will and all his intent how much of it was his own doing."[151] Thus *No Country for Old Men* continues an investigation that McCarthy began several books previously. The novel's emphasis on the consequences of choice and on the unknowability of the future that one's actions will precipitate, precisely because of the presence of other people making other choices in the world, serves to subvert the reader's expectations of a happy ending. In a world of chance such a thing cannot be presumed, let alone demanded, which may well be the point McCarthy is making: Why do we expect the happy ending of our preconceived retributive justice?

There may be echoes of Shakespeare's *King Lear* here:[152] Sheriff Bell is like King Lear, both being like readers who in their old age know only one type of story in which there is an assumed happy ending. Both encounter younger characters—Chigurh and Edmund, respectively—who live beyond the constraints of moral convention and who know, and can instigate, a darkly different story. Thus McCarthy (as Shakespeare did before him) challenges the reader who, like Bell, is wont to assume the inevitability of retributive justice:

> We expect a final showdown between heroes and villains, between strong and weak. Instead, we get untidy conclusions, in which heroes and villains die, always without glory and regard-

> less of whether or not we feel the fate fits. Almost no character in either work can be said to get what he or she deserves.[153]

Evidence of this includes the redheaded hitchhiker whose encounter with Moss seals her untimely fate; the dead crone found by Wells whose death was a result of the gunfight between Moss, Chigurh, and the cartel; and the car crash in which Chigurh is involved.[154]

This last incident is crucial to understanding the book. It shows that Wells had misunderstood Chigurh when he castigated him for thinking that he was "outside of everything."[155] The irony of the car crash's randomness befalling the bringer of random violence should not be overlooked, but it was not wholly random, as the quietly insistent philosophy of Chigurh (and the Border Trilogy) implies. Bell's subsequent enquiries reveal that the vehicle that crashed into Chigurh's car was driven by teenagers who had been taking drugs and had ignored traffic signals.[156] Thus, although unexpected to Chigurh and not initiated by his own past actions, it was not entirely inexplicable. Moreover, if Chigurh had left Carla Jean's house some moments earlier or later he would have avoided it. Even though Chigurh is emblematic of a chaotic principle in the world, he must, if he is right in thinking that the world acts on principles set into motion by the choices—and the consequences of those choices—of all in the world, himself be subject to those selfsame determining principles that he espouses when gazing through the dying eyes of his victims into their very souls, watching their life ebb away.

As already noted, there is an otherness to Chigurh that recalls the Joban descriptions of Behemoth and Leviathan. Like Leviathan, Chigurh is proud (Job 41:34), looking down on others and treating them with a contemptuous disdain. Like Behemoth, he is uncatchable (Job 40:24), as his wraithlike vanishing from the book after the car crash demonstrates. Bell's opening monologue, taking place after the book's events have transpired, states that "somewhere out there is a true and living prophet of destruction and I dont want to confront him. I know he's real. I have seen his work. I walked in front of those eyes once."[157] Leviathan-like, when threatened and cornered, such as in the motel room by Moss, Chigurh does not plead with his captor (cf. Job 41:3): "The man didnt even look at him. He seemed oddly untroubled. As if this were all part of his day."[158] As Moss discovers soon after this episode, "any hope of capturing it [him] will be disappointed" (Job 41:9), for Chigurh, although wounded, maintains his relentless pursuit of Moss, summarily executing any who stand in his way.[159] It is as if no weapon can halt him (Job 41:26-29), a sentiment shared by the man who hires Wells to hunt Chigurh down.[160]

RETURN TO UZ

Anton Chigurh, Judge Holden in *Blood Meridian*, and the grim triune in *Outer Dark* are representative of a troubling and confusing chaotic presence in the world, the origins of which are unknown, but whose presence must be reckoned with. In writing these characters in this Joban-inflected manner, McCarthy conveys a sense of their lurking danger and unpredictability, thereby enabling the reader to apprehend the possibility of such a presence within her own world. McCarthy is uninterested in the etiological quest to rationally explain their presence, bypassing any account of the origins of these agents of chaos. Moreover, by leaving their fate unresolved he shows a corresponding disinterest in their end. They are a given that must be reckoned with, an inevitable aspect of McCarthy's fictional creations.

This is helpful when coming back to the book of Job. It is too easy for the reader to be co-opted into a certain way of thinking about the world by the insistent logic of Job's rhetoric—and we tend to side with Job because we "know" that the comforters are chastised at the book's end, and we do not wish to align ourselves with them—that God must be brought to task for his misgovernance of the world. However, God is uninterested in attending to Job's complaints of mistreatment and injustice. The poetic paeans to Behemoth and Leviathan imply that God's mode of governance cannot be judged by human assumptions concerning justice. God subtly shifts the ground beneath Job's feet, ignoring his questions about justice and directing him to consider these creatures instead.[161] Crucially, *how* God said this to Job is as important as *what* he said: rather than merely stating it in a banally didactic retort, God implied it lyrically through his extravagant meditation on Behemoth and Leviathan. Their crowning climax to the divine speeches show that God's delight in creatures such as these, whose repulsiveness to humans is descriptively evident, subverts the arrogant anthropocentrism that molds human thinking. Creation is a miracle that cannot be fully comprehended within its natural and moral spheres, yet God invites Job—and the reader—to delight in it regardless, apprehending its thrilling wonder.[162] Within the book the divine speeches—by demonstrating how these frightening creatures have a role within God's creation, however incomprehensible to humanity—show that God's justice is not served by the extermination of all that humans perceive to be unjust.[163]

If creation is not solely to serve humanity and if everything within it is not ordered to suit humanity, then God must be free to populate his creation with whatever creatures God sees fit, regardless of human preconceptions. Read this way, chapters 40–41 constitute a divine admission that chaos exists in the world, although under God's control. Like Annie Dillard at Tinker Creek, Job is gifted a proper appreciation of creation through the divine speeches, and as for Dillard paradox was central to that appreciation, so too for Job there is the mystery of Behemoth and Leviathan's seemingly invasive otherness being permitted and endorsed by God.[164] If Behemoth, "the first of the great acts of God" (40:19), is under God's control, then how much more all subsequent creation, however dangerous and threatening it may appear? It is important for Job—and subsequent generations—to realize that God *can* control chaos, as his corralling of the Sea demonstrates, but that God might not do so in a way that corresponds to human expectation and is solely for human benefit. That which appears to humans as chaotic, troubling, and transgressing in God's good creation is nevertheless a part of creation and not inimical to God. Therefore nobody should imagine himself immune from it: "You've got to bear it in mind that nobody that ever lived is specially privileged; the axe can fall at any moment, on any neck, without any warning or any regard for justice."[165] The good world God made is one in which both positive and negative possibilities, anthropocentrically speaking, are built into it. These possibilities are not rampant and unleashed but, like the Sea, controlled and restrained. The chaos embodied by Behemoth and Leviathan is a chaos that does not need to be defeated or conquered by God but is celebrated by him.

Job sought to create a world of value and meaning that would explicate his own experience, but such a quest is ultimately fruitless because of the necessary presence of chaos at the boundaries of life. Chapter 28 adumbrates this liminal focus by stating that wisdom is perceived in God's act of corralling and ordering those created phenomena that appear wild and formless:

> God understands the way to it,
> and he knows its place.
> For he looks to the ends of the earth,
> and sees everything under the heavens.
> When he gave to the wind its weight,
> and apportioned out the waters by measure;
> when he made a decree for the rain,
> and a way for the thunderbolt;
> then he saw it and declared it;
> he established it, and searched it out. (Job 28:23-27)

The dominant mythological backdrop to the divine speeches is not the *Chaoskampf* battle, but the less common tradition that creation involved the setting of boundaries for the sea (Ps 104:5-9; Prov 8:29; Jer 5:22).[166] God is the king of creation, and God is therefore free to graciously bestow existence and a place in creation to whatever God wishes, whether human, Leviathan, or the Sea. This gift of a place in creation also includes the gift of freedom to choose how to behave within creation, which necessarily entails the possibility of great harm. However, God the king is also God the judge who sees all, attends to all, and will judge all, and the free place in creation given to any entity is not without limit or boundary: God places constraints on all, whether human, Leviathan, or the Sea.[167] Nothing—and nobody—exists beyond God's encompassing sovereignty.[168]

Through the divine speeches Job apprehends the legitimacy of Behemoth's and Leviathan's presence in God's creation, which is exemplified by his repentance in 42:6.[169] This "repentance," or "change of course," is not of a specific transgression but of a wrong way of comprehending the world.[170] Job had erred in assuming that Behemoth and Leviathan were trespassing in creation and that his encounter with them indicated poor governance on the part of God. The divine speeches enabled him to realize that such entities need not be feared, for they are safely constrained by God's providential sovereignty. Moreover, Job apprehends that a fearful life that seeks to avoid encountering them is not viable. This is not a pessimistic fatalism, however, for Job returns to life changed by all he has experienced, seen, and heard of God's delight in freedom. God is free, God owes Job nothing, and all that Job has comes through the grace of God, and all that Job has is maintained by the grace of God. Within that grace there is extravagance, and Job displays a commensurate extravagance in his epilogic life.

The divine speeches are a legitimate theological response to Job's complaint. Although the book of Job does not expand on the initial differentiation between the natural and moral causes of Job's sufferings (the fire from heaven and the great wind, and the Sabean and Chaldean raiders), the presentation of Behemoth and Leviathan can be read as the divine acknowledgment of the existence in creation of both created unpredictability (Behemoth) and the consequences of human sinfulness (Leviathan). This is all the explanation that Job gets, and, although less than he wanted, it is all that he needs.[171] While not an explanation of chaos' presence, it is an admission of it. However, the metaphorical suggestiveness of the presentation of Behemoth and Leviathan means that both are understood as being under the providential sovereignty of God and thereby restrained in their capacity to incite fear and terror in Job.

This reality is what Job has to live both with and in, under God's *mišpāṭ* (מִשְׁפָּט) of order, boundary, freedom, and judgment. The world is not safe, but it is ordered. God presents Behemoth and Leviathan to Job in order to teach him that there is a chaotic otherness within creation, the presence of which he must acknowledge. This chaos is under God's control, but the mechanism of this control remains unexplained. Such a view requires Job (and the reader) to accept that God does not order his creation purposes around his—or anyone's—personal comfort or whim, and so a less anthropocentric viewpoint will inevitably emerge. Moreover, to teach Job about creation is also, implicitly, to teach him about God, for new insights into how creation is run will entail a new apprehension of God's majestic sovereignty in ordering and governing creation.

CONCLUDING REFLECTIONS

McCarthy's literary worlds are beautifully and powerfully realized evocations of a Joban creation in which there is a seemingly rampant chaos that—from the human perspective—has neither purpose nor pattern. It cannot even be said that the grim triune, Judge Holden, and Anton Chigurh *always* bring about harm to the human subjects that encounter them, for there are times when they show indifference, or even tender care. But their presence is a given in his literary landscapes. These chaotic characterizations are imaginative portrayals of Behemoth and Leviathan in Tennessee, the Southwestern Mexican borderlands, and West Texas much as C. S. Lewis' *That Hideous Strength* is an imaginative interpretation of the Christian final end of the ages in a quiet English university town. McCarthy's repeated insistence on the givenness of this dangerous and unpredictable chaos asks the reader to consider her assumptions regarding the nature of the world in which she lives, and whether such chaos is indeed a given presence. Importantly, Behemoth and Leviathan are not trespassing into God's good creation, just as the triune, Holden, and Chigurh are not "foreign" to their fictional worlds.[172] Behemoth and Leviathan exemplify the truth that "trouble comes" in but a moment and changes things forever, and the travails brought about by their chaotic unpredictability are a necessary consequence of the freedom with which God has endowed creation. Having been gifted this new epistemological outlook, Job can reenter the world with a new apprehension of its possibilities and a new outlook in relation to those possibilities: he needs neither to be paralyzed in inaction by fear of what might befall him nor to blindly continue as he was before his life was disturbed so inexplicably and unpredictably.

5
The Possibility of Hope

BETWEEN THE IDEALIZED AND THE REAL

> He was a man with no plans for going back the way he'd come nor telling any soul at all what he had seen.[1]

> "I shall go the way from which I shall not return." (Job 16:22)

In a world of unpredictable chaos, what place can there be for any kind of hope? In both McCarthy's novels and the book of Job there is indeed hope, but it is not a hope that life will be what it once was. Cornelius Suttree knows that to go back is not possible. No, for Suttree hope is found by progressing into whatever the future might bring, not by regressing to an idealized past. So too Job, although speaking about what he thinks will be his imminent death,[2] conflates hope with onward movement, even though the landscape into which he advances is unknown and, possibly, frightening. Such a view of "hope" is, admittedly, nebulous but, on the converse, to fail to move or to be brought to inaction by circumstance is to cede ultimacy to that circumstance. To hope—to move on—is to deny that circumstance has the last word and to insist on the possibility of change, even if there are no rational grounds for doing so. In McCarthy's books this change can be positive as well as negative, leading to a worse situation than beforehand. However, the possibility of moving into a worse situation is no argument against movement. To remain motionless and inert is the hopeless response, and to move is the response of hope. The destination is not what marks out the movement as hopeful; it is the act of moving itself.[3]

McCarthy's novels tend not to end with a return to the status quo that prevailed at the novel's start, or for its duration. His novels characteristically conclude with a character on the cusp of something new and different, looking forward: in *The Road* the boy is taken into the bosom of a welcoming family unit; in *No Country for Old Men* Sheriff Bell awakens from his dream into a new day of possibility, reassured by the oneiric presence of his father. "You go to sleep now. I'll see you in the morning,"[4] Billy in the Border Trilogy is told by Betty, whose gracious stabling of him enables Billy to acquire a peace that has brought respite from his previous troubles: tomorrow will dawn, and with it freshness and newness. In *Blood Meridian* the hole-digging man progresses across the plain, thereby allowing all who follow in his wake to move on; and in *Outer Dark* Rinthy's quest is over, having found the child for whom she had sought for so long, and—in contrast to the trapped Culla—she is able to start a new journey, with new possibilities.

This forward movement is also a motif in the book of Job. When Job reenters social life in the epilogue, he does not return to a life previously lived, but he steps forward into a new mode of existence. It is striking that the desert- and salt-flat-dwelling animals mentioned in chapter 39—the wild ass, the wild ox, the ostrich, and the horse—all share a tendency for forward movement without return (39:4-5, 8, 12, 14, 22). This echoes Job's desire for forward movement (10:21; 16:22; 23:8a), and contrasts with the comforters' encouragement of Job to go *back* by returning to God (22:23): "Job and the animals share in this bold exercise of freedom to go where the culturally conditioned cannot."[5] Thus the concern of the book of Job is not to return to how Job's life was, but to find a way *forward* through the turmoil brought upon him. The book abandons neither Job nor the reader in a salt marsh of hopelessness and fatalistic resignation to the pointless absurdities of chaotic oppression. Rather, it portrays Job's ultimately glad acceptance of life lived *despite* this chaos, refusing to be diminished or constrained by it, as enabling his ongoing life. This reflects McCarthy's declinature to abandon his readers on an ash heap of despair in the face of the world's unpredictability.

Without a robust grasp of the nature of this wondrous world—in all its chaotic complexity and latent possibilities—life can be terrifying. The individual becomes mired in the demand for vindication and justice that characterized the dialogic Job. Such an approach allows no movement: forward movement comes through recognizing that there is chaos—whether Behemoth and Leviathan or the cannibalistic road gangs, Anton Chigurh, Judge Holden, and the grim triune—that impinges on human existence and frequently goes unexplained; forward movement requires a refusal to be constrained by chaos' possibilities; forward movement rests on the faithful confession that in this chaotic freedom there is God above it, beyond it, and with us in it, and that therefore there is also hope.

THE ROAD

In *The Road* a father and son—the man and the boy—wander through a landscape ravaged by some unknown global catastrophe. It is a world in which fauna and flora are almost entirely absent, seemingly gone forever.[6] This is a world formless and void, perhaps indicating the potential of the hubristic overreach of humanity's sinful nature to uncreate.[7] McCarthy does not elucidate what caused this wasteland but the man recalls that

> The clocks stopped at 1:17. A long shear of light and then a series of low concussions. He got up and went to the window. What is it? she said. He didnt answer. He went into the bathroom and threw the lightswitch but the power was already gone. A dull glow rose in the window-glass.[8]

This implies some sort of nuclear winter, although it is unclear whether it was initiated by antagonistic conflict or industrial accident.[9] The barren landscape it generated, unillumined by sunlight, is a pastoral analogy to the unenlightened darkness of almost all whom the man and boy encounter. As they travel through this "cauterized terrain," with its "grainy air," and anachronistic agricultural remnants, "everything dead to the root," along with countless "mummied dead," with "flesh cloven along the bones, the ligaments dried to tug and taut as wires," scavenging food wherever they can find it, seeking any vestige of edibility, they seem to be the last living beings.[10] But no, others are abroad too:

> In the pantry were three jars of homecanned tomatoes. He blew the dust from the lids and studied them. Someone before him had not trusted them and in the end neither did he and he walked out with the blankets over his shoulder and they set off along the road again.[11]

These nameless others should not be attracted: "They squatted in the road and ate cold rice and cold beans that they'd cooked days ago. Already beginning to ferment. No place to make a fire that would not be seen."[12] The man fears the perpetrators of a violence the corpses of which he has seen frequently. McCarthy contrasts "those first years" in which

> the roads were peopled with refugees shrouded up in their clothing. Wearing masks and goggles, sitting in their rags by the side of the road like ruined aviators. Their barrows heaped with shoddy. Towing wagons or carts. Their eyes bright in their skulls. Creedless shells of men tottering down the causeways like migrants in a fever land,

with the inevitable predaciousness of human on human: "Within a year there were fires on the ridges and deranged chanting. The screams of the murdered. By day the dead impaled on spikes along the road."[13]

The nature of this threat is clarified in a portentous flashback in which the boy's mother tells the man: "Sooner or later they will catch us and they will kill us. They will rape me. They'll rape him. They are going to rape us and kill us and eat us and you wont face it. Youd rather wait for it to happen. But I cant. I cant."[14] So certain is she of this end that she kills herself.[15] This world of inhuman cannibalistic threat and utter depersonalization is all the boy knows. Unborn when the catastrophe struck, he is incognizant of dams, Coca-Cola, state roads, his own father's pre-paternal life, and the sounds of diesel trains.[16] Inevitably the man and boy encounter the violence-wielding road gangs: "They came shuffling though the ash casting their hooded heads from side to side. Some of them wearing canister masks. One in a biohazard suit. Stained and filthy. Slouching along with clubs in their hands, lengths of pipe."[17] A struggle ensues and the man kills one of the vulturous gang, who is then dismembered and eaten by his fellows.[18]

As they wander deeper through this "blackened jackstraw land," their hope ebbs away, and the father, whose awareness that the boy's survival depends on his own to the extent that he repeatedly contemplates his capacity for filicide, instructs the boy in blowing his own brains out.[19] They grow incautious, investigating a house the basement of which is a living human larder and almost becoming ensnared themselves.[20] They wander through deserted and desolate towns, increasingly resembling the minacious cannibals they seek to evade: "They came upon themselves in a mirror and he almost raised the pistol. It's us, Papa, the boy whispered. It's us."[21] Despite the father's assurances to the boy that there are "other good guys," their presence is undetectable and the people they encounter seem to be foreboding or devious, drawing out of the man a hardness that, in seeking to protect the boy, only erases the distinction in the boy's mind about what separates the good guys, who help people, and the bad guys, who do not.[22] The man becomes terrified of encountering anyone, fearful of what might ensue, and such caution is well-learned, for the unpredictability of daily life in this "ashen scabland"[23] is consistently threatened by sudden violence:

> As they passed the last of the sad wooden buildings something whistled past his head and clattered off the street and broke up against the wall of the block building on the other side. He grabbed the boy and fell on top of him and grabbed the cart to pull it to them. It tipped and fell over spilling the tarp and blankets into the street. In an upper window of the house he could see a man drawing a bow on them and he pushed the boy's head down and tried to cover him with his body. He heard the dull twang of the bowstring and felt a sharp hot pain in his leg.[24]

As the novel closes, the father becomes unable to guarantee his son's survival and dies, whereupon the boy meets and is taken in by a bearded veteran claiming to be a "good guy," along with his female companion.[25]

In *The Road* harmful chaos is not personified in a single agent, as in the other novels discussed above, but is something that has permeated the anthropology of virtually all whom the man and boy encounter, such that anyone could be the instigator of threat and violence toward them. Furthermore, in this novel the Behemothic chaos of created unpredictability is more prominent than in the others, although accompanied by a typically McCarthyite Leviathanic ferocity.

However, it should not be assumed that the chaos of McCarthy's fictional worlds is solely the bringer of calamity and peerless brutality. Of all his novels, it is *The Road* that insists on the statistical logic of chaos bringing boon as well as doom: the man and boy are curiously blessed with good "luck."[26] Despite the book's matchlessness in portraying the results that arise from the terrifying emptiness of the human heart, as paralleled in the emptiness of the world through which they pass, it contains irruptions of grace that are paralleled by the goodness of certain characters in the book. The optimistic potential of this nascent hopefulness has been discussed by various critics: to some it is there, but weak, as if McCarthy offered barely more than a flickering glimmer,[27] which hints that the text—reminiscent of *The Pilgrim's Progress* in its fictional and moral landscape—has a "weak metaphysical goodness."[28] Others proclaim the novel's hope more strongly,[29] seeing this particularly in its final pages.[30] As his most recent (to date) published novel, *The Road* may constitute the culmination of all McCarthy's work, which, retrospectively over McCarthy's entire oeuvre, declares the presence of God in a world tragically bereft of hope.[31] Conversely, there are those who insist on a pessimistic reading, reading the boy's encounter with the man and woman at the end as portentous, wondering whether the boy will be cared for or consumed by the travelers who welcome him so warmly.[32]

However, a pessimistic reading of the novel, and its ending, ignores the steady flow of gracious chaos that trickles through the book, culminating in this adoptive scene. The man and the boy's travels include plenty of inexplicable and unpredictable disturbances that are beneficial. Early on "in an old batboard smokehouse they found a ham gambreled up in a high corner. It looked like something fetched from a tomb, so dried and drawn. He cut into it with his knife. Deep red and salty meat inside. Rich and good,"[33] and later the father finds a can of Coca-Cola for the boy. The seemingly exanimate earth of an old woodland bespeaks the natural world's incessant fruitfulness as the man finds a cluster of morels. In an evacuated farmstead they find a sachet of grape powder, fresh water, and apples.[34] In a country house's yard the man unearths the opening to a subterranean bunker as full of fruitful goodness as the living larder was of fetid flesh: "Crate upon crate of canned goods. Tomatoes, peaches, beans, apricots. Canned hams. Corned beef. Hundreds of gallons of water in ten gallon plastic jerry jugs. Paper towels, toiletpaper, paper plates. Plastic trash bags stuffed with blankets."[35] This becomes a makeshift domestic base for them to launder their clothes, bathe, and barber themselves.[36] Further south they chance upon an antebellum mansion, with a kitchen containing "several dozen quart jars . . . Green beans. Slices of red pepper standing among the ordered rows. Tomatoes. Corn. New potatoes. Okra."[37] A beached boat is scavenged, and its contents prove useful almost immediately.[38] Thus when the reader arrives at the book's denouement she is as prepared for the hospitality of the veteran and the warmly enveloping maternity of his companion as she is for the man's inevitable succumbing to some phthisic illness.

This adoptive ending can be read humanistically, in which it is *human* community that is the only hope.[39] However, this is insufficiently precise, for the novel portrays two different kinds of community: the predatory community of the cannibalistic vagrants and butchering jailers, and the community of the man and the boy, who attempt to preserve the old-time ethics of the road: love of family and kindness to strangers.[40] Yet this latter community is itself wanting, for it is insular. The father cannot bring himself to extend hospitality in practice because he is fearful of what the stranger might represent.[41] While the boy wants to be a "good guy" unconditionally, by befriending and tangibly helping the people they meet, such as the lightning-struck vagabond, the little boy he thinks he sees in an abandoned house, Ely, and the thief, the fear-filled man wrestles with this.[42] He is so consumed with responsibility for preserving his son that his heart has no room for the other, whereas the boy is consumed with responsibility for doing the right thing, not just speaking about it. This is why the boy rebuts the father's claim that "you're not the one who has to worry about everything," by replying, "Yes I am . . . I am the one."[43] The only way that the man can ensure the boy's safety is by dying, thereby releasing him from the paternal grip and allowing the boy to find a community of true neighbor love.[44] It has been claimed that *The Road* upends the McCarthyite tendency for fathers to be conspicuous by their failure to instill in their children a decent social ethic, but this is incorrect.[45] In trying to protect the boy, the man constrains him and fails to truly educate him. Against this insular community of the man and boy is the truly for the other community of the veteran, the woman, and their children, all of whom encounter the boy at the end of the book. In their hospitable embrace of the boy they represent a true community, one based on and enlivened by risky interpersonal love and kindness.

The Road, like McCarthy's earlier works, portrays the world as a place in which there lurks considerable Leviathanic danger, an encounter with which may occur at any time and have unknown consequences. Although the references to this in *The Road* are not specifically Joban, this chaotic threat may be understood as being on the same continuum as that embodied in the grim triune, Judge Holden, and Anton Chigurh. However, *The Road* sounds a note of hope that accompanies the presence of true unpredictability: as it may bring danger, it may also bring blessing. This note is adumbrated by the repeated references in earlier novels, which will be discussed below. Such optimistic hopefulness thereby forbids a collapse under the portentous possibilities that we might assume are the only outcomes that chaos will bring (such was the mother's mistake).

The Road, with its irruptions of grace, enables the reader to apprehend that the chaos of creation is not something that necessarily and only entails tragedy. Although the novel makes repeated reference to the man and boy trudging through a sempiternal world of ash-caparisoned emptiness, the book moves us to focus not on the shadowy figures that lurk in the omni-swaddling ash but on the risky exuberance of living amid such etiolation.[46] In this way the book corresponds to the divine speeches in Job. These—and God's specific signaling of Behemoth and Leviathan to the despairing Job—are not designed to crush Job but to enable him to apprehend the world, in all its unpredictable wonder and with all its myriad possibilities, in a new way. Furthermore, Job's apprehension of this is possible only through the presentation of Behemoth and Leviathan to him. Thus they serve a didactic purpose that allows Job to see beyond the horror of what he has experienced and lead him to a fresh, hopeful understanding of humanity's place in creation.

Although *The Road* draws this gracious hopefulness to its fullest expression, it is present in McCarthy's other works (although expressed in different ways), where it goes frequently unrecognized due to critical focus on their violence and all which that is thought to suggest. One way in which this gracious hopefulness is expressed in *The Road* is through the man and boy's self-designation as "carrying the fire," which at the novel's close is explicitly linked to the notion of being "good guys."[47] Given the plausible suggestion that McCarthy's work comprises "one long variously fabled story," this explicit connection thus explicates a theme that has been running through much of his oeuvre, that of the "invocation of the age-old but nevertheless vital imagery of light and darkness," in which "images of fire, light or a candle flame continually suggest the possibility of goodness or hope set against the world's metaphysical darkness."[48]

NO COUNTRY FOR OLD MEN

Toward the end of *No Country for Old Men*, Sheriff Bell recounts a dream he had in which his father was "carryin fire in a horn the way people used to do."[49] This dream is the second of two important episodes in the book's closing pages that permit—perhaps even endorse—a hopeful reading of this stripped-down novel's apparently bleak investigation of kind deeds gone wrong in a world that depicts the insatiability of industrialized narco-economics and its consequent abnegation of human feeling.[50]

Anton Chigurh, whom the dogged Sheriff Bell has been methodically tracking throughout the bulk of the book, has proved elusive. Wraithlike, he has slipped through the aging Bell's forensic fingers.[51] What is the reader to make of this? Does it mean that Bell must resign himself to the implacability of Chigurh, as Job does to God? If so, the book has no hope in its ending, for unlike Job "the Sheriff's resignation . . . does not result in his restoration."[52] However, a reading of Job that emphasizes *restoration* misses the point, for Job in the epilogue is more than just a Job restored to his previous lifestyle. He is a Job who has apprehended something from the divine speeches that leads him to a new understanding of how to live in the world. An emphasis on the restoration element of the epilogue is overly simplistic and reductive, and it misses much else that the epilogue says. The restoration of Job is less important than the changed outlook that Job has on life and his place in it. Thus the question to be asked is what outlook Sheriff Bell ultimately has on the world.

At the end of the novel Sheriff Bell thinks himself vanquished:

> It was a cold blustery day when he walked out of the courthouse for the last time . . . He'd felt like this before but not in a long time and when he said that, then he knew what it was. It was defeat. It was being beaten. More bitter to him than death. You need to get over that, he said.[53]

But within this self-admonition there remains the possibility of transformation. The next three pages of the novel comprise the last of the thirteen italicized sections that candidly reveal Bell's inner thoughts. These italicized sections are undated, making their relation to the text problematic, but the first and last of these should be located after the book's main events have transpired, as Bell admits to Chigurh remaining uncaptured. Furthermore, the thirteenth such section records memories and thoughts that take place subsequent to the rest of the book. Two features of this section are of interest: first, Bell's consideration of an old stone trough and, second, the aforementioned dream he recounts.

The trough had caught Bell's attention once:

> I dont know how long it had been there. A hundred years. Two hundred. You could see the chisel marks in the stone. It was hewed out of solid rock and it was about six foot long and maybe a foot and a half wide and about that deep. Just chiseled out of the rock. And I got to thinkin about the man that done that. That country had not had a time of peace much of any length at all that I knew of. I've read a little of the history of it since and I aint sure it ever had one. But this man had set down with

> a hammer and chisel and carved out a stone water trough to last ten thousand years. Why was that? What was it that he had faith in? It wasnt that nothin would change. Which is what you might think I suppose. He had to know bettern that. I've thought about it a good deal. I thought about it after I left there with that house blown to pieces.[54]

The trough endures although the house to which it was adjoined is gone, and so it symbolizes to Bell the lasting good that can be wrought in the midst of that changeableness. Although change is the only constant, some things, such as the stone trough, do endure. The craftsman who shaped it knew that the world was a world of change, but that change and all it would inevitably bring in its wake did not gainsay his steady work. Thus there is merit in good work for its own sake, although it cannot prevent the encroaching change that must come. There is a hope of lasting worth for one's work: "And I have to say that the only thing I can think is that there was some sort of promise in his heart."[55]

Bell's simple hope that his career as a lawman might make the world a better place has been shaken by his involvement in the hunt for Chigurh, and the wake of mindless violence that Chigurh engineered. Bell realized that he could not "pull everybody back in the boat," or guarantee their safety, and so has lacked a sense of meaning: "I always thought I could at least someway put things right and I guess I just dont feel that way no more. I dont know what I do feel like."[56] But although he is unable to identify with the promise-full stonemason, he recognizes that his is a good attitude to have and that realization is the first step toward a new outlook on life: "And I dont have no intention of carvin a stone water trough. But I would like to be able to make that kind of promise. I think that's what I would like most of all."[57] Thus it appears that Bell is moving to a new vision.

McCarthy prefers entering his characters' consciousnesses through dreams rather than waking thoughts, which suggests that Bell's dreams must carry some meaning.[58] It has been argued that on an authorial level the dreams constitute "the passing of the Oedipal turn in McCarthy's works," meaning that McCarthy thinks his own voice can now be heard.[59] Certainly Bell's views in the italicized internal monologues, as well as his conversations and comments in the main body of the text, superficially bear a striking resemblance to those that McCarthy has himself espoused.[60] However, it should not be assumed that this famously reticent author has unmasked himself here, speaking through Bell, for "McCarthy has never previously appeared to use a character in isolation as his own mouthpiece," and the resemblance between Bell and McCarthy is considered sketchy at best.[61] It is unlikely that Bell's dreams, which are the last words of the novel, are only meaningful in authorial terms, if at all. Similarly unconvincing is the claim that they provide no more than grains of relief or constitute little more than a chimeric delusion of hope that is but an empty shell.[62] Rather, they are evidence of a continuing acceptance of his place in this world, despite its change and uncertainty.

Speaking about his father, Bell recounts:

> I had two dreams about him after he died. I dont remember the first one all that well but it was about meetin him in town somewheres and he give me some money and I think I lost it. But the second one it was like we was both back in older times and I was on horseback goin through the mountains of a night. Goin through this pass in the mountains. It was cold and there was snow on the ground and he rode past me and kept on goin. Never said nothin. He just rode on past and he had this blanket wrapped around him and he had his head down and when he rode past I seen he was carryin fire in a horn the way people used to do and I could see the horn from the light inside of it. About the color of the moon. And in the dream I knew that he was goin on ahead and that he was fixin to make a fire somewhere out there in all that dark and all that cold and I knew that whenever I got there he would be there. And then I woke up.[63]

An understanding of this dream must take into account the novel's rich description of Bell's relationship with both his grandfather and his father.[64] Bell's grandfather, Jack, is the person in whose footsteps Bell seeks to follow. Both were sheriffs at the same time, and Bell "never did mind bein like him."[65] Jack was the person Bell most admired and sought to emulate, and against whom he evaluated his own successes and perceived failures. Specifically, the cowardice that Bell thinks he showed in World War Two is something he cannot imagine Jack demonstrating. Therefore Jack is a better man than he, and nothing that Uncle Ellis tells him about Jack can make Bell change his mind.[66] Bell's father was not a lawman but a horse trader who died in middle age. In the eyes of the world, in Bell's eyes and, Bell presumes, in Jack's eyes he was someone in comparison with whom Bell came out well. He could be taciturn and impatient, and was neither profound nor articulate, yet he encouraged Bell to be content and at peace with himself, advice that the younger Bell did not heed. Nevertheless, Bell concludes that he "never broke nothin in me and I owe him more than I would of thought."[67] With this background in mind it is likely that the money Bell loses in the first dream refers to those simple paternal values that Bell "might of strayed from . . . as a younger man."[68] He is no better or worse than his father, as the second dream shows. In this dream Bell is alone and in darkness, symbolizing the defeat he felt on quitting his job. His being overtaken by his father, who is the illuminator of the dark and uncertain future, suggests that the simple truths his father instilled in him are what can still provide comfort and hope in a changing and uncertain world.

Thus the dreams and the meditation on the stone trough both emphasize hope, which is expressed as possibility. The former underlines a conviction that the changeability of the world need not lead to despair and a loosing of all moral moorings, for there remains the possibility of hope. The latter nudges Bell toward a place in which he can believe in the worth of his honest service to the law, despite the loose ends that remain in the uncatchable Chigurh. While these optimistic soundings are not realized as fully as they are in *The Road*—neither Bell nor Moss encounter irruptions of grace in the way that the father and the boy do—they are undeniably present in *No Country for Old Men*.

THE BORDER TRILOGY

There are several notes of hope in the Border Trilogy that combine to create a subtle yet harmonious chord that sounds quietly but steadily through its three novels. *Cities of the Plain* adumbrates the marital harmony that crescendos in *No Country for Old Men* by testifying to the conjugal good of marriage when an unnamed old man tells Billy that: "There aint been a day passed in sixty years I aint thanked God for that woman. I never done nothin to deserve her, I can tell you that. I dont know what you could do."[69] This is one of several passages that suggest an optimism about marital love and familial affection, indicating that this novel marks a subtle shift in McCarthy's oeuvre.[70] Furthermore John Grady Cole, described as the closest McCarthy comes to an ideal American man, repeatedly "defies the oncoming physical and metaphysical darkness by defending the vulnerable, wronged, and innocent," whether human or animal.[71] Although his moral code fails to engender the expected end, the Border Trilogy shows that there is worth, nobility even, in quietly doing one's best in the world.[72] In addition to these chimes of grace there are two further notes that sound more clearly the hopefulness inherent within the trilogy: the motif of sunrise, and the books' investigation into the possibility of meaningfulness in life.

In the Border Trilogy, sunrise suggests newness and freshness, thereby implying hopefulness. In *All the Pretty Horses* John Grady Cole watches "the new country as it shaped itself out of the darkness below them," and in response to a question from his companion Rawlins avers that sunrise is a consistent fixed certainty within the world until Judgment Day.[73] This response implies that sunrise is part of God's providential ordering and management of the world. Sunrise has an almost magical ability to transform the world into dazzling brilliance: it makes the desert shine, and in the Edenic setting of the Hacienda Señora de la Purísima Concepción—with its "species of fish not known elsewhere on earth and birds and lizards and other forms of life as well all long relict"[74]—Cole and Rawlins ride out in the early morning, delighting in the alchemical transmutation wrought by the sunrise:[75] "They'd ride out along the ciénaga road and along the verge of the marshes while the sun rose riding up flights of ducks out of the shallows or geese or mergansers that would beat away over the water scattering the haze and rising up would turn to birds of gold in a sun not yet visible from the bolsón floor."[76] Frequently in the book John Grady Cole is described as watching the sun rise, which suggests it is a source of hope and strength for the travails he will encounter.[77]

In *The Crossing*, this association between hopefulness and the growing dawn is made more explicit, both descriptively and in its striking repetition. Here, dawn is suggestive of an entirely fresh creation: "the sun ballooned like boiling glass up out of the plains of Chihuahua to make the world again from darkness."[78] This act of re-creation is no mere consequence of a heliocentric astronomy but suggests a metaphysical implication, as several characters attest. A blind man twice tells Billy that the world is daily made anew by God, something reiterated by a gypsy whom Billy encounters toward the end of the book.[79] These references to the world apply less to the physical tectonics and geological ingredients that comprise the planet's matter and more to the sense of existential meaning that McCarthy suggests is needed to navigate through life. It is in this way that the world is invisible to men, only knowable as existing in men's hearts, and therefrom narrated into existence.[80] By connecting this existential understanding of "world" to the sunrise and a daily act of divine re-creation, McCarthy locates existential meaning in the sphere of God's gracious bestowal of a continuing creation in which to live. This is reinforced at the book's end as Billy "woke in the white light of the desert noon," in which "small birds had wakened in the roadside desert bracken and begun to chitter and to flit about."[81] However, there is an unfittingness to this world, in which birds should only wake at dawn, and in which

> he looked again at the road which lay as before yet more dark and darkening still where it ran on to the east and where there was no sun and there was no dawn and when he looked again toward the north the light was draining away faster and that noon in which he'd woke was now become an alien dusk and now an alien dark and the birds that flew had lighted and all had hushed once again in the bracken by the road.[82]

Billy's wandering has brought him within range of the first nuclear test at Trinity site, and it is the artificial dawn of humanity's nuclear capability that had awoken him.[83] Nevertheless "after a while the right and godmade sun did rise, once again, for all and without distinction."[84] Thus this book must be read as ending on a note of hope for, despite the human potential for mass destruction and despite all that Billy has experienced and witnessed in his manifold crossings, the guarantee of dawn is a guarantee of hope for the world without and for Billy's world within.

The third book of the trilogy, *Cities of the Plain*, despite the absence of this sunrise-hope motif, concludes the entire trilogy on a note of profoundly meaningful hope by tying together two strands of investigation that have recurred throughout all three books: the disparity between the ideal and the real, and the possibility of meaning in life. The books discuss whether it is possible to realize one's ideal "dream" and explore whether ordered meaning is inherent to life or is narratively, and retrospectively, created. Moreover, they investigate who it is that can create this order.

Within the trilogy there is a recurrent theme of the difference between the dream of something and the reality of that same thing.[85] In *All the Pretty Horses* John Grady Cole recalls seeing a painting of horses "copied out of a book," yet "no such horse ever was that he had seen"—something confirmed by his grandfather, who dismisses them as "picturebook horses."[86] A similar idea lies behind Rawlins' comment that there are fewer cattle in Mexico than he had expected.[87] The Dueña Alfonsa, Alejandra's aunt, tells John Grady Cole that when she was young she thought "that the desire was the thing itself." However, that naive optimism evaporated in the heat of the revolutionary terrors she witnessed, and she reminds John Grady that "the world is quite ruthless in selecting between the dream and the reality, even where we will not. Between the wish and the thing the world lies waiting."[88] Thus the first novel of the trilogy suggests that the dream is not the reality, and cannot be.

This idea is revisited in *The Crossing*, particularly the first part, in which Billy's childhood encounter with a wolf has an almost epiphanic character that sets the course of his later life and about which he never speaks.[89] The legacy of this secret lupine encounter is the only plausible reason for Billy's snap decision to rehouse the wolf in Mexico rather than returning home with it to Cloverdale, as he told an old farmer he would.[90]

> An hour down the road he stopped for a long time. He was at Robertson's cross-fence. Ahead an hour's ride lay Cloverdale and the road north. South lay the open country. The yellow grass heeled under the blowing wind and sunlight was running over the country before the moving clouds. The horse shook its head and stamped and stood. Damn all of it, the boy said. Just damn all of it. He turned the horse and crossed through the ditch and rode up onto the broad plain that stretched away before him south toward the mountains of Mexico.[91]

Billy is driven by an idealistic impulse of returning the wild she-wolf to the trackless lands of her natural range. But inevitably the world lies waiting between the wish and the reality, and Billy ends up having to euthanatize the wolf to rescue her from the cruelty of a Mexican baiting pit: "He stepped over the parapet and walked toward the wolf and levered a shell into the chamber of the rifle and halted ten feet from her and raised the rifle to his shoulder and took aim at the bloodied head and fired."[92] In executing the wolf, he murders his own dream.

Cities of the Plain finally unites Billy and John Grady. In this book the pimp Eduardo gives Billy a veiled warning to pass on to John Grady:

> Men have in their minds a picture of how the world will be. How they will be in that world. The world may be many different ways for them but there is one world that will never be and that is the world they dream of. Do you believe that?[93]

Sure enough, John Grady has a mental fantasy of his future life with Magdalena, the prostitute that he dreams of manumitting from Eduardo and living with in the cabin he is renovating.[94] Inexorably, given the prevalence of this theme, the world—in the baleful person of the mincing Eduardo and his obsequious henchmen—once again intervenes to prevent his dream from becoming a reality:

> The girl to whom he'd sworn his love forever lay on the last table. She lay as the rushcutters had found her that morning in the shallows under the shore willows with the mist rising off the river. Her hair damp and matted. So black. Hung with strands of

> dead brown weed. Her face so pale. The severed throat gaping bloodlessly. Her good blue dress was twisted about on her body and her stockings were torn. She'd lost her shoes.[95]

Throughout the Border Trilogy there recurs the suggestion that the tragedy of human life is the attempt to realize the unrealizable dream. However, at the end of *Cities of the Plain*, in a passage that is uncharacteristically precisely punctuated (at least by McCarthy's usual standards of not bounding subordinate clauses clearly with commas), the drifter whom the wandering Billy meets tells him that

> the story of the world, which is all the world we know, does not exist outside the instruments of its execution. Nor can those instruments exist outside of their own history. And so on. This life of yours is not a picture of the world. It is the world itself and it is composed not of bone or dream or time but of worship. Nothing else can contain it.[96]

The world of human existence, which in *The Crossing* is narrated by its actors, constitutes the whole world of meaning and action for those same actors. There neither is nor can be any other world than that which is realized and encountered in this realization. It is not a picture that Billy has made of the world or a picture to which he must conform the "real" world. Therefore, for Billy "to accept the real, to accept life as it is and not the ideal one hopes it will be, is to love fate, to worship this life rather than some transcendent but imaginary one."[97] This idea is foreshadowed in the encounter that Billy has with the *ciego* and his wife. Having impressed on Billy the importance of realizing that men like Wirtz exist—although nobody can explain why[98]—the blind man describes how the blind cannot choose how they will encounter the world, for "everything was abruptly at hand."[99] In such an immediate world the temptation is to remain motionless for fear of harm, but that is not living. To cease to move is to have the world vanish, for its jarring collisions are inescapable if one is to live within it.[100] In the light of the *ciego*'s admission to his first "comforter" that he had always been blind,[101] this suggests that people who encounter cruelty or chaotic tragedy must not cede to it their momentum for life. The blind man's experience was that in his all-consuming blindness "there also was a ground and there one must begin."[102] His condition of blindness was not the last word on him, as the three "comforters" he met helped him to see. This is why he tells Billy that although one cannot clearly know why things befall people—although we might not see either God's goodness or the good God and although the cruelties of Wirtz and others like him appear to gainsay that goodness—we can, and must, listen.[103] It is through listening to others and hearing their stories that the realization comes that all is dust, even those experiences of utmost cruelty and horror. And through this realization comes the warning against "mistaking these things for the real," when they are not, for perhaps they are no more than "obstacles to be negotiated in the ultimate sightlessness of the world."[104] This is not a denial of the fact of painful and potent experiences, and the pain that they bring. It is, however, to suggest that there is hope to be found in the here and now, through attending to one's life as it is. The procrastination of hope until the world conforms to an ideal dream of it is inadequate to the task of enabling a person to find meaning in the present.

This connects with the second strand that is tied up by the epilogue, that of the quest to find meaning to one's life. The "dream" is to imagine that there is a plan, an order to life that one must follow, but the world's reality means that such a fantastic reverie is not the case. In *All the Pretty Horses* the Dueña Alfonsa states her uncertainty about the possibility of locating life's meaning and her belief that there is no fate-setting agent in life. In *The Crossing* Billy attempts to impose meaning onto what has happened to his brother Boyd by wanting to believe that the *corrido* that he repeatedly hears is about Boyd, when it is not. Billy must cease to look for meaning and accept the life he has and get on with living it. *Cities of the Plain* reinforces the ideas built in the previous two novels by its references to the inextricable "net" of life, which problematizes choice.[105] The drifter tells Billy that

> in the middle of my life . . . I drew the path of it upon a map and I studied it a long time. I tried to see the pattern that it made upon the earth because I thought that if I could see the pattern and identify the form of it then I would know better how to continue.[106]

But the map he drew was unclear and could provide no certain course for the future, for it could be read to mean many different things. Thus the trilogy appears to have brought the reader to a place of hopelessness, in which we are unable to choose our own way in life and are thus unable to find any meaning in the events of our lives. However, in the book's final pages the elderly Billy is taken in by a family and stabled in a guest room.[107] After a disturbing dream, Billy awakens to find Betty, the mother, sitting beside his bed. He tells her about Boyd:

> She patted his hand. Gnarled, ropescarred, speckled from the sun and the years of it. The ropy veins that bound them to his heart. There was map enough for men to read. There God's plenty of signs and wonders to make a landscape. To make a world.[108]

The map, which the drifter's account had suggested was unreadable to the protagonist, is readable nevertheless to others. Furthermore, the world of existential meaning can be derived from the carnal materiality of Billy's life. Thus the book suggests that we cannot map, weigh, or order our own lives; this falls to others.

Here McCarthy is close to Hannah Arendt's ideas about action in *The Human Condition*. Arendt argues that "in acting and speaking, men show who they are, reveal actively their unique personal identities."[109] However, the "who" revealed in this way is usually obscured from the actor himself. Arendtian ideas emerge throughout the trilogy, such as in McCarthy's suggestion that all human acts occur in "a vast and endless net" that limits human choice.[110] It is unlikely that McCarthy intends "acts" to mean any or every active human behavior. It is more plausible that he would agree with Arendt, for whom action is more than mere "doing" and speech is more than mere "talking," that "acts" are actions that both achieve and communicate something.[111] Arendt suggests that all speech and action takes place against the backdrop of a web of interpersonal relationships that are inextricable from human community.[112] This "web" is the subjective, intangible disclosure of the subject to the "common interest" objective reality that does not merely conjoin people with one another but veritably binds them together.[113] The new thing initiated by speech and action against this web "eventually emerges as the unique life story of the newcomer, affecting uniquely the life stories of all those with whom he comes into contact." Thus our actions and our speech construct our identity in this web. Arendt continues: "It is because of this already existing web of human relationships, with its innumerable, conflicting wills and intentions, that action almost never achieves its purpose," an idea echoed in the Border Trilogy.[114] Billy is asked by a *ganadero* (ranch hand), "Where is the remedy that has no unforeseen consequence?" The *ganadero* continues: "You do not know what things you set in motion . . . No man can know. No prophet foresee. The consequences of an act are quite often different from what one would guess."[115] This recalls Arendt's idea that the consequences of an act cannot be circumscribed because each act occurs within this web, or net, such that every action generates further actions, and causes further activating interactions, and so on through the interconnecting web like ripples on a vast pond.[116]

However, while this web or net suggests an unknowable and unpredictable future, it also enables the story of a life to be told. This life story is not narrated by the story's subject, for he is not the author of his life because he does not make it by deliberate and careful choice. He cannot, for he lives within this web of choices and possibilities, and the story of his life journey within it is recognized by others, not by himself: "In other words, the stories, the results of action and speech, reveal an agent, but this agent is not an author or producer."[117] Billy's life story cannot reveal an author who has constructed Billy's life, but it can reveal Billy as the hero of it, and thereby is Billy's "who-ness" revealed, albeit to others and not to himself.

In the tender and touching scene between Billy and Betty, McCarthy fictionalizes the Arendtian idea that "the character and content of the . . . story . . . can reveal itself only when it has ended."[118] The "map enough" of Billy's hands may be insufficient for him to read, but it is sufficient for Betty, for although Billy is the subject of his life, Betty "reads" his life in such a way as to generate genuine meaning from it. Thus the Border Trilogy ends on a grace-filled note of hope, and this hope is to do with place as well as possibility. Billy, perennially at risk of being alone,[119] has found a family. He is not alone, and it is because he is not alone in the world that his life can be found meaningful. Betty can see Billy as he cannot see himself, and she can present to Billy who he really is. This enables Billy to come to a sense of himself that would have been impossible had he continued to withdraw from the vulnerabilities of human community. Betty's gracious and loving gentleness is necessary for Billy to find the peace that had eluded him for so long: "The other sees the patterned picture we cannot see ourselves, because it is legible only to others and so our only hope is that it will be pictured back to us as promise or as pardon."[120]

BLOOD MERIDIAN

It is conventional to read both *No Country for Old Men* and *Blood Meridian* as more or less devoid of hope.[121] As the former contains more than a mere murmur of hope, so too does the latter. Although this blood-soaked masterpiece's narrative is propelled by the figure of Judge Holden, whose presence permeates the book from its opening to its closing chapter, he is notably absent from the book's epilogue, which is narrated in a style that separates its mere five sentences from the rest of the text. Thus it may be read as a counterpoint to all that the judge has proclaimed throughout the book. In its entirety it reads:

> In the dawn there is a man progressing over the plain by means of holes which he is making in the ground. He uses an implement with two handles and he chucks it into the hole and he enkindles the stone in the hole with his steel hole by hole striking the fire out of the rock which God has put there. On the plain behind him are the wanderers in search of bones and those who do not search and they move haltingly in the light like mechanisms whose movements are monitored with escapement and pallet so that they appear restrained by a prudence or reflectiveness which has no inner reality and they cross in their progress one by one that track of holes that runs to the rim of the visible ground and which seems less the pursuit of some continuance than the verification of a principle, a validation of sequence and causality as if each round and perfect hole owed its existence to the one before it there on that prairie upon which are the

> bones and the gatherers of bones and those who do not gather. He strikes fire in the hole and draws out his steel. Then they all move on again.[122]

This is certainly an opaque passage, particularly given the syntactical shift from the plainly descriptive first two sentences to the long central sentence's ambiguity, suggested by the phrases "they appear" and "which seems," as well as its use of complexifying similes, which do not refer to a clearly demarcated subordinate clause. Nevertheless, the epilogue is meaningful, as other critics have suggested,[123] and it is quietly hopeful.

It is important that the novel, whose full title is *Blood Meridian, or, The Evening Redness in the West*, begins its epilogue not with the titular crepuscular twilight, but with a dawn. As in the Border Trilogy, this suggests the hopeful promise of a new day. Whereas *The Crossing*'s ending suggests that the inhumanity of humans, implied by the nuclear test, is relativized and subverted by the rising of the "right and godmade sun," so too here the inhumanity of humans, ably and memorably depicted throughout the blood-spattered novel, is subverted and relativized by the epilogic dawn that promises hope and a new start. This hopefulness is further suggested by the title's intertextual allusion to *Moby Dick*. In chapter 96 ("The Try-Works"), the narrating Ishmael connects redness to the "artificial fire" that "makes all things look ghastly." However, there is hope in the coming morrow, when "in the natural sun, the skies will be bright."[124] The redness that comprises *Blood Meridian*'s sanguinary violence is like the artificial fire of Melville's Try-Works that casts a portentous pall over the world: although superficially terrifying, it is artificial and not indicative of the true nature of life. Thus *Blood Meridian*'s epilogue begins on an almost imperceptible note of hope, which is suggested by the novel's very title.

Furthermore, this hopeful note is gently amplified as the epilogue continues. The epilogue is constructed chiastically, thereby locating the central idea as the most important one. This is true of the epilogue as a whole, and the central third sentence itself, as illustrated in the scheme following:

A (first sentence): In the dawn there is a man progressing over the plain by means of holes which he is making in the ground.

B (second sentence): He uses an implement with two handles and he chucks it into the hole and he enkindles the stone in the hole with his steel hole by hole striking the fire out of the rock which God has put there.

C (third sentence)

C 1: On the plain behind him are the wanderers in search of bones and those who do not search

C 2: and they move haltingly in the light like mechanisms

C 3: whose movements are monitored with escapement and pallet

C 4: so that they appear restrained by a prudence or reflectiveness which has no inner reality

C 5: and they cross in their progress one by one that track of holes that runs to the rim of the visible ground

C 4': and which seems less the pursuit of some continuance than the verification of a principle,

C 3': a validation of sequence and causality

C 2': as if each round and perfect hole owed its existence to the one before it there

C 1': on that prairie upon which are the bones and the gatherers of bones and those who do not gather.

B' (fourth sentence): He strikes fire in the hole and draws out his steel.

A' (fifth sentence): Then they all move on again.

The first and fifth sentences (A and A') are parallel, for both contain movement. The second and fourth sentences (B and B') both concern the hole-maker's ignition of the rock, although the second sentence's content is abbreviated in the fourth. The third sentence (C) has no parallel, and is thus highlighted as the key sentence. Within that central sentence there is yet a further chiasm: C1 and C1' both mention those who search for bones and those who do not, and the location in which they exist ("the plain" and "that prairie"); C2 and C2' both contain comparatives ("like" and "as if"); C3 and C3' contain a suggestion of mechanistic determinism; C4 and C4' introduce the already mentioned hesitancy by using suggestive verbs ("they appear," "which seems") that muddy the descriptive waters. This leaves C5 as the syntactic element with no parallel; thus, we identify it as being the interpretative key for the third sentence and the entire epilogue: the steady traverse of the postholes by the wanderers. This is reinforced by McCarthy's use of the word "cross," which indicates both this chiastic structure and the place in this long sentence when the focus shifts—or crosses over—from the wanderers to the postholes.[125]

The importance of forward movement is reinforced by McCarthy's deliberate obfuscation of the text through the use of similes and suggestive verbs. The wanderers move *like* mechanisms, but it is unclear if their movement is indeed solely mechanical. They *appear* restrained by an unreal caution but are not explicitly said to be so restrained. What is plain is that "they cross in their progress one by one that track of holes that runs to the rim of the visible ground." The track of postholes *seems* to be predetermined and necessary *as if* each hole had required the existence of the one following, but this is not necessarily so. Therefore, the only unambiguous part of the sentence is the central portion, describing the plainsmen's *steady movement toward the horizon*. As the structural center of the chiasm, and therefore the key part for discerning meaning, it suggests that *forward movement* is the key idea in the epilogue.

This movement is associated with fire in the first, second, fourth, and fifth sentences: it is the kindling of the fire that permits the passage of the following wanderers. As already mentioned, the motif of "carrying the fire" is important in both *No Country for Old Men* and *The Road*, but within *Blood Meridian* the mention of the man striking fire out of the rock alludes back to the judge's comments to the kid in the Fort Griffin bar:

> A man seeks his own destiny and no other, said the judge. Will or nill. Any man who could discover his own fate and elect

> therefore some opposite course could only come at last to that selfsame reckoning at the same appointed time, for each man's destiny is as large as the world he inhabits and contains within it all opposites as well. This desert upon which so many have been broken is vast and calls for largeness of heart but it is also ultimately empty. It is hard, it is barren. Its very nature is stone.[126]

The judge declares that the desert is hard and rocky, devoid of life. But the desert of which he speaks is not the cauterized terrain of the American Southwest that he and the kid have been traversing. Rather it is the desert of autonomy and freedom of choice that comprises the deterministic world the judge preaches. This is the hard, stony truth that is so unshakable as to break all those who will not receive it.[127] The judge asserts the emptiness and meaninglessness of seeking one's own destiny in a deterministic life, which is a tacit argument for his embrace of savagery. However, in the epilogue the progressing man strikes fire—something illuminating and warming—from the rock, which refers to the hardness of this life. In a helpful article Jordan Carson argues that the novel constantly associates the kid with fire, symbolizing moral autonomy, whereas Holden embodies text and the quest for textual supremacy.[128] The kid's resistance to Holden's allure therefore "upholds moral autonomy as a foundation for constructing a meaningful personal narrative."[129] Carson argues that this kid-fire connection is relevant to the epilogue, in which the man is engaged in the preliminary stages of fence building by which means *all* the travelers may move on. Thus he too sees the importance of the kindling of the fire with permitting the ongoing passage of the wanderers.

Fire does indeed seem to stand for moral autonomy, but whereas the judge in Fort Griffin declared a determinism that was inescapable, the epilogue portrays a counter to this view by finding fire—moral autonomy—within the very stoniness of the constraints of life itself. This stony life, which appears inescapably fatalist, is the raw material from which God intends the human exercise of moral autonomy. This divine connection is suggested because it is a fire that "God has put there," which benefits others. This neighborly concern, which may seem out of place, is adumbrated earlier in the novel, when the judge tells the story of a man who is told by a traveler that "he was a loss to God and man alike and would remain so until he took his brother into his heart as he would take himself in and he come upon his own person in want in some desert place in the world."[130] An individual is of no use to his brother or neighbor unless he welcomes the other into his heart. Furthermore, unless he does so that individual is of no use to God. Thus the kindling of fire *in order that others may progress* connects to this neighborly openheartedness. So fire stands for the moral autonomy that enables us to constrain our lives as we wish, demarcating and bounding some areas and not others, and to construct our own narratives of what is meaningful and therefore worth our pursuit of it.[131] Therefore, the motifs of movement and fire that frame the central portion of the chiastic epilogue are also harmonics of hope—a hope that one's own life might benefit others—that suggest an optimistic departure from the novel.

OUTER DARK

Of all the books discussed so far this might seem to be the hardest in which to find hope. At the novel's end Rinthy wanders into a glade of "dust and ashes," containing the incinerated remains of the tinker's trade as well as the costal charrings that were once her child.[132] Her journey appears to stop there, but Culla's is incessant for "in later years he used to meet a blind man, ragged and serene," and in Culla's final appearance in the book he converses with this blind man before continuing along a road that leads to a swamp. Culla retraces his steps, passing again the blind man, who is steadily shuffling toward this mire. Culla does not warn him but reflects that "someone should tell a blind man before setting him out that way."[133]

Nevertheless, there is some small measure of hope in the book.[134] It is notable that both Rinthy and Culla's final scenes are in ashen lands. In these ash lands Rinthy moves "in a frail agony of grace," but Culla is "shambling, gracelorn."[135] Thus there is a subtle distinction between them: although they are both, Job-like, among dust and ashes, their futures are as different as the past paths that led them to these places. It is simply not the case that the novel holds out neither guidance nor hope for either Culla or Rinthy.[136] There may not be guidance but there is hope, at least for Rinthy.

Rinthy's journey has been one of seeking an ending, and in the glade she finds peace because she has found the site of her dead child, the very thing she set out to locate and wreathe with flowers before discovering that Culla had tricked her into thinking him dead. She has found her child "and so her journey ends with a sign of communion, our 'little sister' here 'cradled in a grail.'"[137] Rinthy has arrived and found "closure," in modern parlance, and in her arrival is the possibility of subsequent movement into the new, and this is the hope that the novel suggests is hers.[138] By contrast, Culla's journey is one of flight, seeking an evasion, not an ending.[139] The only peace possible for him is to admit that which he seeks to escape: a confession of his complicity. There will be no peace for Culla until he owns the responsibility he seeks to evade and names the sins he has committed.[140]

In addition, for two reasons it seems unlikely that there is any hope of redemption for Culla.[141] First, McCarthy begins the final chapter by stating that "in later years he [Culla] *used* to meet a blind man."[142] The choice of "used to meet" rather than "met" suggests that Culla is trapped in a circular life so that he repeatedly meets this blind man. Second, there is a connection between the novel's closing scene and its opening, unitalicized one, in which Culla is awoken from a dream:

> There was a prophet standing in a square with arms upheld in exhortation to the beggared multitude gathered there. A delegation of human ruin who attended him with blind eyes upturned and puckered stumps and leprous sores. The sun hung on the cusp of eclipse and the prophet spoke to them. This hour the sun would darken and all these souls would be cured of their afflictions before it appeared again. And the dreamer himself was caught up among the supplicants and when they had been blessed and the sun begun to blacken he did push forward and hold up his hand and call out. Me, he cried. Can I be cured? The prophet looked down as if surprised to see him there amidst such pariahs. The sun paused. He said: Yes, I think perhaps you will be cured. Then the sun buckled and dark fell like a shout. The last wirethin rim was crept away. They waited. Nothing moved. They waited a long time and it grew chill. Above them hung the stars of another season. There began a restlessness and

> a muttering. The sun did not return. It grew cold and more black and silent and some began to cry out and some despaired but the sun did not return. Now the dreamer grew fearful. Voices were being raised against him. He was caught up in the crowd and the stink of their rags filled his nostrils. They grew seething and more mutinous and he tried to hide among them but they knew him even in that pit of hopeless dark and fell upon him with howls of outrage.[143]

At the novel's end the blind man tells Culla:

> I heard a preacher in a town one time, he said. A healin preacher wanted to cure everbody and they took me up there. They was a bunch of us there all cripple folks and one old man they did claim had thowed down his crutches and they told it he could make the blind see. And they was a feller leapt up and hollered out that nobody knowed what was wrong with. And they said it caused that preacher to go away. But they's darksome ways afoot in this world and it may be he weren't no true preacher.[144]

It is uncontroversial to assert that the blind man's account is a second telling of Culla's dream.[145] Thus Culla's passage through the novel ends with a return to his beginning in it. It is Culla's journey that is cyclic, as evidenced by the word "used" to refer to the meeting with the blind man:[146] in his beginning is his end, and the end of all his exploring is to arrive again where he started, albeit *not* seeing it afresh.[147] Culla is caught in an inescapable cycle that is signaled by the opening dream, which is steadily realized as the novel progresses.

In the dream, the dreamer—that is, Culla—is "caught up among the supplicants," something that the text underscores as he runs from Rinthy "bearing his clenched hands above him threatful, supplicant, to the mute and windy heavens."[148] McCarthy's choice of the word "supplicant" suggests a deliberate reference back to the dream. The dream's fulfillment is also signaled by the outraged hog drovers whose attempts to lynch him Culla only narrowly avoids, recalling the "restlessness and muttering" that the oneiric crowd vocalizes before harrying the dreamer.[149] Finally, Culla's unredeemable nature is disclosed by the dream prophet who affirms Culla's potential for cure. This prophet is false, for his prophecy of the crowd's healing during the tenebrous eclipse is unfulfilled. Therefore, his claim that Culla may be cured is likewise false, and Culla is consigned to a hopeless "gracelorn" end.

Outer Dark does end with the possibility of hope—of closure and therefore the potential opening of something new—but this possibility is not extended to all the main characters in the book. The tinker's hanged body turns in the breeze; the grim triune are absent (like Chigurh, and like the judge); Culla's perennial evasion of responsibility ensures his ongoing unredeemability; but Rinthy finds peace.

HOPE IN JOB?

Endings are important aspects of literary works, and McCarthy's novelistic endings routinely contrast with much of what has preceded them, and leave the reader with a sense of hope and possibility for the future. It is this forward-looking hopeful note, not the cacophony of the chaos that precedes it in his novels, that the reader takes away from the books.

The book of Job likewise ends with a forelooking, but it is easy for readers of this strange text to either skip over the epilogue completely, or skim-read it such that careful attention is not paid either to what it does or what it does not say. When this happens, the overriding impressions that one receives from the book constellate around frustration, confusion, despair, and injustice. Chaos indeed appears to have the last word as Job is paid off by God at the last to shut him up. But if the book is read to the end, then—like McCarthy's novels too—chaos is seen not to be ultimate. For all that the presentation of Behemoth and Leviathan to Job in the divine speeches is a climactic event that helps the reader in her reading and interpretation of the book, the book of Job does not end with this consideration of terrifying and dangerous zoological power. In Job 42:7-17 there is a return to the prose style of the first two chapters, but this stylistic return is not indicative of a narratival backward step, as if Job "steps back into the world of the prologue to the book, the world of naïve folk-tale.'"[150] This would be a retrograde step, going *back* to collect the broken pieces of his former life in order to pick up where he left off, and it would render the book's message ultimately hopeless because cyclical. However, if the epilogue, like McCarthy's epilogues, describes a movement onward, then there are grounds for reading Job as a hopeful book.

The divine speeches communicate to Job through both content and form so that Job apprehends something hitherto unrealized regarding the creation in which he lives. Job has glimpsed a creation that is both prodigal and profuse, just as Annie Dillard did while at Tinker Creek. He cannot unsee it but must take it into account in his own life. If the divine speeches, through careful use of metaphor, suggest a world of bounded threat and disregard for human convention, then how does Job's subsequent behavior demonstrate that he has understood this? Job had disdained and denounced his world in chapter 3's birthday-curse:

> Let the day perish in which I was born,
> and the night that said "A man-child is conceived."
> Let that day be darkness!
> May God above not seek it, or light shine on it. (3:3-4)

But three inconspicuous and seemingly insignificant features of the epilogue's closing verses reveal how the world that Job reentered is remade by God "through his [i.e., Job's] imagination, before his eyes."[151]

The first sign that Job has apprehended the untamable riskiness within the world is that he throws caution to the whirlwind by fathering further children, risking that he might again need to grieve untimely death. Chapter 1's risk-averse portrait, exemplified by Job's protective preemptive sacrifices on behalf of his feasting children (Job 1:5), is gone: Job cannot guarantee his children's safety. Furthermore, Job's whole attitude to his children has changed: their position in the inventory of Job's wealth suggests this. Whereas in chapter 1 they were the sign of God's blessing, preeminent in Job's property portfolio, in chapter 42 they appear almost as an afterthought, indicated by the NRSV's casual "He also had." Children are not some commodity to be paraded as signaling blessing but a gift to be treasured. There is risk and there is threat, but Job is no longer cowed by such things.

The second indication of Job's new outlook is that his beautiful and beautifully named daughters are designated as legatees alongside their brothers. Although 42:15's quietly subversive bequest is easily overlooked, it implies a new ethical compass. Job has apprehended that the world's conventions need not be slavishly upheld. He is free and may do as he wishes, regardless of the social norms that guide inheritance law (cf. Num 27:7).[152] This is a godly act of gratuitous and reckless extravagance.[153]

The third clue is the telling absence of slaves in the restored Job's inventory, which shows that Job has apprehended something about social hierarchy and its inherent injustice. Chapter 1:2-3 carefully enumerates his wealth: 7,000 cattle, 3,000 camels, 500 yoke of oxen, 500 she-donkeys, and numerous servants. Chapter 42:12-13 recounts his restored estate: 14,000 sheep, 6,000 camels, 1,000 yoke of oxen and 1,000 she-donkeys. If we have not drowned in the doubling of chapter 1's numbers, then the "numerous servants" should be conspicuous by their absence. However, many interpreters focus on the doublings to the detriment of any comment on the servants' omission.[154] Yet this dearth of domestic servitude is striking, and shows that Job has realized that in a world wherein all belongs to God—even Leviathan—no human may belong to another. It could be argued that, through the book's mention of Job having had "very many servants" (1:3), many of whom would have died as a direct result of their servitude to him (1:15-17),[155] Job should be charged with complicity in perpetuating societal structures that are oppressive and unjust and as a result of which untimely death is visited on those less well-off than he. However, there is no censure of him for his slave-ownership; he is "blameless and upright" at the start of the book (1:1, 8), and remains thus even after the tragedy of the death of some of his servants (2:3). Furthermore, the epilogue portrays a Job who continues to wield social power—after all, he is still a wealthy landowner and patriarch (42:12-13)—but who wields that power altogether differently: he is fearless and free, gracious and gratuitous. The book subtly problematizes attitudes toward servitude that would be considered normal in the world of the book, and for many of those for whom it has subsequently been received as Holy Scripture.[156] Therefore the book shows Job as someone whose experience of chaos brings about a change in him that has societal benefits. He does not perpetuate his patriarchal privileges at the expense of others but moves away from thralldom, thereby indicating a new outlook, characterized and imbued by action that is gratuitously free, or "without cause." This idea of acting *ḥinnām* (חִנָּם), or in a way that transcends rational explanation, runs through Job. In 1:9 the satan asks God if Job fears him *ḥinnām* ("for nothing"), and in 2:3 God tells the satan that the satan's questions moved God to destroy Job *ḥinnām* ("for no reason"). In Job 9:17 Job charges God with having multiplied his wounds *ḥinnām* ("without cause"). In the epilogue Job has realized that God's freedom is such that God acts in accordance with only it, and is beholden to no human expectation or demand. As God has acted to Job with *ḥinnām*, so now Job acts toward others with a similar *ḥinnām*.

These three unobtrusive features in the epilogue indicate that Job has apprehended from the divine speeches something new about the world in which he lives and his own place within it. The speeches have this transformative effect on Job not because of any information presented or any bullying insistence that Job ought to "put up and shut up," but through the use of metaphor to convey truths to Job that could only be expressed in those ways: the precise literary form used in these speeches is what enables Job to apprehend the otherwise incomprehensible. The divine speeches in Job should be read as a signal demonstration of God's good grace that moves Job to disavow the dust and ashes (Job 42:6; cf. 2:8) to which he had felt himself reduced (30:19) and reenter life in the awareness that the chaotic element that exists within the world—the Behemothic fire from heaven and great wind from the desert and the Leviathanic Sabean and Chaldean raiders—remains indisputably there but is no longer something to be feared, for grace remains.

ONWARD INTO, AND WITH, GRACE

Yes, agree both McCarthy and Job, chaos is an unpredictable and inexplicable irruption of disturbance into human lived experience. However, suggests McCarthy, that lived experience is as likely to be disturbed by an irruption of grace and surprising good luck as it is by the looming threat of Behemoth and Leviathan. In *The Road*, when the man and the boy stumble upon a bunker filled with "the richness of a vanished world," there is a fourfold repetition of "Oh my God."[157] This may indicate nothing more than surprise, but the scene suggests that such bounty is taken to be the provision of a God long assumed to be absent from this world. McCarthy enables the reader to apprehend her own place in the world as one of risk and open possibility to *any* eventuality, negative or positive. We have no rights to expect anything and so all is grace, and thankfulness for this grace of God is clearly articulated in McCarthy's fiction, although a minor-key theme.

Such grace is there in *No Country for Old Men*, apparent for those with the eyes to see in Bell's reflections on the stone trough and his dreams of his father. Yet it also gentles the hard and tough prose of the novel at other points, too. Although the book depicts Sheriff Bell's increasing sense of lostness in the violent world that Chigurh typifies, it is a lostness that would be utter were it not anchored so soundly in marriage. The book's subtle approval of marriage, which is foreshadowed in *Cities of the Plain*, is highlighted by Sheriff Bell's repeated tender references to his wife, Loretta, as well as the touching descriptions McCarthy gives of those simple acts that show their love.[158] Bell is sustained throughout by this familial love, and his comment that "I wish I had her ease about things," coupled with the depiction of Loretta as the stable center of Bell's life, depicts the marital state as a source of gracious hope and good in a chaotic and unpredictable world. Sheriff Bell is still seeking the authentic existence that Loretta already enjoys.[159] She is alive in a way that Bell is not yet, and her contented authenticity is the steadfast anchor that enables Bell to develop his own authenticity. Thus this work, both in its closing section and its insistent reference to the good of Bell's marriage, suggests to the reader that the Joban ash heap is not the ultimate dwelling place. While the book of Job does not state or even imply that Job is sustained through his tragedy by his wife's support,[160] it is noteworthy that in the epilogue he is once again in the bosom of his family, seeing several generations. Family—including brothers, sisters, and children, and also, therefore, his wife—continues to be an important component of Job's epilogic life.

If everything is grace, then the recipient of that grace has no claim on the shape in which that gift of grace is received. This is something that the Border Trilogy enables the reader to apprehend, by underscoring the truth that the grounds for the hope that one's life will be meaningful lie not in its degree of conformity to some externally fantasized ideal but in the living of that life in all its daily responsibilities. This corresponds to Job in that while Job complained to God of his ill-treatment at God's hands, he was unable to find life meaningful: Job believed that the grace of God had to be presented thus and so, in a particular manner demanded by Job. Part of the purpose of the divine speeches was to show the falsity of the ideal to which Job had been insisting that God conform. But once Job had been shown that the world was run utterly differently to his assumed ideal, and that God's grace was *God*'s grace—and therefore given to Job as God saw fit, not as Job demanded—Job repented of the false conceptions of creation and of God within which he had been trying to corral God. This repentance became the crucial event that enabled him to reenter life and find meaning once more. For both Job and Billy Parham this meaningfulness is located in the ongoing grace of the living of one's life.

The grace of God is properly radical and subversive, calling into question the assumed norms and patterns within which life is lived and presumed to be the "proper" living of it. *Blood Meridian* asserts the God-intended necessity of individual moral autonomy for the sake of others, which corresponds to the epilogic Job's exercise of moral autonomy in electing to live a life that is untrammeled by societal convention. In choosing to have more children and in choosing to bequeath to his daughters and in choosing to cease to own slaves, Job displays an autonomy that is not self-centered but graciously benefits others in profoundly political ways. In *Blood Meridian* the plainsman kindles fire that others may progress, and in this McCarthy enables the reader to apprehend that the arrogant blustering of Judge Holden does not have the last word: in a world of unpredictability the importance of forward-looking, grace-impelled moral autonomous choices in defiance of that unpredictability are paramount.

But what of *Outer Dark*? Can grace be said to be resident in this malevolent landscape? There are several mentions of grace in the book. Before Culla jumps off a cliff to escape from the pig drovers who are muttering about lynching him, he rudely tells the Reverend who intervened in this attempted gibbeting to go about his business elsewhere. To this the Reverend replies that "a feller mires up so deep in sin after a while he don't want to hear nothin about grace and salvation. Not even a feller about to be hung dead."[161] This underscores Culla's graceless life, as does the Reverend's recounting of a sermon he preached to a blind man who wanted to curse God for his sightlessness: "The grace of God don't rest easy on a man. It can blind him easy as not. It can bend him and make him crooked. And who did Jesus love, friends? The lame the halt and the blind, that's who; Them is the ones scarred with God's mercy. Stricken with his love."[162] Culla is arrogantly upright, defiantly unbowed by the grace of God, but by contrast Rinthy, "delicate as any fallow doe," enters the charnel house of a clearing in which her journey ends: "in a frail agony of grace she trailed her rags through dust and ashes."[163]

Rinthy alone of all the characters finds grace, Rinthy whose love and pain are conjoined, and, moreover, whose pain comes from her taking the risk of being vulnerable to love.[164] And this grace is explicitly placed in an intertextual tension with the "dust and ashes" of Job 42:6. Job's "repentance" is best understood as "changing a course of action" or "moving on" from the "dust and ashes" that had both characterized Job's location and defined his stance before God (30:19; cf. 2:8; 10:9; 16:15). It is grace that enables Rinthy to pass *through* the dust and ashes of the clearing, and it is grace that enables Job to move *on* from them into a new life of "for naught" (*ḥinnām*) openhanded gratuity. Grace is neither an absence of tragedy nor a protection from it, but a life-giving potential that allows an individual to experience tragedy's full force and yet remain unbowed by it. Thus Rinthy—this little sister—rests, sleeping peacefully in the place where her child perished. Thus Job must have taken his wife to himself again and loved her fully and freely. The way of grace-empowered hopefulness is also the way of love and kindness, which is ineluctably the way of vulnerability and pain.

This grace shines through in the gentle welcome and storying of Billy's life by Betty, and her Christlike offer of a glass of water to Billy;[165] in the powerfully defiant exercise of moral autonomy that refuses to grant the last word to Judge Holden's arrogant declamations; and in the subtle endorsement of Rinthy's love and kindness.

CONCLUDING REFLECTIONS

McCarthy's fiction presents the reader with a world in which chaos is not the final word. Life in a world of unpredictability need not be lived in a fearful, small, constrained manner. Worth and meaning in life are still possible. The book of Job does likewise. The epilogic Job comes to realize that his life is not constrained by human expectation but only by the limits of his own imagination as to the extent of *ḥinnām*. As grace has been freely shown to him, so too is he free to show grace to whomsoever he wishes, howsoever he chooses.

6
Of Theodicy and Transformation
McCARTHY AS THEOLOGIAN

> He seemed to be making for the river with her but in the loose sand he lost his footing and they fell and he knelt there in the rain over her and held his two fists at his breast and cried to the darkness over them all. Oh God I caint take no more. Please lift this burden from me for I caint bear it.[1]

> "By his power he stilled the Sea;
> by his understanding he struck down Rahab.
> By his wind the heavens were made fair;
> his hand pierced the fleeing serpent.
> These are indeed but the outskirts of his ways;
> and how small a whisper do we hear of him!
> But the thunder of his power who can understand?"
> (Job 26:12-14)[2]

What is the ultimate divine answer to the cries of history's hurting sufferers? Suttree's anguished howl, which foreshadows that of the nameless father in *The Road*,[3] is and has been the cry of countless millions. At the last, when the tears flow and the wounds bleed, are God's ways so far beyond the human mind as to be incomprehensible, or is there some way in which the trials of Job can be held alongside the claim that the chaotic Sea has been stilled?

McCarthy depicts something of the nature of chaos in the violence, blood, dust, malevolence, and cruelty that run through his novels. This chaos—an unpredictable and inexplicable disturbance into human lived experience—is *inexplicable* insofar as the human mind can never fully understand why it is permitted to exist in creation, all the more so given the possibility of its negative aspect staining human life in such a profound and painful way. But inexplicable does not mean sovereign. McCarthy is clear that such inexplicable chaos is not ultimate, nor does it negate the possibility of a life lived well, meaningfully and—yes—with and in grace. Therein lies hope. The book of Job similarly makes clear that the chaos that had irrupted into Job's ordered life might appear to be "king over all" (41:34), but it is not. It is subordinate to the sovereignty of the loving God to whom its presence in creation is explicable, but on whom there is no moral claim to explain its presence to his creation. Therein lies hope.

This inexplicable element is *chaos* insofar as, no matter what defenses one might try to erect against its negative consequences through wealth, wisdom, or moral uprightness, it remains utterly outside human control. In McCarthy, the terrifying psychopathic violence of the grim triune, Judge Holden, and Anton Chigurh cannot be gainsaid by attempted arrogation, fearful obfuscation, or pyrrhic confrontation. It is a given and it must be recognized as such. Although McCarthy shows no interest in constructing a generalized theodicy, his recurring explorations of how to live in this world in which there is inexplicable and dangerous chaos suggests a theodicean interest, and to this extent McCarthy may be classified as a writer whose novels have a theological contribution to make.

THE ENTERPRISE OF THEODICY

Theodicy's endeavor to reconcile the existence of a God who is all wise and all powerful with the sheer weight and depth of evil in the world is an attempt to square the circle of David Hume's clear and decisive reasoning, itself based on Epicurus:

> Why is there any misery in the world? Not by chance, surely. From some cause then. Is it then from the intention of the deity? But he is perfectly benevolent. Is it contrary to his intention? But he is almighty. Nothing can shake the solidity of this reasoning. So short, so clear, so decisive . . .[4]

However, this definition may be nuanced helpfully by insisting that theodicy should not seek to justify God for the presence of evil but the presence of suffering.[5] It is possible, then, to distinguish between theoretical theodicies—which attempt to give an objective answer to the problem of evil by seeking to answer questions such as "How can evil be comprehended? Is the existence of God compatible with the existence of evil?"—and practical theodicies, which focus on God's involvement in suffering and overcoming evil by asking, "What does God do to overcome evil? What should we do, as his creatures, to overcome evil?" The "problem of evil" must be treated as one of particulars—historical and contextual—and so it cannot be solved universally. This helpfully reminds would-be theodiceans that attention must be paid to the specifics of the situation, because without any practical consequence pertaining to how pain and misery should be overcome, theological assertions—even though they may inspire such "spiritual" benefits such as prayer, confession, and empathy—are little more than empty words.[6]

Sadly, it is unusual for this practical attention to be paid to the specifics of the human situation of suffering, meaning that theodicies usually contribute little to the question of "How now do we live from here?" Traditional theodicy has been rightly criticized for its academic objectivity and its assumption that the primary issue is explanatory when for most people suffering is not a cerebral puzzle but a pastoral lived reality. Such an etiological answer is likely to provide scant relief, being little more than a symptom of post-Enlightenment hubris that implies the "problem of evil" is soluble. Moreover, the whole enterprise of theoretical theodicy derives from a post-Enlightenment culture that assumes science and reason can explain or answer everything.[7]

The questions of theodicy are perhaps better framed not as "How can a good and just God permit such a depravity of evil in his creation?" but in terms such as "How do we—how can we—live with the tensions that exist between our convictions of God's love and omnipotence and the realities of the pain and hurt of created life?" Any discussion of philosophical theodicy must be evaluated against the lived realities of evil, so that attention is paid to the question of how to wrestle with evil in both our lives and the lives of others. To the extent that theodicy asks the theologian to be articulate about atrocities, rational and reasonable in the face of the repugnant and repellent, the theologian who engages in it must be mindful of the inevitable paucity of language and thought to provide a fully adequate answer. However, this is no counsel of despair, for "what looks perplexingly blank in the abstract has handholds for our thought when we think about the question in connection with a story."[8] This allows for the intriguing possibility that literary investigations of theodicy can have an important contribution to make by particularizing theological or philosophical stances so that they can be evaluated. This usefulness—perhaps even fittingness—of narrative to theodicy returns us to McCarthy, who is manifestly *not* constructing a theodicy as it is traditionally understood, but who is a theodicean in the same way that the author of the book of Job is: that is, his investigation into the presence of chaos in the world is uninterested in explaining its etiology but is interested in pastorally enabling its victims to live in its aftermath. But this pastoral response requires the acceptance of a conceptual framework in which chaos is a given.

McCarthy is *uninterested* in the explanatory questions of theoretical theodicy, but he clearly *is* interested in examining the pastoral question of how to live in a world in which the actions of others have consequences that impinge on us, either directly or indirectly. In McCarthy's fiction, such living is a thoroughly risky venture, as evidenced by the unnamed inhabitants of villages and towns who are inexplicably drawn into the whirling violence and chaotic savagery wrought by the grim triune, Holden, Chigurh, et al. to such devastating end. McCarthy's use of literary Gothic is one way in which he conveys this.

McCARTHYITE GOTHIC

McCarthy is a Southern writer, if such categorization rests on the writer's philosophical and theological interests more than geographical location.[9] One way in which he tackles these interests that recur throughout his works is by writing from within the Southern Gothic tradition. Many writers have located his work here, particularly his early novels.[10]

The Gothic style can be a way of "confronting our demons and rewriting our origin myth," as William Faulkner does in his Yoknapatawpha

County novels, and as McCarthy does in his Appalachian novels.[11] Such works combine an allegorical style, which is inflected with notes of horror and palpable dread and unease, with historically plausible settings that critique the assumed conventions of "normal" life by exposing social ills—such as racism, wealth inequality, injustice—in order to highlight repressed social anxieties. Recurring motifs of Gothic literature include crumbling and rotting buildings enmired in squalor, unremittingly hard and apparently hopeless settings, and deviant or emotionally twisted and damaged protagonists, all of which inhabit a clearly Southern setting "to evoke both terror and horror, to externalize the emotional distress that attends social transformation, and to connote the perversity inherent in human nature."[12]

However, McCarthy moves beyond Southern Gothic and into the overlapping realm of the grotesque, in which the familiar is defamiliarized and distorted in order both to highlight the violence within it and name the bruised and bloodied victims on whose justice-denied bones that myth is constructed.[13] By using the grotesque the author can shine a light onto, and examine more directly, issues relating to evil and sin, as exemplified by the work of Flannery O'Connor. O'Connor argues that because the world of most readers is one in which theological concerns are marginalized or circumvented, the author is at odds with many of them: "This means frequently that he may resort to violent literary means to get his vision across to a hostile audience, and the images and actions he creates may seem distorted and exaggerated to the Catholic mind."[14]

McCarthy follows O'Connor in using the grotesque such that it forms a characteristic feature of his writing. In doing so he does not merely equalize human and nonhuman referents but mutates the everyday into something otherworldly in order to reveal something of its mysterious essence. This allows McCarthy to highlight human wickedness and brokenness, and their attendant consequences, in such a way that the reader is forced to recognize that from which they would otherwise turn away or withdraw. McCarthy's use of the grotesque to portray human evil—one of the components of chaos—implies its existence as an inescapable fact in the world. This has profound theological consequence, as has been discussed already. Moreover, McCarthy's writing style is such that there is an "excessive, sublime, even dangerous thing within the beautifully lyrical text" that enables "the terror or horror to take effect" in the reader.[15] McCarthy's work enables the reader to apprehend from his fiction certain truths, often impalpable and nebulous, that cannot be expressed in a more straightforward fashion. Although the Appalachian novels are seen as the most Gothic, elements of this style are also found in *Blood Meridian* and the Border Trilogy.[16]

McCARTHY'S THEODICEAN ENTERPRISE

If one were to ask who "we" are in McCarthy's fictional worlds, one would be unlikely to answer that "we" are any of the protagonists. Far more likely that "we" are the peaceable Mexican "Indians" savagely attacked and scalped by Glanton's marauding gangs in *Blood Meridian*, the redheaded hitchhiker or the elderly crone killed—one deliberately, the other accidentally, but both unnecessarily—in *No Country for Old Men*, the nameless farmhand or the ferryman in *Outer Dark*, or one of the shuffling amputees in *The Road*'s living larder. The presence of chaotic entities in McCarthy's world is a given, and so the questions he asks are not explanatory ("how did we get here?") but pastoral ("how do we live here?").[17]

McCarthy is a practical theodicean, if he is one at all, and his engagement with the questions of theodicy is one which does not set the question of "How do we live in the light of this?" against some abstract calamity but asks it in the midst of a life of confusion, pain, hardship, distress, and unpredictability, and is utterly dismissive of attempts to answer the question that will not attend to the particularities of that turbulent life. McCarthy is more like the Caborcan hermit than the Huisiachepican priest, insistently asking how human beings may live in a world in which there is created unpredictability and the consequences of human sinfulness that appear to make meaningless any attempt at living well. In this he reflects literature's ability to reveal the culture's concerns, interests, and presuppositions, as well as asking those specific theological questions with which the culture is wrestling. McCarthy's fiction provokes the theological guild to resist slipping into easy philosophizing, as well as revealing that this question of how to *live* is one of the foremost concerns in the culture at large.

Sketching a McCarthyite "Theodicy"

McCarthy's literature not only challenges theologians to articulate how to live in a chaotic world, but also it explores theological ideas, weaving together different threads to give a rich and dense picture of this unpredictable world. Although teasing these apart risks ripping the overall picture, it is important to consider the picture that McCarthy presents to his readers. This is not to say that McCarthy is deliberately engaging in theological argument, merely that in exploring the nature of the world, and the place of humans within it, he is considering issues with which theology overlaps.

The first theological thread concerns the place of humanity, as evidenced in McCarthy's use of optical democracy, which underscores that the human subject is not central. This is a theological claim that overlaps with Augustine's Aesthetic view that every created thing has an appointed place within which it is good. This can be hard to discern, but even when we can discern no benefit we should not conclude that there is none, or that creation is at fault.[18] Thus Augustine critiques an overly subjective anthropocentric viewpoint that has too narrow a view of the effects of a thing, seeing these solely in terms of their impingement on human life. Within the Judeo-Christian tradition, it is God—not the human subject—who is central, and, properly speaking, God is free to do as God wishes: "In both Judaism and Christianity the recognition that anything may happen to one is extremely important." However, for many believers "there is a deep tendency in us to resist what it says, namely, that we are not people to whom the cosmos owes anything."[19]

McCarthy would be in firm agreement with this, as he gives his readers no reason to assume that their way through life should be one of ease and comfort; after all, none of his characters live such a blessed life. McCarthy can therefore be located alongside thinkers such as John Swinton and Kenneth Surin, who identify an anthropology shaped by the dominance of post-Enlightenment subjective individuality as the impetus for constructing theodicies, along with an uncritical assumption of humanity's capacity to eradicate those things that cause suffering as time progresses. McCarthy's epigraphic use in *Blood Meridian* of a newspaper article reporting on the excavation of a human skull showing evidence of having been scalped bolsters the point: there is no "progress" in human nature here.

In *The Crossing*, one of McCarthy's characters states that

> men wish to be serious but they do not understand how to be so. Between their acts and their ceremonies lies the world and in this world the storms blow and the trees twist in the wind and all the animals that God has made go to and fro yet this world men do not see. They see the acts of their own hands or they see that which they name and call out to one another but the world between is invisible to them.[20]

This highlights how the human gaze is unable to see outside itself. However, to be serious demands the seeing of the world as it is, beyond human naming and artifice. The true nature of the world is that storms *do* blow and trees *do* twist in the wind: there is a dynamism to the world that goes unrecognized and unappreciated for as long as the human gaze will not extend beyond the purview of human interest. The world of twisting trees and driving winds is nevertheless there, although currently unseen. It is invisibly present and will remain unapprehended and incomprehensible for as long as it continues to go unrecognized. Looking beyond human utility and adopting a non-anthropocentric viewpoint will not erase the sufferings encountered during life in this world, but it may invite a consideration of the possibility that the world does not revolve around oneself. Thus what McCarthy's optically democratic world encourages is the apprehension that the human subject is not the center of the world.[21] She has no special privileges in the world, neither by virtue of being a human being nor by being herself, as is quietly suggested by the book of Job, for instance in 38:25-27:

> Who has cut a channel for the torrents of rain,
>   and a way for the thunderbolt,
> to bring rain on a land where no one lives,
>   on the desert, which is empty of human life,
> to satisfy the waste and desolate land,
>   and to make the ground put forth grass?

The world is not managed to benefit humans alone, still less to benefit one man from Uz. Job, in his railing against God, shows how hard this is to accept.

The second thread concerns governance, and explores the theological question of whether, even if God does not owe his human creatures anything, he is bound to act toward his animal creatures in a certain way. The Joban world is one in which ostrich eggs may be trampled underfoot (39:13-15), and the fresh blood of slaughtered prey sates the hawk's young (39:26-30).[22] Correspondingly, McCarthy's fictional worlds depict hardship in both the human and animal spheres: small birds are windblown onto a cholla bush's impaling thorns, or shot; dogs are run down, or attack one another; horses are executed, stabbed, bludgeoned to death, snakebitten, go mad, and die.[23] Augustine's Aesthetic view has been criticized for leaving "unillumined a large part of the mystery of animal pain,"[24] meaning that Augustine may be charged with disregard for such suffering; by extension, the charge can likewise be leveled against McCarthy.

Certainly there is in McCarthy none of the liberal concern regarding the pain and suffering of the animal world that is found in some writers who attempt to construct a "cosmic theodicy." McCarthy's fictional universe is one in which "nature is random, contingent, blind, disastrous, wasteful, indifferent, selfish, cruel, clumsy, ugly, struggling, full of suffering, and, ultimately, death";[25] yet it is nevertheless beautiful in this. Thus McCarthy disagrees with those theologians who, while acknowledging the vast difference between "the suffering of an animal being torn apart by other animals with the deliberate, freely chosen torture of a human by other humans," believe that "the problem in terms of the goodness of God is of the same kind."[26] For McCarthy the life of creatures—including humans—inevitably includes suffering and death, and there is no apparent moral dimension to this facet of creaturely existence. Death understood as a natural limitation is not of itself evil but is a part of this good world, however baffling this may seem. This echoes the thought of Barth,[27] as well as those theologians for whom God's providential care of creation includes both law and chance: "it is God who has chosen to allow a degree of unpredictability, open-mindedness, and flexibility in the world God continues to hold in existence and through whose process God continues to create."[28]

This providential holding-together constitutes a third thread, which is represented in McCarthy by *The Crossing*'s threefold mention of a "matrix" in life.[29] That such an unusual word is used in three distinct passages by an author whose choice of language is very careful suggests an authorially intended connection. Such a connection is indeed there; the matrix is the web of life from which no creature may extricate itself:

> He touched the cold and perfect teeth. The eye turned to the fire gave back no light and he closed it with his thumb and sat by her and put his hand upon her bloodied forehead and closed his own eyes that he could see her running in the mountains, running in the starlight where the grass was wet and the sun's coming as yet had not undone the rich matrix of creatures passed in the night before her. Deer and hare and dove and groundvole all richly empanelled on the air for her delight, all nations of the possible world ordained by God of which she was one among and not separate from.[30]

This matrix is McCarthy's expansion of the Arendtian web such that it now contains not only interpersonal relationships necessary for common life but also all creatures and all causal chains and intersections thereof that might, from the human perspective, be thought to demonstrate mere chance. Not so, for "not chaos itself lay outside of that matrix."[31] That this matrix of life contains chaos does not mean that the matrix itself is random or happenstantial for "the matrix was not so easily defined," because "things were rightly named its attributes which could in no way be counted back into its substance."[32] The indefinable matrix contains within it possibilities and permutations that one might attribute to it but without needing to lay claim to the matrix's substance being composed of such occurrences.

Within a wider McCarthyite worldview it is legitimate to say that the apparent meaninglessness and randomness of animal suffering in this world is most emphatically *not* an indication of any essential coldness or uncaring hardness. The impaled birds chirping piteously from the cholla bush are neither a sign of moral failing nor of God having created a defective world. If this description of McCarthy's position is accurate, then it approximates to the thought of Thomas Aquinas, for whom there is no question of creation conforming to a "good" pattern, for there was no pattern before creation took place.[33] Thus insofar as God created a world in which small songbirds may be blown by the wind onto the spikes of a desert cactus, horses may be driven wide-eyed and teeth-baringly mad by snakebite, and dogs may be brutally killed, God has not created a poor world. Rather, God has created a world in which God accepts responsibility for such chance occurrences, crushed ostrich eggs notwithstanding.[34]

The word "chance" illumines a fourth thread in McCarthy's theologically imaginative picture. The role of chance is a characteristic constituent of McCarthy's fictional landscapes. While Hume's critique of natural religion assumes uncritically that misery cannot be the result of chance, McCarthy insists that it is. Hume uses chance to describe events whose causes cannot be discerned, which therefore seem independent of causality.[35] For Hume such an occurrence is inconceivable, and so those events to which we give the appellation chance are not *real* chance, merely events the causes of which remain unknown. Therefore chance is a term indicative of philosophical laziness, much as the term "mystery" in theology can be used as an excuse for neglecting deeper and more accurate investigation. However, it is entirely reasonable to refer to a situation in which our knowledge is too limited to predict an outcome with certainty as chance: there can be epistemic, or experiential, chance and to call it chance is no lazy option.[36] Furthermore, it is precisely this sort of occurrence that McCarthy's characters routinely encounter and that causes much of their suffering and distress, for they are inextricably part of a web of life such that the actions of others impinge on them. Therefore, part of the reason for misery in McCarthy's world *is* by chance, if chance is understood in this way (as the subjectively unforeseen consequences of the choices of others). Moreover, this understanding of chance enables McCarthy to sidestep the age-old debate regarding moral evil's origin. Whence it came is an etiological question that McCarthy is simply uninterested in answering. It is a fact of humanity's existence that people will do unspeakable things to one another, as *Blood Meridian*'s epigraph attests: Behemoth and Leviathan are in creation, and McCarthy—contra theodiceans more generally—appears supremely uninterested in categorically identifying the nature of this chaotic other as either privative or radical evil. That is not to say that human moral discernment is either impossible or a fool's errand, merely that McCarthy's interest is in living in the immediate aftermath of an encounter with Leviathan.

In McCarthy's worlds it is entirely by chance that characters encounter the chaos of the triune, Holden, or Chigurh. Just as in Job the origins of Leviathan, Behemoth, and the Sea are not explicated but assumed as being within the responsibility of God, so too the origins of these characters remain unexplored and unexplained. They are a given fact in the world, just as Behemoth and Leviathan are. This does not mean that their presence is necessary for God to bring good out of their encounters with unfortunate wretches; McCarthy appears uninterested in squaring that circle. But given the inescapability of such chaotic entities, McCarthy's fiction underlines the importance of realizing that anything is possible. This is, in part, due to God's magnificent untamability: no matter how deep His grace and mercy in drawing close to us, God remains—must always remain, else we fall into idolatry—the ineffable Subject who cannot be bound or mastered.[37] Such an uncontainable Presence is the overt God of McCarthy's books, whose will is inscrutable and whose ways are unknowable: "It was his experience that God could not be spoken for and that men with wicked histories often enjoyed lives of comfort and that they died in peace and were buried with honor."[38] Thus the world presided over by this God is one of chaotic possibility through which any actor may encounter the unforeseen "anything." McCarthy's fiction pushes the reader to see her own place in the world as one of risk and open possibility.

This possibility of negative experiences is admitted by Job in 3:25-26. Although these verses have been interpreted as referring to Job's belief that any new trial he can conceive will befall him,[39] it is more likely that they show that Job always knew that his prosperity was finely balanced, and might be lost at any time.[40] The turmoil that he knew was possible has now been realized. Such an understanding of one's place involves more than mere intellectual comprehension. Acceptance of the chaos of the world involves a *religious* dimension that allows the transcendence of the attempted imposition of "a system of checks and balances that will make everything alright for us in the end."[41] So to apprehend that anything can befall us is to refute the claim to sacrosanct immunity, to set aside the sense of a right to cosmic—or divine—guarantee of favor.

The final thread is that recognizing anything can happen must include the acknowledgment that unpredictability can bring blessing as well as hardship. Humans have no right to expect anything and so all is grace, and thankfulness for this grace of God is clearly—but quietly—articulated in McCarthy's fiction. It is often voiced by those who are older, perhaps recognizing that such a viewpoint cannot be taught or passed on easily, but is something hard-won that must be lived into incrementally over long years.[42] All is within God's hand, and all is grace, even in the chaos and darkness: "the corn grows by the will of God and beyond that will there is neither corn nor growing nor light nor air nor rain nor anything at all save only darkness."[43] Later on a Mexican café proprietor, whose age is implied by his great courtesy, "said that it was good that God kept the truths of life from the young as they were starting out or else they'd have no heart to start at all."[44] In the context of the novel this pertains to John Grady and Rawlins' naivety, but seen in the current of this oeuvre-wide elderly wisdom, it stands as a testimony to the hard facts of life: all is from God's hand, and all is grace, even in the chaos and darkness.

Such an apprehension of God's grace in life is no mere fatalistic resignation. This grace-recognizing response of faith entails "a requirement to love the fact that God has given life with its contingencies to human beings. This love is gratitude for existence."[45] The gratitude voiced in McCarthy's fiction corresponds to the epilogic Job's willingness to risk further loss and grief by having further children. The Lord had given to Job and the Lord had taken away from him, yet the Lord remains free to bless and give again and Job is able to enjoy good things solely because God in his grace has bestowed them on him as free gifts. Job receives them as such, and his attitude to his newfound wealth is profoundly different from this new realization.

Reflections on McCarthy's "Theodicy": Human *Being*

This "theodicy" that is present within McCarthy's novels presents the reader with a sort of theological anthropology: a conception of what it means to be human. In his novels, humans live in a world within which they comprise but one ingredient among many. The part that humans play is no more and no less important than that of a desert flower or an insect. This claim both chastens anthropocentric assumptions and also accords great significance to the rest of the world, with which humans comprise a vast interconnected matrix. The extant world is greater and more magnificent than humans are wont to think, and any attempt to impress meaning on this magnificence is little more than an act of hubris that is doomed to failure, for it is predicated on the ability to raise the human gaze above the matrix in order to allocate meaning to its complexities, as if one were God and could understand it. The world is not like that.

This anthropology can be seen running through the book of Job also. Both Job and his comforters erred in assuming that they knew how creation operated, but this errant assumption led them to different conclusions: while Job presumed to tell God how to run God's own creation, the comforters (including Elihu) presumed to tell Job what their preconceptions coerced them into believing was true of Job. In different ways, both Job and the comforters attempted to elevate themselves above God's creation in order to make pronouncements about how it should be managed. This is an anthropology that the reader of Job should likewise come to terms with, else he might err in assuming that what was true of Job must be true for himself also, as if God were bound to act toward all who suffer in a particular way. However, that is not the case. If Job was but one element of an interconnected matrix that included the mountain goats and the deer and the onager and the wild ox and the ostrich and Behemoth and Leviathan, and was therefore owed no special privilege from God, then the same is true for the reader of Job. To that extent—and to that extent only—can Job validly be considered an everyman. Once the reader realizes this, then the expectation of a Joban theophany that "resolves" the situation is held up for what it is: an attempt to corral

God within a preconceived *colindancia* that denies God's own essential freedom *in se*.

That this theological anthropology of what human *being* comprises is articulated by both McCarthy's fiction and the book of Job is one thing. But there is another issue: How should human *living* be construed within an unpredictable world? Superficially, it would seem that fatalism is the only valid response to such an inexplicable and chaotic creation. Is that the conclusion one should draw, or is there something deeper at play?

Reflections on McCarthy's "Theodicy": Human *Living*

Works of literature can exert a formative effect on the reader. They do this by providing imaginative illustrations of "how to live" or, more deeply, investigating the consequences of certain philosophical or theological positions—as, for instance, Dostoyevsky does in the characters of Alyosha and Ivan in *The Brothers Karamazov*. However, literary works can also effect an illocutionary formation:[46] they can exert a morally formative potential that is inextricable from the works themselves.

Flannery O'Connor recognized this capacity of literature, and argued that a book's message is inseparable from the book itself, for in all artistic creation the work is more than its abstracted meaning.[47] Therefore to read a novel solely to mine it for some moral example is to miss the point, for the story is not merely the clothing that must be removed to comprehend the central ethical point. Stories primarily work through imagination, but they also give rationality, albeit in such a way that these rational facts are inseparable from, and derive their meaning from, the interpretative story. This means that the author "demonstrates something that cannot possibly be demonstrated any other way than with a whole novel," so that the narrative form is inextricable from the message.[48] Therefore to "use" literary art instead of "receive" it, in an attempt to allow it to "add" to our lives is fruitless: only by receiving art can it "add" to us.[49] The authorial vision can only be appreciated fully—and it can only have its effect on the reader—when the reader fully enters the narrative world of the novel and journeys through it as it is.

On this reading, the form of a work of literature is as important in communicating to the reader as its content, although the reader may be unaware of this. Such implicit influence is precisely why novels are important for moral development, for "an influence which cannot evade our consciousness will not go very deep."[50] The message, and the medium in which the message is communicated, are indivisible. This is true of the Joban divine speeches, the meaning of which is inseparable from the metaphorical language in which that meaning is generated, and it is also true of McCarthy's writing. Therefore, his literary output is not only wrestling with theodicean issues pertaining to inexplicable chaos, but also it is subtly advocating a way of living in the world in which chaos runs rampant.

McCarthy, like the author of Job, locates his literary creations within a world of assumed unpredictability and investigates how to live in its shadow. He eschews an explicit authorial position in favor of allowing four distinct stances to coexist in mutual interrogation, inviting readerly evaluation. This is reminiscent of Dostoyevsky, who invites similar engagement in *The Brothers Karamazov*. Although the different anthropological offers McCarthy presents seem as confused as Job's different viewpoints, they are not. Just as the author of Job subtly directs us to seeing the divine voice as bringing the necessary means to Job for continuance of life, so too does McCarthy distinguish between these offers. The characters who embody these different approaches experience very different end points in the novels, and their character arcs contain an implicit exploration of the consequences of such viewpoints, and therefore a didactic thread of moral formation: herein lies McCarthy's judgment on the different offers of how to live in a world of chaos.

Trying to Control Chaos

The first offer is to attempt to control worldly chaos by riding its turbulent wave for selfish ends. This is illustrated in many of his works: in *Blood Meridian* there is Judge Holden who lords it over the created order with hubristic arrogance; *Cities of the Plain*'s ruthless *cuchillero* Eduardo slashes his way to the top of the pimping pile, stripping the world of religious mystery and treating it as a barren emptiness to be filled by those with sufficient strength of will, like himself; *No*

Country for Old Men's Anton Chigurh attempts to impress on this chaos a mechanistic determinism of which he is self-appointed agent; and in *The Counselor* Malkina is revealed to be the puppeteer irresistibly directing the ends of almost all the other characters. For each of these forceful figures, strength of will, cunning, and ruthlessness are the qualities needed to survive the world.

However, McCarthy consistently subverts the seemingly "strong" characters' claims to supremacy and control. Malkina is subject to the same violent chaos from which she has reaped temporary benefit. Chigurh's claims lie as shattered as his arm by the unexpected car crash that marks his exit from the book's narrative. Eduardo's preening butchery is brought to a bloody end in a dirty Juárez alleyway. Even the mesmerically nimble Judge Holden is absent from *Blood Meridian*'s optimistic epilogue. Thus McCarthy skillfully skewers the pretension that the way to live in an unpredictable world is to attempt to tame it for oneself.

Mystifying Chaos

The second proposal that McCarthy offers is that of awed mystification, in which the unpredictability of life is infused with an abstruse purpose that leaves the subject powerless to do anything save genuflect before it. *Blood Meridian*'s Tobin, the ex-priest member of the scalp-hunting Glanton gang, exemplifies this. Tobin it is who tells the kid about the judge, expiating in awestruck tones on Holden's manifold skills and talents. Tobin it is who tells the kid that each and every gang member had met the judge before joining Glanton's mob. Tobin it is who tells the kid in breathless admiration how the judge wrought the gang's salvation by transmuting bat guano, volcanic sulfur, and the men's own urine into gunpowder. Tobin it is who warns the kid not to enquire after the judge too keenly.[51] He beholds chaos' wondrous freedom, but steps fearfully, wary of rousing it from slumber.

As Malkina, Holden, and Chigurh's attempts to dominate the chaotic world in which they live is rejected, so too is this mindless mystification. Tobin's helplessness is rejected as the vacuity of his viewpoint is revealed when the judge's malevolence turns against him. Although palpably terrified of the judge, Tobin is paralyzed, unwilling to put his soul at hazard by direct engagement.[52] Repeatedly Tobin beseeches the kid to shoot Holden, before fading from the novel's gaze, his fate bruited by the judge's ominous rumors.[53]

Combating Chaos

The third approach—combating chaos—is exemplified by John Grady Cole in the Border Trilogy. In his uncompromising stance against injustice and his softhearted love for Magdalena, the epileptic prostitute in Eduardo's bordello, he offers a courageous and defiant response to malevolent chaos, staring it down and fighting it in defense of the weak.

Yet John Grady Cole's reckless courage is—surprisingly, perhaps—not endorsed. Yes, he is autonomous, brave, and considerate, but in the climactic knife fight with Eduardo, representing Cole's attempt to defeat chaos, he pays a prohibitively high price for his courage. Although Cole guts Eduardo, he cannot effect the rescue of Magdalena. While noble, he fails to illustrate how to *live* in the world, remaining merely a portrait of how to stand—and fall—in protest at it, signifying McCarthy's authorial repudiation of this approach. Cole's stance offers little hope for those who lack either the moral fiber or the opportunity to fill Leviathan's skin with harpoons, or die trying.[54]

Taking Chaos as a Challenge to Endure

McCarthy's fourth offer is represented by various characters throughout his books, such as *No Country for Old Men*'s Sheriff Bell, the Border Trilogy's Billy Parham,[55] and *The Road*'s boy. They are saddened and bewildered by the unpredictability of the world but see it neither as something to which they should fatalistically acquiesce (as Tobin does) nor as something to be single-handedly defeated (as John Grady Cole does). Rather, they accept it as a challenge to endure, drawing on their human situatedness to do so and attempting to live kindly in its shadow.

The baffled acceptance of Sheriff Bell and Billy Parham—McCarthy's imaginative illustrations of what a good life might look like—comprises the anthropological offer that the reader is left with. But this is no "last man standing" argument. There are hints throughout McCarthy's work that suggest his endorsement of this stance. First, a recurring theme in the Border Trilogy is the distance between the ideal and reality, as well as the foolishness of attempting to live in the former in denial of the latter. McCarthy suggests that the real world of human existence constitutes the whole world of meaning. There can be no other world than that which is realized and encountered; wishing for a less chaotic world, in which safety and blessing are guaranteed, is fruitless: "To move is to abut against the world."[56] There is an unpredictability to creation that will not be gainsaid. Therefore, it is necessary for Bell and Billy—and the reader—to accept the real world as it is, on its own terms, and to live life within this acceptance. This is not a political statement that encourages a refusal to protest against social injustice and oppression, or that legitimizes the denial of speech to those who have been victimized. Rather, it is a recognition that this world as it is constitutes the only arena for living. One cannot wait until the world conforms to a better fantasy of it before one dare take the risk of living. To live within the acceptance of the world as it is does not mean that one should be sheepishly constrained by its injustice or venality. Moreover, it is precisely through taking the risk of living in the world as it is that one can contribute to the sometimes necessary work of shaping that world into a more just iteration, or the apocalyptic work of revealing to those in power—who would rather not see the world as it truly is—the nature of the false fantasy world they inhabit and seek to impress on others. So, while the risk of living may involve protest and resistance to oppression, it cannot be a waiting on the sidelines until the world has become more just or inclusive or however one wishes it should be.

A second hint of endorsement is found in McCarthy's foregrounding of the importance of simple kindnesses.[57] McCarthy's novels contain many small acts of charity and simple hospitality that the reader may miss through the lack of any authorial emphasis of them, and McCarthy underscores the noticeable gratitude that characters in the novels feel toward such acts:

> He mounted up and rode out down the little dusty street nodding to those he passed on his way. Riding like a young squire for all his rags. Carrying in his belly the gift of the meal he'd received which both sustained him and laid claim upon him.

> For the sharing of bread is not such a simple thing nor is its acknowledgement. Whatever thanks be given, however spoke or written down.[58]

Not only does McCarthy see value in simple hospitality, but also he understands that these simple kindnesses ricochet through people's lives. Sometimes they can generate more kindness, as when Billy is asked why he stopped to help some Mexicans repair a punctured tire. He replies:

> Its just that the worst day of my life was one time when I was seventeen years old and me and my bud—my brother—we was on the run and he was hurt and there was a truckload of Mexicans just about like them back yonder appeared out of nowhere and pulled our bacon out of the fire. I wasnt even sure their old truck could outrun a horse, but it did. They didnt have no reason to stop for us. But they did. I dont guess it would even have occurred to em not to. That's all.[59]

Or they can lead to a very different outcome,[60] such as Llewellyn Moss' fateful decision to take water to a dying Mexican cartel member, which he justifies to Carla Jean by saying "Im fixin to go do something dumbern hell but I'm going anyways."[61] He goes because every life is important, every life matters: "Everbody is somethin."[62] That rash act of kindness is all that is needed to give his pursuers the necessary information to hunt him down. Similarly, his kindness to the redheaded hitchhiker leads only to her gruesome death;[63] kindness may produce a harvest of future kindness, but it may not. Whatever the end result, goodwill and kindness are things to be honored and not taken for granted. These gratuitous acts quietly flow like a stream through the blistered and harsh landscapes traversed by the books' protagonists. Nevertheless, their effect on McCarthy's characters is considerable, suggesting that they should not be overlooked: "He said it was a mistake to discount the goodwill inherent in the old man's desire to guide them for it too must be taken into account and would in itself lend strength and resolution to them in their journey."[64] They are worthy in themselves, regardless of their unknown end, and they are worthy despite being able neither to shield the altruist from the world's unpredictability nor to compensate him for the sufferings that he has experienced or the cruelties he has seen.

A third hint is McCarthy's portrayal of the sustaining importance of human community for locating life's meaning. The Border Trilogy problematizes human attempts to find meaning in life by showing them to be artificial constructs, and by underscoring the inextricability of human actions from those of others, thereby questioning free choice. This is seen in the epilogue of *Cities of the Plain* in which Billy is welcomed by Betty and her family, and in whose gentle company he finds the home he had lost and the meaning that had so long eluded him. For Billy, meaning and purpose are not found apart from the risk of human situatedness but in its midst. The same is also true of the boy in *The Road* who must trust that the veteran is truthful. Similarly for Bell, Loretta's stability and fidelity to him indicate that the meaning he seeks may yet be found in the perennially risky country of marriage.

McCarthy's novels suggest that human community is necessary for locating life's meaning, but it is also the locus for demonstrating the meaningfulness of that newly received life. Neither the boy nor Bell or Billy return to life as it was once lived. It is as if their understanding of what life comprises, and the shape that it takes, has been amplified or embellished by their journeys. Their prior lives had been lived within certain assumed constraints, and some of these constraints were downright oppressive to their experience of what life was: this is how life is, and you just need to put up with it. But both the boy and Bell show a covert resistance to acquiescing to their situation's norms, and Billy is enabled to do likewise. *The Road* depicts the boy as knowing only the society engendered by his father, which is profoundly insular and claustral. Yet the boy shows a determined refusal to perpetuate the societal norm of suspicious neighbor-mistrust demonstrated by his father. At the veteran's approach the boy begins to retreat into sylvan solitude but hesitates. Despite his father's dying warning to take no risks, the boy, who is cold, hungry, and alone, courageously and fearlessly chooses to do precisely that with the scarred, wall-eyed stranger and in so doing he breaks with his societal constraints.[65] In *No Country for Old Men* Bell refuses to capitulate to an overwhelming hopelessness at Chigurh still being at large in the world. Such hopelessness is reflective of the assumption that a sheriff's success lies in his capturing psychopaths, not allowing them to escape. Bell's self-reproach at feeling defeated and his resolve to "get over that" begins with his meditation on the stone trough and the steady endurance of the man who had carved it. This resolve leads him to reflect in the novel's opening pages (which should be located after the book's events have taken place) that "there is another view of the world out there and other eyes to see it and that's where this is goin. It has done brought me to a place I would not of thought I'd of come to."[66] This other view is one in which an individual's worth is not measured by external notions of success; Bell knows that the world would esteem him as more successful than his father, but he will not yield to that judgment. Bell's encounter with Chigurh's terrifying presence has led him to a new outlook in which worth is not measured by success nor defeat by failure. Thus he too resists the easy acquisition of societal assumptions that oppress and demean.

Each of these characters is effecting as much change as they can within those areas in which they have influence, and is therefore resisting the dominant and oppressive narratives of self-preservation or the equation of worth with success. Billy is more complex. He has a youthful idealism in *The Crossing*, which is still present in *Cities of the Plain* but is there attached to John Grady, "the all-American cowboy."[67] Billy blames himself for John Grady's death, just as he blamed himself for Boyd's.[68] In despair Billy embarks on his nomadic lifestyle, convinced that "in everything that he'd ever thought about the world and about his life in it he'd been wrong."[69] But in the epilogue Betty's adoptive stabling of Billy provides a sense of meaning for him, which subverts Billy's earlier hopelessness. The novel ends with Billy coming to terms with a sense of this new life, meekly accepting Betty's appraisal of him, thereby able to resist his self-told narrative of failure and worthlessness that would constrain him in powerlessness. Therefore McCarthy's "endorsed" characters all demonstrate a resistance to external assumptions of how the world works, and thereby to societal oppression.

For the boy, Bell, and Billy, the warm welcome of human community enables their social power to be recalibrated and reconfigured such that they no longer live constrained by the expectations of specific other people, or by society in general. They are liberated from that which oppressed them.

LIVING WELL AT THE END OF JOB

The reader who turns from McCarthy to Job will find a similar offer of how to live in a world wherein Leviathan and Behemoth may yet wreak their turbulent havoc. As McCarthy subtly endorses a way of life that acknowledges chaos' presence and yet lives well despite it, so too does the author of Job subtly hint in the epilogue at what is not said explicitly.

Both Sheriff Bell and Billy Parham had to lay down the attempt to wrestle the reality of the world into conformity with the ideal that they desired it to have, and so too did Job have to accept that the way he thought the world should be run was not the way in which God chose to run it. This is what constitutes Job's repentance: the setting aside of the idolatry of the ideal and the acceptance of the reality of creation being what it is: ostriches dealing cruelly with their young, egrets sucking up the blood of their prey (39:16, 30). Job must move beyond the ideal and accept creation as it is, on its own divinely governed terms, and live life within this acceptance, even though the troubling presence of Behemoth and Leviathan remains.

The acts of gracious kindness that run through McCarthy's works are signs of a life lived according to principles of neighborly generosity, for neither selfish nor utilitarian ends, and they open the reader's eyes to the epilogic Job's kindness. Having realized that the creation in which he dwells is this sort of creation, Job is released from his position on the sidelines of life from where he has insisted that the world should work along lines other than those that God has graciously decreed for it, and so Job is free to bestow grace onto others. This can be seen in his daughterly bequest, which is an act of gratuitous kindness, appropriate to the unpredictable creation in which he now realizes he lives.

McCarthy's implicit suggestions of the importance of human community for sustaining this way of living in the world is also reflected in the book of Job. We may imagine Job sustained and helped in his new way of living in creation by those brothers and sisters who visited him and ate bread with him (42:11). However, Job himself plunges deeper into the mutual obligations and covenants of love that family life entails by fathering further children. Seven sons and three daughters—these last both beautiful and beautifully named—cement Job's reentry into the parental riskiness of human society.

In addition, Job's involvement in the structural power politics of society is also recalibrated. Far from acceptance of the world as it is leading to a little life of personal and political quietism, constrained by the societal status quo, Job's acceptance of the grandeur with which God graciously governs creation leads his epilogic self to wield his social power in a way different from his portrayal in the prologue. By ceasing to own slaves he resists participation in the societal evils of slave ownership and by bequeathing so lavishly to his daughters he resists expected norms that implicitly oppress and marginalize. The actions he takes within the realm of life over which he has influence have profound consequence and are a subliminal—and substantial—critique of the assumptions operative within the book's ambiguously located patriarchal setting. Job's understanding of social power is reworked by the grace of God, as was that of Sheriff Bell, Billy, and the boy. But Job goes further, for not only is he transformed, but also his transformation brings about liberation and transformation for others.

FINAL REFLECTIONS

McCarthy helps us to see beyond our own preconceptions regarding Job to what the book also speaks of: a creation that is bafflingly unpredictable to humanity due to the presence of inexplicable chaos, by which human lived experience is irruptively disturbed. In the book of Job, a creation within which Behemoth did not bask and Leviathan did not loom would not be the creation in which Job lives, regardless of how much Job himself might have wished it to be so. Yet the negative dimension of this chaos is neither something that need be feared nor something that need constrain the human endeavor: life is meaningful in spite of chaos' unpredictability, and life can be meaningful again for those who have survived its onslaught and trust God. This humble acceptance of the nature of the creation in which life is lived is the key to the possibility of meaningful life within it. To live well, one must first acknowledge that one cannot gain mastery of chaos (with its attendant positive and negative consequences), and this must then be accompanied by a determination to live well—showing kindness, generosity, and a rootedness in the many levels of community responsibility—in spite of its presence. This broad understanding is articulated in the works of Cormac McCarthy and in the book of Job, and McCarthy's novels serve the theological reader by enabling the apprehension of a Joban admission of the etiological explanatory question, and an answer to the pastoral question that arises from it.

Suttree's burden—that he found so unendurable—is not lifted from him, and neither is the nightmarish burden of living in a world of unpredictability lifted from us. The vision of the night resolves, but its chaotic terrors need not paralyze; a recognition of them can indeed yield new behavior. The chaotic Sea is still there, albeit stilled. There is a power greater than its turbulence, and its tempestuous waves are not ultimate. The chaos of Behemoth and Leviathan exists in creation, and this must be acknowledged in order to be able to live in its shadowy light, carrying the fire onward, both for oneself and for others.

Notes

INTRODUCTION

1 For further exploration of these four themes see, respectively, V. M. Bell, *The Achievement of Cormac McCarthy* (Baton Rouge, La.: Louisiana State University Press, 1988); Leo Daugherty, "Gravers False and True: *Blood Meridian* as Gnostic Tragedy," in *Perspectives on Cormac McCarthy*, ed. Edwin T. Arnold and Dianne C. Luce (Jackson, Miss.: University Press of Mississippi, 1999); P. Mundik, *A Bloody and Barbarous God: The Metaphysics of Cormac McCarthy* (Albuquerque: University of New Mexico Press, 2016); Dianne C. Luce, *Reading the World: Cormac McCarthy's Tennessee Period* (Columbia: University of South Carolina Press, 2009); Carole Juge, "The Road to the Sun They Cannot See: Plato's Allegory of the Cave, Oblivion and Guidance in Cormac McCarthy's *The Road*," *The Cormac McCarthy Journal* 7, no. 1 (2009): 16–30; Robert L. Jarrett, *Cormac McCarthy* (New York: Twayne, 1997); and William Prather, "'Like Something Seen Through Bad Glass': Narrative Strategies in *The Orchard Keeper*," in *Myth, Legend, Dust: Critical Responses to Cormac McCarthy*, ed. Rick Wallach (Manchester, U.K.: Manchester University Press, 2000).

2 Brian Evenson, "McCarthy and the Uses of Philosophy in the Tennessee Novels," in *The Cambridge Companion to Cormac McCarthy*, ed. Steven Frye (Cambridge: Cambridge University Press, 2013), 54. G. Guillemin, *The Pastoral Vision of Cormac McCarthy* (College Station: Texas A&M University Press, 2005), 142 argues that McCarthy's works are "polyglot mosaics that lend themselves to discussions of specific themes and aspects but resist comprehensive surveys."

3 John Cant, *Cormac McCarthy and the Myth of American Exceptionalism* (New York: Routledge, 2008), 13.

4 These are present in McCarthy's earlier works, but Michael Lynn Crews, "The San Marcos Archives: *Blood Meridian* and the West," in *Cormac McCarthy in Context*, ed. Steven Frye (Cambridge: Cambridge University Press, 2020), 288–98 argues that *Blood Meridian* marked a decisive shift by deliberately foregrounding them. The post–*Blood Meridian* novels then continue these philosophical investigations and rest on their foundations in it.

5 Rick Wallach, "Editor's Introduction: Cormac McCarthy's Canon as Accidental Artifact," in *Myth, Legend, Dust: Critical Responses to Cormac McCarthy*, ed. Rick Wallach (Manchester, U.K.: Manchester University Press, 2000), xv.

6 For example, Mitchell Ploskonka, "'See the Wild Man Two Bits': James Robert, Disability and Personhood in *Blood Meridian*," *The Cormac McCarthy Journal* 16, no. 1 (2018); Luke William Mills, "American Faerie: Medieval Fairy Lore in Cormac McCarthy's *Blood Meridian*," *The Cormac McCarthy Journal* 17, no. 1 (2019); and Craig A. Warren, "Drawing a Blank: Illustrating 'the Kid' in Cormac McCarthy's *Blood Meridian*," *The Cormac McCarthy Journal* 18, no. 1 (2020): 3–25.

7 A useful introduction to critical engagements of McCarthy may be found in Stacey Peebles, "Cormac McCarthy: A Critical History," in *Cormac McCarthy in Context*, ed. Steven Frye (Cambridge: Cambridge University Press, 2020).

8 It should be noted that when the discourse of theology is mentioned, whether by appeal to "theology," "theologians," or "theological circles," etc., I mean specifically *Christian* theology. I suspect that there will be overlap with other theological traditions, but I am not qualified to discuss these. Furthermore, by Christian theology I include study of the Scriptures, dogmatic reflection on the content of those Scriptures, and the task of communicating the meaning of those Scriptures to a wider audience.

9 All of which is to say that any act of interpretation is not a simple matter, as readers bring their own preconceptions, assumptions, and values with them to the task of interpretation. R. Gordis, *The Book of God and Man: A Study of Job* (Chicago: University of Chicago Press, 1965), v; Luis Alonso-Schökel, "God's Answer to Job," in *Job and the Silence of God*, ed. Christian Duquoc and Casiano Floristán (Edinburgh: T&T Clark, 1983), 45; J. A. Wharton, *Job* (Louisville, Ky.: Westminster John Knox, 1999), 158; and S. E. Balentine, *Job* (Macon, Ga.: Smyth & Helwys, 2006), 628 all highlight this as an issue when reading the book of Job. D. J. A. Clines, *Job 1–20* (Nashville, Tenn.: Thomas Nelson, 1989), xlvii does likewise, but he adds that this is not something that can be evaded. Moreover, he encourages a deliberate engagement of those assumptions with the text itself: "One will recognize that the text may

have little concern with such matters, but if they are a serious concern to the reader they may be legitimately put on the agenda for interpretation, that is, the mutual activity that goes on between text and reader."

10 U. Simon, *Atonement: From Holocaust to Paradise* (Cambridge: James Clarke, 1987), 6.

11 Stanley Hauerwas, *Dispatches from the Front: Theological Engagements with the Secular* (Durham, N.C.: Duke University Press, 1994), 56.

12 See F. W. Dillistone, *The Novelist and the Passion Story* (London: Collins, 1960); F. W. Dillistone, *The Christian Understanding of Atonement* (Welwyn, U.K.: James Nisbet, 1968); and N. A. Scott, *The Broken Center: Studies in the Theological Horizon of Modern Literature* (New Haven, Conn.: Yale University Press, 1966).

13 For example, Robert Detweiler, "Theological Trends of Postmodern Fiction," *Journal of the American Academy of Religion* 44, no. 2 (1976); L. Ryken, *Triumphs of the Imagination: Literature in Christian Perspective* (Downers Grove, Ill.: InterVarsity, 1979): J. Coulson, *Religion and Imagination: "In Aid of a Grammar of Assent"* (Oxford: Oxford University Press, 1981); A. H. T. Levi, "The Relationship between Literature and Theology: An Historical Reflection," *Journal of Literature & Theology* 1, no. 1 (1987); and D. Jasper, *The Study of Literature and Religion: An Introduction* (London: Macmillan, 1989).

14 See Simon, *Atonement: From Holocaust to Paradise*; K. Paffenroth, *In Praise of Wisdom: Literary and Theological Reflections on Faith and Reason* (New York: Continuum, 2004); Rowan Williams, *Dostoevsky: Language, Faith, and Fiction* (London: Continuum, 2008); R. C. Wood, *Literature and Theology* (Nashville, Tenn.: Abingdon, 2008); T. J. Basselin, *Flannery O'Connor: Writing a Theology of Disabled Humanity* (Waco, Tex.: Baylor University Press, 2013); Robert Alter, *Pen of Iron: American Prose and the King James Bible* (Princeton, N.J.: Princeton University Press, 2010); and R. C. Wood, *The Gospel according to Tolkien: Visions of the Kingdom in Middle-Earth* (Louisville, Ky.: Westminster John Knox, 2003).

15 Paffenroth, *In Praise of Wisdom*, xii.

16 Coulson, *Religion and Imagination*, 4 says that theological truths are "most convincingly expressed . . . when they are successfully translated into the language of literary imagination." See too Paffenroth, *In Praise of Wisdom*, xi.

17 Coulson, *Religion and Imagination*, 3–5.

18 Rowan Williams warns against the temptation to constrain theology by foreclosing its possible conversation partners. He specifically highlights the temptation for theologians to insist that all partners must converse with the same critical precision to which they themselves aspire, thereby neglecting conversational language in a more imaginative idiom. This,

he avers, "risks breaking off one of the most crucial conversations he or she is likely to be involved in, conversation with an idiom deliberately less controlled, more concerned with evocation and suggestion." See Rowan Williams, *On Christian Theology* (Oxford: Basil Blackwell, 2000), 9.

19 Robert Alter and Frank Kermode, "General Introduction," in *A Literary Guide to the Bible*, ed. Robert Alter and Frank Kermode (London: Fontana, 1997), 2 argue that "the Bible is probably the most important single source of all our literature."

20 U. Simon, *Story and Faith: In the Biblical Narrative* (London: SPCK, 1975), 116.

21 Simon, *Story and Faith*, 121.

22 John Barton, "Déja Lu: Intertextuality, Method or Theory," in *Reading Job Intertextually*, ed. Katharine Dell and Will Kynes (New York: Bloomsbury, 2013), 14 distinguishes between two senses in which the term is used theologically: "soft" intertextuality investigates influence and connection, whereas "hard" intertextuality denotes a way of perceiving the world, and therefore contributes to theories of political importance regarding the ownership of a text's meaning. However, even the term's originator, Julia Kristeva, although holding to the "hard" understanding, nevertheless engaged in the "soft" questions of which texts had influenced an author.

23 Barton, "Déja Lu," 12 is clear about this: "Writers bring to the act of writing everything they have previously read (heard, seen); readers bring the same baggage to the act of reading. No two readings will be the same, any more than any two pieces of writing will be the same, because everyone is 'situated' at a particular place within the environing culture and its history."

24 Alter, *Pen of Iron*, 3.

25 Alter, *Pen of Iron*, 5.

26 Williams, *Dostoevsky*, xi.

27 Eliot had a "residually Christian morality," while Hardy had a "continuing respect for the underlying sense of Scripture." See Norman Vance, "George Eliot and Hardy," in *The Oxford Handbook of English Literature and Theology*, ed. Andrew Hass, David Jasper, and Elisabeth Jay (Oxford: Oxford University Press, 2007), 490–93. See too Levi, "Relationship between Literature and Theology," 17, who states that "indeed in modern times it is quite difficult to find an author acknowledged as seriously major who has not sought to engage theological orthodoxy." Compare also J. Barnes, *Nothing to Be Frightened Of* (London: Vintage, 2009), 1: "I don't believe in God, but I miss Him."

28 Jasper, *Study of Literature and Religion*, 31.

29 Barth's magnum opus, *Church Dogmatics*, begins with this statement: "Dogmatics is a theological discipline. But theology is a function of the Church" (*CD* I/1, 3).
30 See *CD* IV/1, 110–36.
31 Alter, *Pen of Iron*, 4.
32 *CD* I/1, 81.
33 Barth says that insights deriving *extra muros ecclesiae* are neither the complete and full truth of the one Word nor mere partial truth, for "the one truth of Jesus Christ is indivisible." Rather, their veracity is "a particular refraction which is as such still a faithful reflection of it as the one light" (*CD* IV/3.1, 123). This refraction may be particularly unusual, so that it might be superficially unclear how these "true words" have a connection to the truth of Jesus Christ; nevertheless, that connection will be there if they are indeed "true words."

1 OF DARKNESS AND DEFINITION

1 Cormac McCarthy, *Suttree* (London: Picador, 1980), 459.
2 *TSL*, 14–15.
3 It has been suggested that the "this" of "Who is this that darkens counsel by words without knowledge?" (Job 38:2) refers to Elihu, not Job. See Karl G. Wilcox, "'Who Is This . . . ?' A Reading of Job 32:2," *Journal for the Study of the Old Testament* 23, No. 78 (1998): 87–88 and C. L. Brinks, "Who Speaks Words without Knowledge? A Response to Wilcox and Bimson," *Journal for the Study of the Old Testament* 35, no. 2 (2010): 200 for this view; and John J. Bimson, "Who Is 'This' in 'Who is This . . . ?' (Job 38:2): A Response to Karl G. Wilcox," *Journal for the Study of the Old Testament* 25, No. 87 (2000): 126–27 for a critique of it.
4 In referring to the book of Job as "a tale" I am not passing judgment on the historical factuality, or lack thereof, of the book's account of Job's experiences. On this issue, J. H. Walton, *Job*, NIV Application Commentary Series (Grand Rapids: Zondervan, 2012), 25 says that "we lose nothing by accepting Job's story as historical and we gain nothing by concluding that he is a fabricated, fictional character." However, he notes that ancient authors often built stories around epic figures of the mythical past, so that one need not insist on a literal historicity.
5 *TSL*, 27.
6 *TSL*, 95.
7 As M. Broncano, *Religion in Cormac McCarthy's Fiction: Apocryphal Borderlands* (New York: Routledge, 2014), 9, describes it.
8 *TSL*, 139. The verb "dangling" suggests strings connected to some sort of marionette, an idea that recurs in *ATPH*, and is likely a reference to Plato, *The Laws*, trans. T. J. Saunders (London: Penguin, 1975), 31, 246–47.

9 Cant, *Myth of American Exceptionalism*, 258.

10 Nahum N. Glatzer, "Introduction: A Study of Job," in *The Dimensions of Job: A Study and Selected Readings*, ed. Nahum N. Glatzer (Eugene, Ore.: Wipf and Stock, 2002), 1–4. The covenant name YHWH is used throughout chapters 1 and 2, and in chapters 38–42, but in the dialogues only occurs at 12:9 and 28:28. Clines, *Job 1–20*, 294–95 argues that the phrase "hand of YHWH" was a popular idiom inserted by the poet as a refutation of the common cliché. J. E. Hartley, *The Book of Job* (Grand Rapids: Eerdmans, 1988), 208–9 takes the view that it is a scribal error influenced by this common phrase.

11 For a comprehensive list of works influenced by Job, see D. J. A. Clines, *Job 38–42* (Nashville, Tenn.: Thomas Nelson, 2011), 1377–464.

12 Gabrielle Oberhänsli, "Job in Modern and Contemporary Literature on the Background of Tradition: Sidelights of a Jewish Reading," in *Reading Job Intertextually*, ed. Katharine Dell and Will Kynes (New York: Bloomsbury, 2013), 277–78.

13 Glatzer, "Introduction," 17–20.

14 For example E. Wiesel, *The Trial of God (as It Was Held on February 25, 1649, in Shamgorod)* (New York: Schocken, 1979), in which the drama is set in a specific place and time. Although Shamgorod is fictitious, it represents many small communities in Poland and the Ukraine decimated by vicious pogroms during the Khmelnytsky Uprising of 1648–1657. The play's subtitle specifies the date as the February 25, 1649: Purim, when the defeat of Haman's plot to annihilate the Persian Jews is commemorated. Traditionally Purim was marked by levity, feasting, mask-wearing, and a *Purimschpiel*, a comic dramatization of Haman's scheming and Esther's bravery. In specifying so clearly the play's setting and date Wiesel grounds in a certain time and place specific issues that others might be tempted to address in a merely hypothetical manner. The play demands a concrete engagement with these issues that, despite being set in 1649, originated in Wiesel's experiences in Auschwitz and so transcend their historical situation.

15 M. Larrimore, *The Book of Job: A Biography* (Princeton, N.J.: Princeton University Press, 2013), 221 notes that "Job's protest spoke to the moment like no other biblical voice, but what was one to do with his ultimate submission to a blustering God?"

16 Oberhänsli, "Job in Modern and Contemporary Literature," 276.

17 Oberhänsli, "Job in Modern and Contemporary Literature," 281.

18 Oberhänsli, "Job in Modern and Contemporary Literature," 283.

19 Larrimore, *Book of Job*, 65.

20 Larrimore, *Book of Job*, 65.

21 Larrimore, *Book of Job*, 133–34 (emphasis added).

22 Larrimore, *Book of Job*, 134.

23 Larrimore, *Book of Job*, 19.
24 Glatzer, "Introduction:," 4.
25 Cited in Clines, *Job 38–42*, ix.
26 J. Clinton McCann, Jr., "The Book of Job and Marjorie Kemper's 'God's Goodness,'" in *Reading Job Intertextually*, ed. Katharine Dell and Will Kynes (New York: Bloomsbury, 2013), 296; cf. Larrimore, *The Book of Job: A Biography*, 242.
27 This is noted by, but not endorsed by, M. H. Pope, *Job: Introduction, Translation and Notes* (New Haven, Conn.: Yale University Press, 2008), lxxiii; Clines, *Job 1–20*, xxxviii; T. Longman, *Job* (Grand Rapids: Baker Academic, 2012), 462.
28 R. Frost, *A Masque of Reason* (Oxford: Alden, 1948), 12–23.
29 L. Wilson, *Job* (Grand Rapids: Eerdmans, 2015), 213.
30 One could claim the existence of a third category, structural evil. This refers to the existence of uncritically and often subconsciously assumed and widely perpetuated preconceptions or ideas that sustain oppression and injustice through the agency of institutions rather than individuals. In this project, structural evil will not be treated as a separate category because it ultimately derives from human agency. However, that is not to downplay its importance. The Black Lives Matter movement, which came to the fore during the time of writing, has alerted many in the West to the importance of critically evaluating the structural and systemic ways in which evil is perpetuated.
31 From Carver's poem "Lemonade" (R. Carver, *All of Us: The Collected Poems* [London: Harvill, 1997], 287). D. J. A. Clines, *Job 21–37* (Nashville, Tenn.: Thomas Nelson, 2006), 1036 notes that Job's speech "is wrapped in nostalgia, in a conjuring up of blissful days."
32 E. F. Davis, *Getting Involved with God: Rediscovering the Old Testament* (Plymouth, Mass.: Cowley, 2001), 122.
33 C. Ash, *Job: The Wisdom of the Cross* (Wheaton, Ill.: Crossway, 2014), 435.
34 Contra Clines, *Job 38–42*, 1241.
35 *NCFOM*, 4.
36 *COTP*, 265; cf. *TC*, 327.
37 *COTP*, 267.
38 James Dorson, "The Judaeo-Christian Tradition," in *Cormac McCarthy in Context*, ed. Steven Frye (Cambridge: Cambridge University Press, 2020), 121. See too James Keegan, "'Save Yourself': The Boundaries of Theodicy and the Signs of *The Crossing*," *The Cormac McCarthy Journal* 1, no. 1 (2001); John Vanderheide, "Sighting Leviathan: Ritualism, Daemonism and the Book of Job in McCarthy's Latest Works," *The Cormac McCarthy Journal* 6 (2008); and Richard Walsh, "(Carrying the Fire on) No Road for Old Horses: Cormac McCarthy's Untold

Biblical Stories," *Journal of Religion and Popular Culture* 24, no. 3 (2012).

39 Dianne C. Luce, "Cormac McCarthy and Albert Erskine: The Evolution of a Working Relationship," *Resources for American Literary Study* 35 (2010): 328.

40 Although there are other interests in McCarthy too. For example, Platonism and existential Christianity.

41 Bell, *Achievement of Cormac McCarthy*, 1–2.

42 Bell, *Achievement of Cormac McCarthy*, xiii.

43 *OD*, 251.

44 Cant, *Myth of American Exceptionalism*, 174–76; Steven Frye, "Histories, Novels, Ideas: Cormac McCarthy and the Art of Philosophy," in *The Cambridge Companion to Cormac McCarthy*, ed. Steven Frye (Cambridge: Cambridge University Press, 2013), 7–8; and M. L. Potts, *Cormac McCarthy and the Signs of Sacrament: Literature, Theology, and the Moral of Stories* (London: Bloomsbury, 2015), 29–44.

45 See, respectively, Frye, "Histories, Novels, Ideas," 7–8; Cant, *Myth of American Exceptionalism*, 174–76; Potts, *Signs of Sacrament*, 29–44.

46 Frye, "Histories, Novels, Ideas," 8.

47 Dan Flory, "Evil, Mood, and Reflection in the Coen Brothers' *No Country for Old Men*," in *Cormac McCarthy: All the Pretty Horses, No Country for Old Men, The Road*, ed. Sara L. Spurgeon (London: Continuum, 2011), 126.

48 Cant, *Myth of American Exceptionalism*, 78.

49 Cant, *Myth of American Exceptionalism*, 113 (emphasis added). See too Madison Smartt Bell, "A Writer's View of Cormac McCarthy," in *Myth, Legend, Dust: Critical Responses to Cormac McCarthy*, ed. Rick Wallach (Manchester, U.K.: Manchester University Press, 2000), 10; Steven Frye, *Understanding Cormac McCarthy* (Columbia: University of South Carolina Press, 2011), 5.

50 Russell M. Hillier, *Morality in Cormac McCarthy's Fiction: Souls at Hazard* (Cham, C.H.: Palgrave Macmillan, 2017), 3. The influential reading of Daugherty, "Gravers False and True," 159–71 understands gnosticism as arising from humanity's common experience of the world as evil, and apparent alienation from it. Citing as evidence of gnosticism in *Blood Meridian* the book's mention of Anareta (thought to be a life-destroying planet), Judge Holden's attempts to achieve full suzerainty, and the epilogue's depiction of a mass of blind, barely living humanity who are little more than automatons unaware of the mystery inherent to life, in this reading the epilogic man striking fire is the revealer of gnosis, alone in a world in which the majority do not even realize that there is a divine. Cf. John E. Sepich, *Notes on Blood Meridian: Revised and Expanded Edition* (Austin: University of Texas Press, 2008), 164, n. 5.

51 Frye, "Histories, Novels, Ideas," 5–6.
52 *BM*, 326.
53 Allen Josephs, *On Cormac McCarthy: Essays on Mexico, Crime, Hemingway and God* (Wickford, R.I.: New Street Communications, 2016), 10–12.
54 Luce, *Reading the World*, viii.
55 Luce, *Reading the World*, 71–72.
56 Luce, *Reading the World*, 67; cf. McCarthy's comments to Oprah Winfrey: "I like to think it's about the boy and the man on the road, but obviously you can draw conclusions about all sorts of things from reading the book, depending on your taste." The video is available at https://www.youtube.com/watch?v=y3kpzuk1Y8I; accessed October 24, 2018.
57 Luce, *Reading the World*, ix.
58 Sepich, *Notes on Blood Meridian*, xix; cf. Richard B. Woodward, "Cormac McCarthy's Venomous Fiction," *The New York Times Magazine*, 1992.
59 Woodward, "Cormac McCarthy's Venomous Fiction."
60 Evenson, "McCarthy and the Uses of Philosophy," 58.
61 Broncano, *Religion in Cormac McCarthy's Fiction*, 3.
62 Frye, *Understanding Cormac McCarthy*, 12 identifies these questions as concerning "the existence of God, the possibility of finding purpose in self-sacrifice, and the reality of love."
63 Carol A. Newsom, *The Book of Job: A Contest of Moral Imagination* (Oxford: Oxford University Press, 2003), 3–31.
64 For an interesting comparison of Berry and McCarthy, see T. Edmondson, *Priest, Prophet, Pilgrim: Types and Distortions of Spiritual Vocation in the Fiction of Wendell Berry and Cormac McCarthy* (Eugene, Ore.: Pickwick, 2014).
65 As Cant, *Myth of American Exceptionalism*, 175 claims.
66 See Frye, *Understanding Cormac McCarthy*, 2–3 for a brief summary; and Edmondson, *Priest, Prophet, Pilgrim*, 62–115 for a more detailed examination.
67 David Kushner, "Cormac McCarthy's Apocalypse," *Rolling Stone*, 2007.
68 Woodward, "Cormac McCarthy's Venomous Fiction."
69 On his Catholic background, see Frye, *Understanding Cormac McCarthy*, 3; and Cant, *Myth of American Exceptionalism*, 8.
70 Woodward, "Cormac McCarthy's Venomous Fiction."
71 Frye, *Understanding Cormac McCarthy*, 3.
72 See Ciaran Dowd, "The Santa Fe Institute," in *Cormac McCarthy in Context*, ed. Steven Frye (Cambridge: Cambridge University Press,

2020) for a discussion of his role there, and how his novels might reflect the research interests of the SFI.

73 Richard B. Woodward, "Cormac Country," *Vanity Fair*, 2005; Kushner, "Cormac McCarthy's Apocalypse."

74 Kushner, "Cormac McCarthy's Apocalypse."

75 Woodward, "Cormac Country."

76 Kushner, "Cormac McCarthy's Apocalypse."

77 Woodward, "Cormac Country."

78 Bell, *Achievement of Cormac McCarthy*, xii.

79 Woodward, "Cormac McCarthy's Venomous Fiction."

80 The interview is available online in many places, for example at https://www.youtube.com/watch?v=y3kpzuk1Y8I; accessed October 24, 2018.

81 Dianne C. Luce, "The Archives and the Tennessee Years II," in *Cormac McCarthy in Context*, ed. Steven Frye (Cambridge: Cambridge University Press, 2020), 287 comments that the archival material on McCarthy "expand[s] our awareness of his circle of friends and acquaintances and give[s] the lie to the thoughtlessly repeated notion that he is reclusive or antisocial."

82 Woodward, "Cormac McCarthy's Venomous Fiction."

83 Woodward, "Cormac Country."

84 Kushner, "Cormac McCarthy's Apocalypse."

85 See Michael Lynn Crews, *Books Are Made Out of Books: A Guide to Cormac McCarthy's Literary Influences* (Austin: University of Texas Press, 2017); Jarrett, *Cormac McCarthy*, 126; and Kushner, "Cormac McCarthy's Apocalypse."

86 Woodward, "Cormac McCarthy's Venomous Fiction."

87 Kushner, "Cormac McCarthy's Apocalypse."

88 C. L. Seow, *Job 1–21: Interpretation and Commentary* (Grand Rapids: Eerdmans, 2013), 1–2.

89 See Daniel J. Treier, *Virtue and the Voice of God: Toward Theology as Wisdom* (Grand Rapids: Eerdmans, 2006), 199–200; cf. Daniel J. Treier, "Theological Hermeneutics, Contemporary," in *Dictionary for Theological Interpretation of the Bible*, ed. Kevin J. Vanhoozer, Craig G. Bartholomew, Daniel J. Treier, and N. T. Wright (London: SPCK, 2005), 792.

90 Barth is clear that Sartre and Heidegger have no knowledge of God, and cannot speak from that vantage point, yet also that "in their atheistic blindness [they] could not escape the problem of God" (*CD* III/3, 344).

91 See James K. A. Smith, *On the Road with Saint Augustine: A Real-World Spirituality for Restless Hearts* (Grand Rapids: Brazos, 2019), for a sustained discussion of how both Sartre and Heidegger were heavily influenced by Augustine's *Confessions*.

92 Garry Wallace, "Meeting McCarthy," *Southern Quarterly* 30, no. 4 (1992): 138.
93 *TCo*, 3–10.
94 *TCo*, 17–40.
95 *TCo*, 165, 174.
96 *TCo*, 10.
97 Jacob Agner, "Salvaging *The Counselor*: Watching Cormac McCarthy and Ridley Scott's Really Trashy Movie," *The Cormac McCarthy Journal* 14, no. 2 (2016): 208.
98 Cf. Job 41:8.
99 *TCo*, 34.
100 *TCo*, 63–64; cf. 58–60, 112–14.
101 *TCo*, 145.
102 *TCo*, 146. This is very different from the advice given to Billy in *COTP* 288.
103 *TCo*, 184.
104 *TCo*, 147.
105 *TCo*, 17.
106 *TCo*, 34–38.
107 Agner, "Salvaging *The Counselor*," 218.
108 Agner, "Salvaging *The Counselor*," 218; Russell M. Hillier, "'Nor Hell a Fury': Malkina's Motivation in Cormac McCarthy's *The Counselor*," *The Explicator* 72, no. 2 (2014): 153.
109 *TCo*, 13; cf. 86, 90–93, 179–80.
110 Agner, "Salvaging *The Counselor*," 210, 214.
111 In this McCarthy's hope is more akin to the biblical concept (as seen in, e.g., Rom 8:23-25; 1 Pet 1:13) than that which is in common currency in contemporary usage. However, it obviously does not rest on the grounds that scriptural hope does.
112 Agner, "Salvaging *The Counselor*," 205.
113 *TCo*, 20.
114 *TCo*, 146.
115 *TCo*, 3.
116 Agner, "Salvaging *The Counselor*," 223.

2 THE FRUITLESSNESS OF PHILOSOPHICAL THEODICY

1 McCarthy, *Suttree*, 307.
2 The argument presented here stands in stark contrast with the view of P. Josyph, *Cormac McCarthy's House: Reading McCarthy without Walls* (Austin: University of Texas Press, 2013), 96, who states that "*Cities of the Plain* may be the best example of bad McCarthy."
3 It is thus unsurprising that Scott Gilbert, "Discourse Theory in *The Crossing*," *The Cormac McCarthy Journal* 1, no. 1 (2001): 38 believes

the novel to be about "the nature of discourse in relation to the nature of the world." Cant, *Myth of American Exceptionalism*, 196 agrees, seeing it as demonstrating how culture comprises the weaving together of many different narratives.

4 *TC*, 137; cf. 50, 139, 243.

5 S. Kierkegaard, *Fear and Trembling; Sickness unto Death*, trans. W. Lowrie (Garden City, N.Y.: Doubleday, 1954), 165.

6 Guillemin, *Pastoral Vision of Cormac McCarthy*, 104; Broncano, *Religion in Cormac McCarthy's Fiction*, 72.

7 Cameron MacKenzie, "A Song of Great Order: The Real in Cormac McCarthy's *The Crossing*," *The Cormac McCarthy Journal* 13, no. 1 (2015): 101.

8 *TC*, 141–62.

9 *TC*, 156.

10 *TC*, 162.

11 Barth does not appear in the index of Crews, *Books Are Made Out*, for example, but Crews is by his own admission looking for "direct references to the names of authors, the titles of books, or clearly attributable quotations" (7) while also admitting that "McCarthy's sources are so seamlessly woven into the fabric of the novels that they are often hard to find" (15). However, it would be entirely unsurprising to learn that McCarthy's famously voracious and wide-ranging reading habits had included Barth.

12 Josyph, *Cormac McCarthy's House*, 69, 261 n.1; *CD* III/3, 298–99; Philip McCosker, "Blessed Tension: Barth and Von Balthasar on the Music of Mozart," *The Way* 44, no. 4 (2005): 81.

13 *CD* IV/3.1, 361.

14 *CD* IV/3.1, 379–82.

15 *CD* IV/3.1, 384–87.

16 *CD* IV/3.1, 389.

17 *CD* IV/3.1, 405. In this, Barth avers, Job "was still a witness to Jesus Christ, to the One who as the suffering, crucified, dead and buried Son of God and Man is the only true Witness, in face of whom the falsehood of man is shown to be mere wind and vanishes as such" (*CD* IV/3.1, 408).

18 *CD* IV/3.1, 416.

19 *CD* IV/3.1, 422.

20 *CD* IV/3.1, 422–25.

21 In *CD* IV/3.1, 430 Barth says that "in the boldest of digressions, He speaks of very different things, of heaven and earth and sea, and more specifically of ordinary and extraordinary specimens from the animal kingdom. He lets these other things speak, and causes them to speak, not in the form of natural theology, but simply and yet eloquently of

themselves. He obviously counts upon it that they belong so totally to Him, that they are so subject to Him and at His disposal, that in speaking of themselves they will necessarily speak of Him and His mystery. He is so sure of them as His creatures—as sure as He is of Himself—that He has only to open the great book of nature and show Job a few pages to be sure at once of the service which the creatures will quite simply render Him in His self-manifestation. They have only to declare their own existence and nature and they speak indirectly but very effectively of Him, not merely indicating His mystery but revealing it."

22 *CD* IV/3.1, 432.

23 *CD* IV/3.1, 434.

24 *CD* IV/3.1, 398.

25 *TC*, 149.

26 *TC*, 150.

27 *CD* IV/3.1, 428.

28 *TC*, 151.

29 *CD* IV/3.1, 404.

30 *TC*, 152.

31 *TC*, 151–52; cf. C. S. Lewis, *A Grief Observed* (London: Faber & Faber, 1961), 8: "The real danger is of coming to believe such dreadful things about him. The conclusion I dread is not 'So there's no God after all,' but 'So this is what God's really like. Deceive yourself no longer.'"

32 *CD* IV/3.1, 402.

33 This continues the allusion to chapter 7 of Job, in which Job complains to God that sleep brings him no comfort for "then you scare me with dreams, and terrify me with visions" (Job 7:13-14). This idea is also repeated by Elihu, who affirms that God can speak to bring clarity through dreams (Job 33:15-18).

34 *TC*, 152.

35 As Crews, *Books Are Made Out*, 156 also agrees.

36 H. Melville, *Moby Dick* (New York: Norton, 2002), 345.

37 This reading is in contrast to that of Mundik, *Bloody and Barbarous God*, 146, who claims that "the weaver god is sinister, obsessed with the task of controlling his creation" and is neither omnipotent nor sovereign. Furthermore, as James D. Lilley, "'The Hands of Yet Other Puppets': Figuring Freedom and Reading Repetition in *All the Pretty Horses*," in *Myth, Legend, Dust: Critical Responses to Cormac McCarthy*, ed. Rick Wallach (Manchester, U.K.: Manchester University Press, 2000), 272 points out, "McCarthy's texts form the same narrative shapes time and time again," and within these shapes, argues Timothy Parrish, "History and the Problem of Evil in McCarthy's Western Novels," in *The Cambridge Companion to Cormac McCarthy*, ed. Steven Frye (Cambridge: Cambridge University Press, 2013), 77, McCarthy is dealing with

"how the world is known and ordered and further how this ordering is made manifest through either works of God or humans." Therefore, it is unsurprising that this idea of the weaver appears in the prologue to *Suttree*, 5 and in the kid's dream in *BM*, 326–27.

38 *TC*, 160.
39 *CD* IV/3.1, 427.
40 *TC*, 160.
41 *TC*, 161.
42 *TC*, 162.
43 *CD* IV/3.1, 431.
44 This is an echo of Ps 84:3 in which "even . . . the swallow" has a place to nest in the temple of God.
45 *TC*, 153.
46 *CD* IV/3.1, 402.
47 *TC*, 154.
48 *TC*, 155–56.
49 *TC*, 156.
50 *CD* IV/3.1, 453.
51 *CD* IV/3.1, 457.
52 *CD* IV/3.1, 430.
53 *CD* IV/3.1, 458.
54 *CD* IV/3.1, 456.
55 *TC*, 155.
56 *TC*, 155.
57 *CD* IV/3.1, 458.
58 Josyph, *Cormac McCarthy's House*, 117.
59 However, Job's wife is conspicuously absent from the dialogues.
60 Critical scholarship has no consensus on this. Many think that there is a kernel of truth somewhere behind the book of Job, but it is also apparent that the author-narrator, like that of Dostoyevsky's novels, has insight into the motivations, inner life, and dialogues of characters that would be impossible for a human author.
61 I have used lowercase for satan here because the Hebrew text uses הַשָּׂטָן (*haśśatān*; "*the* satan"), suggesting that this is a function of one of the members of the divine council, and not the personal evil being of later theology.
62 For a discussion of the theophany, see W. P. Brown, *The Ethos of the Cosmos: The Genesis of Moral Imagination in the Bible* (Grand Rapids: Eerdmans, 1999), 339 and Alex Luc, "Storm and the Message of Job," *Journal for the Study of the Old Testament* 25, no. 87 (2000): 119, n. 20.
63 Job's comforters are correct to declare the fact of God's hidden knowledge. This is stated by Eliphaz (5:9; 15:8) and Zophar (11:6), who declares that God's ways are beyond Job's grasp, "longer than the

earth and broader than the sea" (11:9). Such geographical quantification foreshadows God's questions to Job of 38:5 ("Who determined its [the earth's] measurements . . . or who stretched the line upon it?") and 38:18 ("Have you comprehended the expanse of the earth?"). Zophar's questions to Job are essentially those of God in chapters 38–41, "Who are you?" and "Where were you?" In both cases the point is Job's slender grasp of the realities that God knows intimately. Thus Zophar is speaking correctly, as Eliphaz had done previously. In fact Job has already admitted as much in 9:10, when he declared that God "does great things beyond understanding, and marvelous things without number," the phrase being an obvious, and almost identical, echo of Eliphaz's in 5:9. Where Job has עֹשֶׂה גְדֹלוֹת עַד־אֵין חֵקֶר וְנִפְלָאוֹת עַד־אֵין מִסְפָּר (*'ośeh gĕdōlōt 'ad-ēn ḥēqer wĕnifĕlā'ōt 'ad-ēn misĕpār*) Eliphaz has עֹשֶׂה גְדֹלוֹת וְאֵין חֵקֶר (*'ośeh gĕdōlōt wĕ'ēn ḥēqer*).

The comforters also emphasize God's lofty sovereignty (11:8; 22:12), which foreshadows various parts of chapters 38–39, which are, in some sense, predicated on an assumption of the divine loftiness and sovereignty. It is *this* sovereignty, the divine speeches imply, and the perspective engendered by it, that allows God to demarcate the storehouses of snow and the halls of hail (38:22), lead out the stars (38:31-32), mark the generative seasons of the mountain goats (39:1-3), and watch the migrations of the wild ass (39:8). Perspective is key, and that of God is far superior to that of Job, something that is underscored by God's celebration of the restless and awesome Behemoth and Leviathan. However, God's perspective is also superior to that of the comforters, who had themselves misunderstood God's sovereignty: for Zophar, it indicated the divine impenetrability, whereas for Eliphaz it assured God's impartiality in governing creation.

Finally, the comforters repeatedly connect God's hidden wisdom with his works and ways in creation. According to Eliphaz, one of the "marvelous things" that God effects is the sending of rain (5:10). A cloudburst is not just meteorological but is also theological and Eliphaz is correct to recognize this, for God himself directs Job's attention to consider the divine governance of rainfall in 38:25-28. Although Eliphaz draws the wrong conclusion, seeing God's sending of rain as evidence of his ability to bring life-giving transformation to that which is barren, whereas in God's speeches it is a sign of his non-anthropocentric governance of creation (38:25-28), he was correct to see its relevance. Of all the comforters, Eliphaz's speeches most often contain seeds of truth that flower fully in the divine speeches, as in 15:7-8, when he asks Job if he was "brought forth before the hills." Commentators disagree on the referent, with Longman, *Job*, 225 seeing this as an allusion to Adam as the epitome of wisdom while other commentators, such as

Clines, *Job 1–20*, 349 see it as a reference to an extra-biblical "mythical figure endowed with supernatural wisdom." Traces of the story may also be discerned in Ezekiel's description of the Tyrian king (Ezek 28), and it is also associated with the depiction of Wisdom in Proverbs 8 (see Clines, *Job 1–20*, 349; Carol A. Newsom, *Job* [Nashville, Tenn.: Abingdon, 1996], 449; and Longman, *Job*, 225). Regardless, the point is clear: if Job had been the first man, born at creation's inception, then he would have had deep knowledge of God's secrets; but he was not and so he does not. This idea then blossoms in the first divine speeches: in 38:4 God asks, "Where were you when I laid the foundation of the earth? Tell me, if you have understanding," and in 38:19-21 he presses the issue again: "Where is the way to the dwelling of light, and where is the place of darkness, that you may take it to its territory and that you may discern the paths to its home? Surely you know, for you were born then, and the number of your days is great!"

64 Newsom, *Job*, 450.

65 Despite the claim of J. G. Janzen, *Job* (Atlanta: John Knox, 1985), 237 that God has "an apparently taunting tone" in 38:21.

66 Balentine, *Job*, 646.

67 Janzen, *Job*, 250–51.

68 For example, Christopher Rush's *To Travel Hopefully* (2005), Helen MacDonald's *H Is for Hawk* (2014), and Clover Stroud's *The Wild Other* (2017).

69 Elaine A. Phillips, "Speaking Truthfully: Job's Friends and Job," *Bulletin for Biblical Research* 18, no. 1 (2008): 40–41.

70 It is sometimes assumed that Job's friends, who began by caring for Job as an individual—lamenting with him and sitting with him in silence—were doing well until they spoke. This view can lead to the assumption that any attempt to verbally answer a sufferer is not just foolhardy, but will also be oppressive, for failure is assumed to be inevitable. Thus it raises the pastoral question: "Is it better to stay silent than to speak, given that we're almost certain to speak wrongly?" However, the friends' approach is not coercive but compassionate, beginning with Eliphaz's tentative question of 4:2—"If one ventures a word with you, will you be offended? But who can keep from speaking?"—that simultaneously acknowledges the danger of attempting to articulate an answer and the necessity of not ignoring Job. Eliphaz is stuck in a dilemma; as an advocate of the wisdom tradition, he would rather stay silent (cf. Prov 10:19; 12:23), but softness of heart at the sight of Job's plight overcomes his reluctance to speak. Perhaps he recognizes that to stay silent in the face of such suffering would be to allow suffering to have the last word, and to allow its ultimacy to go unchallenged.

Eliphaz's first word is הֲנִסָּה (*hănissâh*), which Aron Pinker, "A Friend's First Words in Job 4:2," *Vetus Testamentum* 63 (2013): 78–88 argues should be translated as "to try/test/attempt." This is significant, for it shows that his attitude was one of humility. As Janzen, *Job*, 248 recognizes: "Eliphaz at the beginning sensed that he was in the presence of something for which common words and expressions are not adequate. The easy exchange by which people ordinarily traffic between language and experience, converting either into the other, slowed down as he searched for words." This suggests that the comforters performed a self-sacrificial function by entering into dialogue with Job. Although they perceived the dangers of attempting to answer him, they attempted to do so nevertheless. Therefore, to be a responsible friend is to enter into conversation with a sufferer; although one's words may offer little comfort, that is better than saying nothing, which would be a tacit admission of suffering's ultimacy. Thus a friend ought to tread the harder path of sacrificially saying something, even if at the risk of error. As Barth says in *CD* IV/3.2, 780: "Better something doubtful or over bold, and therefore in need of correction and forgiveness, than nothing at all!'"

A second charge laid against the comforters is that they spoke presumptuously by trying to say what only God could say. However, it should not be assumed that a sufferer cannot be comforted and helped by human words. The comforters are not foolish to think that human words can bring comfort and help, for, as Eliphaz says, Job is one who has "instructed many," and "strengthened weak hands," and so Eliphaz is moved to speak in the hope that his words will function to Job as Job's have done to others (4:3-4). The friends could neither know—just as Job could not—of the unusualness of his circumstances, nor what was needed to change them. Thus, while in the case of Job a divine theophany *was* what was required, the comforters are not guilty of trying to say what only God could say.

71 *TC*, 282.

72 Billy is given boiled eggs (*TC*, 283), which recalls the Huisiachepican hermit, who gives Billy scrambled eggs (*TC*, 141–42).

73 *TC*, 285.

74 *TC*, 285.

75 See also Job's remarks in 23:3 ("Oh, that I knew where I might find him, that I might come even to his dwelling!") and in 23:8-9 ("If I go forward, he is not there; or backward, I cannot perceive him; on the left he hides, and I cannot behold him; I turn to the right, but I cannot see him.").

76 *TC*, 285.

77 *TC*, 287.

78 Just before this he hears "a bell that tolled slowly three times and ceased" (*TC*, 289) but is later on told by the stranger that there is no church nearby (*TC*, 290).

This motif of characters hearing a bell tolling recurs throughout the Border Trilogy. In *All the Pretty Horses* John Grady Cole and Lacey Rawlins hear a "bell that tolled and ceased where no bell was" (*ATPH*, 31). In *The Crossing*, Billy hears "a solitary bell that tolled and ceased" (*TC*, 115) after having had a dream of his father. Lastly, in *Cities of the Plain* John Grady Cole hears the "distant toll of bells from the cathedral in the city" (*COTP*, 258) as he lies dying after the knife fight with Eduardo. In each case the tolling of the bells occurs at a moment of liminality. John Grady and Rawlins hear it as they ride like "young thieves in a glowing orchard," slipping into the new possibilities of any of the "ten thousand worlds for the choosing" (*ATPH*, 31). They have left behind the old world of their younger selves and are about to embark on a new chapter, with all its unknown possibilities. When Billy hears it in *The Crossing* he awakes to the horrors of the wolf-baiting pit (*TC*, 116ff.), which marks a threshold between his idealistic younger self and the reality of the world he now inhabits. In *Cities of the Plain* John Grady is dying, and thus inhabits the liminal space between life and death. In each case there is also a connection between the bell and mortality: John Grady and Rawlins are on the cusp of great adventure but death is an inescapable fact for them, whether of Blevins (*ATPH*, 182–83), the *cuchillero* in Saltillo (*ATPH*, 206), or the "death" of John Grady and Alejandra's love. Thus it functions as an omen for the reader that not all will be well. Billy's dream-bell is a warning/signal to the reader that a tragedy has befallen Billy's father, and so it proves to be, and is a portent for what is about to happen to the wolf and to Billy's dream. After the knife fight with Eduardo, the bell is real, at last, and a real reminder of John Grady's mortality, and a portent of his imminent death.

Read against this backdrop, the tolling bell heard by *el ciego* as he seeks his own death indicates a threshold moment for him, and alerts the reader to the fact that the blind man is about to enter into a new experience.

Moving ahead in McCarthy's oeuvre, it is likely that Sheriff Bell in *No Country for Old Men* is named so as to connect to these ideas. He resides in a world in which mortality is a constant presence, and he is also living in a liminal space, confronted with new knowledge about the nature of the world and its horrifying possibilities.

79 *TC*, 289.

80 *TC*, 290.

81 *TC*, 291.

82 *TC*, 292: "There is light in the world, blind man . . . As before, so now."

83 This idea of hope will be developed more fully in chapter 5.
84 *TC*, 296.
85 *TC*, 296.
86 *TC*, 298. This recalls the Huisiachepican hermit telling Billy that he was the priest who had debated with the Caborcan.

3 THE DECENTERING OF THE HUMAN SUBJECT

1 McCarthy, *Suttree*, 5.
2 Cant, *Myth of American Exceptionalism*, 176.
3 Guillemin, *Pastoral Vision of Cormac McCarthy*, 73.
4 *BM*, 3.
5 *BM*, 16.
6 This effect is similar to the approach of Annie Dillard at Tinker Creek, although her technique is different. Crews, *Books Are Made Out*, 166–69 finds evidence that suggests McCarthy has read Dillard.
7 *BM*, 56–57.
8 *BM*, 261.
9 For example in *BM*, 256.
10 Guillemin, *Pastoral Vision of Cormac McCarthy*, 80.
11 *ATPH*, 61.
12 *TC*, 75.
13 *ATPH*, 309.
14 *TC*, 47.
15 *TOK*, 184–86; *TR*, 306–7. Alter, *Pen of Iron*, 172 writes about how in *The Road* McCarthy uses a paratactic style to map the topography of "an order of reality fundamentally alien to the reality in which and for which our shared language has been framed."
16 *BM*, 258.
17 There are twenty-five in chapter 38 and a further fourteen in chapter 39.
18 See S. R. Driver and G. B. Gray, *A Critical and Exegetical Commentary on the Book of Job: The International Critical Commentary* (Edinburgh: T&T Clark, 1921), 324; N. C. Habel, *The Book of Job: A Commentary* (London: SCM Press, 1985), 527; and Clines, *Job 38–42*, 1087–88 for discussions about the meaning of this interrogative onslaught. L. G. Perdue, *Wisdom in Revolt: Metaphorical Theology in the Book of Job* (Sheffield, U.K.: Almond, 1991), 201 thinks that it is "like a school-teacher interrogating a student,'" while Longman, *Job*, 64 reads it as an expression of exasperation, like a teacher with an upstart student. Gordis, *Book of God and Man*, 128 points out that to read the speeches as a naked display of divine intellect and power that demands Job's surrender would be "a stultifying conclusion to a brilliant debate." H. H. Rowley, *Job* (London: Thomas Nelson, 1970), 308 notes that while

there is rebuke in the speeches, that is not their dominant note, which is to encourage Job to humbly submit to God.

19 Pope, *Job: Introduction, Translation and Notes*, lxxx.

20 W. P. Brown, *Wisdom's Wonder: Character, Creation, and Crisis in the Bible's Wisdom Literature* (Grand Rapids: Eerdmans, 2014), 16.

21 Clines, *Job 38–42*, 1090. É. Dhorme, *A Commentary on the Book of Job*, trans. H. Knight (Nashville, Tenn.: Thomas Nelson, 1967), lviii says that they are governed by "a sense of sublimity."

22 Robert Alter, *The Art of Biblical Poetry: Revised and Updated* (New York: Basic Books, 2011), 120–21 contrasts Job's initial speech in chapter 3 with God's initial speech in chapter 38: "In Job's initial poem, various elements of the larger world were introduced only as reflectors or rhetorical tokens of his suffering. When the world is seen here through God's eyes, each item is evoked for its own sake, each existing thing having its own intrinsic and often strange beauty." Job cannot see the external world of creation as anything other than material for his use, but God rejects such an anthropocentric grasping at His creation.

23 Newsom, *Job*, 242.

24 Brown, *Ethos of the Cosmos*, 350; Clines, *Job 38–42*, 1118.

25 Newsom, *Book of Job*, 245.

26 Alter, *Art of Biblical Poetry*, 127 describes how this chapter's depiction of "the nonmoral realm" of the animal world and "the sharp paradoxes it embodies make us see the inadequacy of any merely human moral calculus," whether that of Job's comforters or of Job himself.

27 Brown, *Ethos of the Cosmos*, 365–67.

28 Newsom, *Job*, 632.

29 Newsom, *Job*, 337; cf. Clines, *Job 38–42*, 1088–92.

30 As Alter, *Art of Biblical Poetry*, 129 sees, the decision to have God speak not in the arena of justice, which is the most common metaphor used by Job after chapter 3, but that of creation is important, for it is "a creation that barely reflects the presence of man, a creation where human concepts of justice have no purchase."

31 David Holloway, "Modernism, Nature, and Utopia: Another Look at 'Optical Democracy' in Cormac McCarthy's Western Quartet," *The Southern Quarterly* 38, no. 3 (2000): 194 sees that McCarthy often uses "similes that fail to do the work of similes" by his authorial refusal to use "a clearly designated subordinate clause in which the parallel might be drawn." This then represses the simile deep into a pile of competing detail, adding to, rather than qualifying, the superabundance of objects on view. This hollowing out of the simile then has the further effect of doing away with the notion that any given detail in the scene might be more contingent or of any lesser value than any other detail.

32 *BM*, 56–57.

33 Steven Shaviro, "'The Very Life of the Darkness': A Reading of *Blood Meridian*," in *Perspectives on Cormac McCarthy*, ed. Edwin T. Arnold and Dianne C. Luce (Jackson, Miss.: University Press of Mississippi, 1999), 153.

34 Bell, *Achievement of Cormac McCarthy*, 129 says that "our assumptions about the place of human power over the world are thereby called into question."

35 Holloway, "Modernism, Nature, and Utopia," 199.

36 Shaviro, "'Very Life of the Darkness,'" 153–54 says that "this is not a perspective *upon* the world, and not a vision that *intends* its objects: but an immanent perspective that already *is* the world, and a primordial visibility, a luminescence that is indifferent to our acts of vision because it is always passively at work whatever objects we may or may not happen to look at" (emphasis added).

37 *BM*, 144–45.

38 Guillemin, *Pastoral Vision of Cormac McCarthy*, 79.

39 J. M. Soskice, *Metaphor and Religious Language* (Oxford: Clarendon, 1985), 15 (emphasis added).

40 Soskice, *Metaphor and Religious Language*, 48 says that "what is identified and described is identified and described uniquely by this metaphor. It is in this way that a metaphor is genuinely creative and says something that can be said adequately in no other way, not as an ornament to what we already know but as an embodiment of a new insight."

41 K. Nielsen, *There Is Hope for a Tree: The Tree as Metaphor in Isaiah* (Sheffield, U.K.: Sheffield Academic, 1989), 55.

42 Soskice, *Metaphor and Religious Language*, 69–70; D. Brown, *God and Mystery in Words: Experience through Metaphor and Drama* (Oxford: Oxford University Press, 2008), 56.

43 Brown, *God and Mystery in Words*, 56. We do not suggest that metaphorical language is the only way of transmitting meaning (or even the superior way), nor do we competitively play off literal and nonliteral language, propositional definition, and metaphor. Rather, we recognize that both contribute to a description of, and engagement with, the world. As Eberhard Jüngel, "Metaphorical Truth: Reflections on the Theological Relevance of Metaphor as a Contribution to the Hermeneutics of Narrative Theology," in *Theological Essays 1*, ed. John B. Webster (Edinburgh: T&T Clark, 1989), 68 states, "Metaphor is language which liberates, whereas the definition limits and secures. Both are means of stating more precisely that which is."

44 Clines, *Job 38–42*, 1089.

45 Coulson, *Religion and Imagination*, 44 argues that "our language achieves its greatest range and precision, not in the plain and literal style

of Francis Bacon, but in the densely metaphorical style of Shakespeare and Donne."

46 As argued by Rowan Williams, *The Edge of Words: God and the Habits of Language* (London: Bloomsbury, 2014), 68.

47 *CD* II/1, 115.

48 Metaphor is distinct from a model in that metaphor speaks *language* suggestive of something else, whereas a model regards something in terms of another. See Soskice, *Metaphor and Religious Language*, 51.

49 Some commentators, such as A. Pelham, *Contested Creations in the Book of Job: The World-as-It-Ought-and-Ought-Not-to-Be* (Leiden: Brill, 2012), 112–13; Perdue, *Wisdom in Revolt*, 207; and C. Keller, *Face of the Deep: A Theology of Becoming* (Abingdon, U.K.: Routledge, 2003), 131 conflate these such that the Sea is a rambunctious infant needing to be penned in, as if the Sea were a baby at whose birth God was midwife, or even the offspring of God's own womb. Such an integration is unnecessary and robs the language of its richness and unusual contrasts.

50 Clines, *Job 38–42*, 1054, notes that the noun for swaddling bands, which is unique to Job, and the verb חתל, which is found at Ezek 16:4, "are not specifically related to wrapping up infants."

51 Clines, *Job 38–42*, 1189.

52 Soskice, *Metaphor and Religious Language*, 60.

53 This is seen in the repeated interrogatives of Job 41:1-7.

54 Brown, *God and Mystery in Words*, 8.

55 Brown, *God and Mystery in Words*, 50.

56 Clines, *Job 38–42*, 1188.

57 Janzen, *Job*, 234.

58 Janzen, *Job*, 13.

59 Janzen, *Job*, 246.

60 Janzen, *Job*, 259.

61 Newsom, *Job*, 625–26.

4 THE LOOMING THREAT OF CHAOS

1 McCarthy, *Suttree*, 435–36.

2 *BM*, 145 (emphasis added).

3 *BM*, 258 (emphasis added).

4 Wirtz, the sadistic German officer responsible for the condition of the *ciego* in *The Crossing*, could also be slotted into this lineage.

5 *OD*, 55, 102.

6 *OD*, 37, 135.

7 *OD*, 244–46.

8 Guillemin, *Pastoral Vision of Cormac McCarthy*, 55.

9 *OD*, 17.

10 Bell, *Achievement of Cormac McCarthy*, 34.
11 Even his gaze is disturbingly cold and unsettling. While painting a barn roof he watches a girl move through the farmyard, "the shape of her breasts pulling against the cloth" (*OD*, 96), indicating, perhaps, a sexual voyeurism and leering lustfulness.
12 The claim of Edwin T. Arnold, "Naming, Knowing and Nothingness: McCarthy's Moral Parables," in *Perspectives on Cormac McCarthy*, ed. Edwin T. Arnold and Dianne C. Luce (Jackson, Miss.: University Press of Mississippi, 1999), 47–49 that Rinthy's name is a contraction of Corinthians and his identification of intertextual links between the novel and Paul's first epistle to that church are far-fetched and unconvincing.
13 Lydia R. Cooper, "McCarthy, Tennessee, and the Southern Gothic," in *The Cambridge Companion to Cormac McCarthy*, ed. Steven Frye (Cambridge: Cambridge University Press, 2013), 46.
14 James R. Giles, "*Outer Dark* and Romantic Naturalism," in *The Cambridge Companion to Cormac McCarthy*, ed. Steven Frye (Cambridge: Cambridge University Press, 2013), 97 suggests that it may be that Rinthy is received more sympathetically because while Culla's abandonment of his child is an act of cold cowardice that bespeaks a flight from responsibility, Rinthy is seeking to fulfill hers.
15 Cant, *Myth of American Exceptionalism*, 82.
16 Giles, "*Outer Dark* and Romantic Naturalism," 99.
17 Arnold, "Naming, Knowing and Nothingness," 54.
18 Luce, *Reading the World*, 63 argues that "our experience of the world is always a projection of our inner grace or darkness, and the world of 'reality' is largely subjective." In a similar vein, William C. Spencer, "Cormac McCarthy's Unholy Trinity: Biblical Parody in *Outer Dark*," in *Sacred Violence: A Reader's Companion to Cormac McCarthy*, ed. Wade Hall and Rick Wallach (El Paso, Tex.: Texas Western Press, 1995), 73 argues that the steady disintegration of the italic/regular type structure through the book implies that the evil represented by the triune is not something external and without but resides within, an internal trait. See also Bell, *Achievement of Cormac McCarthy*, 35–36; Giles, "*Outer Dark* and Romantic Naturalism," 104; and Evenson, "McCarthy and the Uses of Philosophy," 55.
19 John M. Grammer, "A Thing against Which Time Will Not Prevail: Pastoral and History in Cormac McCarthy's South," in *Perspectives on Cormac McCarthy*, ed. Edwin T. Arnold and Dianne C. Luce (Jackson, Miss.: University Press of Mississippi, 1999), 35 argues that they are time, reaping the souls of those whose time is up, whereas Cant, *Myth of American Exceptionalism*, 77 sees them as an anti-Trinity, described in nimbused terms, through whom McCarthy launches a "radical and extreme attack on the beliefs and imagery of 'that old time religion.'"

Luce, *Reading the World*, 88 detects in them a deviant Gnosticism, while to Frye, *Understanding Cormac McCarthy*, 29 they represent Fate. Brian Evenson, "Embodying Violence: The Case of Cormac McCarthy," *The Cormac McCarthy Journal* 14, no. 2 (2016): 141 reads them as "embodiments of evil, perhaps called up by Culla's actions," which recalls the assertion of Cooper, "McCarthy, Tennessee, and the Southern Gothic," 45 that they intensify evil, forcing Culla to admit that which he is attempting to hide. Arnold, "Naming, Knowing and Nothingness," 50 sees a connection between Culla and the bearded leader of the grim triune in that neither of them wishes to disclose his name to the other and each of them has forsworn the opportunity to name another, Culla his infant son and the leader the mute member of his vicious party. Thus the unnamed child and the triune's mute function as versions of each other. This is supported by Culla's denial of paternity to his son being the cause of all his subsequent misfortune, which coheres with the suggestion that the unnamed mute "just by *being*, directed Culla to them" (emphasis added). On this reading, it is significant that the baby's death, intended but not performed by Culla, is completed by the triune, specifically the bearded one who represents Culla. Moreover, it is the mute, representing the baby, who feeds on its pumping blood.

20 For the view that they are evil, see Spencer, "Cormac McCarthy's Unholy Trinity," 69–72.

21 *OD*, 3.

22 *OD*, 150; cf. 53, 90, 99, 133.

23 *OD*, 53; cf. 35.

24 *OD*, 133; cf. 99.

25 *OD*, 186.

26 *OD*, 238.

27 While lexicons do not cite Job 40:15 specifically, L. Koehler and W. Baumgartner, *The Hebrew and Aramaic Lexicon of the Old Testament*, trans. M. E. J. Richardson (Leiden: Brill, 2001), 252 give the primary meaning of *hinnēh* (הִנֵּה) as "behold, see" in the sense of "calls attention to the following noun," while F. Brown, *A Hebrew and English Lexicon of the Old Testament, with an Appendix Containing the Biblical Aramaic: Based on the Lexicon of William Gesenius as Translated by Edward Robinson* (Oxford: Clarendon, 1952), 243 gives it as "lo! behold!" when "pointing to persons or things." The נָא is emphatic, "craving a favourable consideration of the fact pointed to by הִנֵּה, and of the request founded upon it" (Brown, *Hebrew and English Lexicon*, 609; cf. Koehler, *Hebrew and Aramaic Lexicon*, 656–57). Thus we follow Clines, *Job 38–42*, 1186–87 in reading *hinneh na* (הִנֵּה־נָא) as explicit encouragement to Job to reflect "on the significance of what

is seen, for the meaning of the divine response will only be discerned beneath the level of the visible."

28 Clines, *Job 38–42*, 1188.

29 Clines, *Job 38–42*, 1201.

30 Driver and Gray, *Critical and Exegetical Commentary*, 1.353; Dhorme, *Commentary on Job*, lix, xciii, 619; E. J. Kissane, *The Book of Job: Translated from a Critically Revised Hebrew Text with Commentary* (Dublin: Richview, 1939), 286, 288; Gordis, *Book of God and Man*, 119–20; R. Gordis, *The Book of Job: Commentary, New Translation, and Special Studies* (New York: Jewish Theological Seminary of America, 1978), xxxi, 558; Clines, *Job 38–42*, 1184, 1192; and J. Gray, *The Book of Job* (Sheffield, U.K.: Sheffield Phoenix, 2010), 68, 489–90.

31 Pelham, *Contested Creations*, 182. See too Hartley, *Book of Job*, 524; Pope, *Job: Introduction, Translation and Notes*, xxii.

32 For example, the argument of Perdue, *Wisdom in Revolt*, which itself builds on the prior work of Hermann Gunkel, "The Influence of Babylonian Mythology upon the Biblical Creation Story," in *Creation in the Old Testament*, ed. Bernhard W. Anderson (London: SPCK, 1984).

33 D. T. Tsumura, *The Earth and the Waters in Genesis 1 and 2: A Linguistic Investigation* (Sheffield, U.K.: Sheffield Academic, 1989), 50, 65, 157–58.

34 Kissane, *Book of Job*, 288; John Bimson, "Fierce Beasts and Free Processes: A Proposed Reading of God's Speeches in the Book of Job," in *Wisdom, Science and the Scriptures: Essays in Honour of Ernest Lucas*, ed. Stephen Finamore and John Weaver (Oxford: Bristol Baptist College and Regent's Park College, 2012), 21.

35 N. Whybray, *Job* (Sheffield, U.K.: Sheffield Phoenix, 2008), 19, 185.

36 Newsom, *Book of Job*, 248, 252; Newsom, *Job*, 614–15.

37 The NRSV follows one of the emendations suggested by Dhorme, *Commentary on Job*, 631–32, and translates this as "under the whole heaven, who?" Gordis, *Book of Job*, 483 states that to translate תַּחַת כָּל־הַשָּׁמַיִם לִי־הוּא as "beneath the entire sky all is mine," is "unexceptional," but "irrelevant in the context." He thus emends לִי־הוּא (*li-hû*) to לֹא־הוּא (*lō-hû*). Clines, *Job 38–42*, 1162 believes that the verse's subject is Leviathan and so emends the text to לֹא אֶחָד (*lō eḥād*).

38 T. E. Fretheim, *God and World in the Old Testament: A Relational Theology of Creation* (Nashville, Tenn.: Abingdon, 2005), 235–36; T. E. Fretheim, *Creation Untamed: The Bible, God and Natural Disasters* (Grand Rapids: Baker Academic, 2010), 79, 89.

39 *OD*, 35.

40 *OD*, 53.

41 Arnold, "Naming, Knowing and Nothingness," 62 describes them as "the same manifestation, extended over time and space," and according

to Giles, "*Outer Dark* and Romantic Naturalism," 102, they "exist in some dimension simultaneously inside and outside physical space. Their crimes are so brutal, so random and unmotivated that they seem to be, at least on one level, agents of an unknowable supernatural force." See too Frye, "Histories, Novels, Ideas," 5.

42 John E. Sepich, "'What Kind of Indians Was Them?' Some Historical Sources in Cormac McCarthy's *Blood Meridian*," in *Perspectives on Cormac McCarthy*, ed. Edwin T. Arnold and Dianne C. Luce (Jackson, Miss.: University Press of Mississippi, 1999), 127ff.; Patrick W. Shaw, "The Kid's Fate, the Judge's Guilt: Ramifications of Closure in Cormac McCarthy's *Blood Meridian*," *Southern Literary Journal* 30, no. 1 (1997): 110.

43 Frye, *Understanding Cormac McCarthy*, 72; Mundik, *Bloody and Barbarous God*, 8, 54–55.

44 Frye, *Understanding Cormac McCarthy*, 67.

45 On literature's concretization of theological and philosophical stances, see Coulson, *Religion and Imagination*; Paul S. Fiddes, "Concept, Image and Story in Systematic Theology," *International Journal of Systematic Theology* 11, no. 1 (2009); and Hans S. Gustafson, "Sacramental Spirituality in *The Brothers Karamazov* and Wendell Berry's Port William Characters," *Journal of Literature & Theology* 27, no. 3 (2014).

46 As suggested by Linda Woodson, "McCarthy's Heroes and the Will to Truth," in *The Cambridge Companion to Cormac McCarthy*, ed. Steven Frye (Cambridge: Cambridge University Press, 2013), 17.

47 Dennis Sansom, "Learning from Art: Cormac McCarthy's *Blood Meridian* as a Critique of Divine Determinism," *The Journal of Aesthetic Education* 41, no. 1 (2007) reads it as an examination of theo-determinism, in which the sovereign God is cause of all, and therefore all actions reveal God's will.

48 *BM*, 6, 8, 84, 98, 125, 136, 206, 231, 253, 344.

49 *BM*, 177; cf. 346.

50 *BM*, 353; cf. 130, 179–80, 200.

51 *BM*, 102.

52 *BM*, 89–91, 178, 342.

53 *BM*, 124, 130, 178, 252–53, 268, 298.

54 *BM*, 130, 147.

55 *BM*, 132–42.

56 *BM*, 123–26, 169–73, 201–2, 252, 287–90, 342–51.

57 *BM*, 202, 273. On McCarthy's treatment of James Robert and disability in *Blood Meridian*, see Ploskonka, "'See the Wild Man Two Bits.'"

58 *BM*, 133.

59 Cant, *Myth of American Exceptionalism*, 167.

60 *BM*, 209.
61 *BM*, 117–18, 134, 140, 147, 182, 208–9.
62 *BM*, 209.
63 *BM*, 148.
64 *BM*, 38, 230, 343–44, 353.
65 *BM*, 6–7, 99–101, 131, 343ff.
66 *BM*, 133.
67 *BM*, 173, 290, 300–301, 308–9.
68 *BM*, 134.
69 *BM*, 346.
70 *BM*, 348.
71 *BM*, 258–59.
72 *BM*, 347.
73 *BM*, 349.
74 Rick Wallach, "Judge Holden: *Blood Meridian*'s Evil Archon," in *Sacred Violence: A Reader's Companion to Cormac McCarthy*, ed. Wade Hall and Rick Wallach (El Paso, Tex.: Texas Western Press, 1995), 128–29.
75 Cassie Polasek, "'Books Are Made Out of Books': Herman Melville's Moby Dick and Cormac McCarthy's Judge Holden," in *They Rode On: Blood Meridian and the Tragedy of the American West*, ed. Rick Wallach (Miami: Cormac McCarthy Society, 2013), 82–94; Mundik, *Bloody and Barbarous God*, 31; Bell, *Achievement of Cormac McCarthy*, 119.
76 Emily J. Stinson, "*Blood Meridian*'s Man of Many Masks: Judge Holden as Tarot Fool," in *They Rode On: Blood Meridian and the Tragedy of the American West*, ed. Rick Wallach (Miami: Cormac McCarthy Society, 2013), 107.
77 Stephen Pastore, "Judge Holden: Yahweh on Horseback," in *They Rode On: Blood Meridian and the Tragedy of the American West*, ed. Rick Wallach (Miami: Cormac McCarthy Society, 2013), 108–11.
78 Broncano, *Religion in Cormac McCarthy's Fiction*, 50.
79 Daugherty, "Gravers False and True," 164; Mundik, *Bloody and Barbarous God*, 32–35.
80 Chris Dacus, "The West as Symbol of the Eschaton in Cormac McCarthy," *The Cormac McCarthy Journal* 7, no. 1 (2009): 8.
81 Cant, *Myth of American Exceptionalism*, 170.
82 Dan Moos, "Lacking the Article Itself: Representation and History in Cormac McCarthy's *Blood Meridian*," *The Cormac McCarthy Journal* 2, no. 1 (2002): 29.
83 Broncano, *Religion in Cormac McCarthy's Fiction*, 52.
84 Jarrett, *Cormac McCarthy*, 81.
85 Iain Bernhoft, "'Some Desperate Entrepreneur Fleeing from a Medicine Show': Judge Holden in the Age of P. T. Barnum," *The Cormac*

McCarthy Journal 10, no. 1 (2012): 27–45; Guillemin, *Pastoral Vision of Cormac McCarthy*, 88.

86 Scott D. Yarbrough, "Tricksters and Lightbringers in McCarthy's Post-Appalachian Novels," *The Cormac McCarthy Journal* 10, no. 1 (2010): 48.

87 Jordan Carson, "Drawing Fire from the Text: Narrative and Morality in *Blood Meridian*," *The Cormac McCarthy Journal* 12 (2014): 22.

88 Guillemin, *Pastoral Vision of Cormac McCarthy*, 85, 96.

89 Sansom, "Learning from Art," 9.

90 Carson, "Drawing Fire from the Text," 23.

91 Stinson, "*Blood Meridian*'s Man of Many Masks," 95.

92 Edwin T. Arnold, "'Go to Sleep': Dreams and Visions in the Border Trilogy," in *A Cormac McCarthy Companion: The Border Trilogy*, ed. Edwin T. Arnold and Dianne C. Luce (Jackson, Miss.: University Press of Mississippi, 2001), 46.

93 This is developed most fully by Potts, *Signs of Sacrament*, 47–51.

94 See Bernhoft, "'Some Desperate Entrepreneur,'" for the full argument.

95 *BM*, 258.

96 *BM*, 266.

97 Arnold, "Naming, Knowing and Nothingness," 66.

98 *BM*, 118 (emphasis added).

99 *BM*, 102: "The judge like a great ponderous djinn stepped through the fire and the flames delivered him up as if he were in some way native to their element." Cf. *OD*, 186.

100 *BM*, 7, 292, 353.

101 *BM*, 342–43.

102 *BM*, 177.

103 *BM*, 148.

104 Job 41:25. Clines, *Job 38–42*, 1146, 1169 takes אֵלִם (*'ēlim*) as a variant spelling of the plural of אַיִל, meaning "ram, chief," and so, by metaphorical extension, hero. For this comparative point, the precise identification of the subject is not determinative.

105 *BM*, 9.

106 *BM*, 344.

107 *BM*, 138.

108 *BM*, 262–64.

109 *BM*, 155.

110 For example, John Vanderheide, "Varieties of Renunciation in the Works of Cormac McCarthy," *The Cormac McCarthy Journal* 5, no. 1 (2005): 34; Robert L. Jarrett, "Genre, Voice and Ethos: McCarthy's Perverse 'Thriller,'" *The Cormac McCarthy Journal* 5, no. 1 (2005): 38–42, 55; and Parrish, "History and the Problem of Evil," 67–75. Linda Woodson, "'. . . You Are the Battleground': Materiality, Moral Responsibility and Determinism in No Country for Old Men," *The Cormac McCarthy*

Journal 5, no. 1 (2005): 8 argues that "both the judge and Chigurh are beyond good and evil," and Yarbrough, "Tricksters and Lightbringers," 50 suggests that Chigurh evokes Holden's occasional coin trickery.
111 Evenson, "Embodying Violence," 137; Frye, *Understanding Cormac McCarthy*, 160; Cant, *Myth of American Exceptionalism*, 70, 91, 95, 116, 185, 189, 205, 248.
112 *NCFOM*, 3–4, 38–40, 62–64, 90–91, 123–24, 158–60, 195–97, 216–18, 248–49, 281–85, 293–99, 303–5, 307–9.
113 Cant, *Myth of American Exceptionalism*, 241; Mundik, *Bloody and Barbarous God*, 262; cf. Kushner, "Cormac McCarthy's Apocalypse." However, it would be odd for McCarthy to suddenly break the habit of a literary lifetime and use a character as his own mouthpiece. Furthermore, this would not seem to fit with the way that McCarthy views his literary works.
114 Cant, *Myth of American Exceptionalism*, 248.
115 Cant, *Myth of American Exceptionalism*, 249; Broncano, *Religion in Cormac McCarthy's Fiction*, 110.
116 Jarrett, "Genre, Voice and Ethos," 37; Walsh, "(Carrying the Fire on)," 344.
117 Mundik, *Bloody and Barbarous God*, 265.
118 *NCFOM*, 52.
119 *NCFOM*, 55.
120 *NCFOM*, 111–12.
121 Woodson, "'. . . You Are the Battleground,'" 8; cf. *NCFOM*, 248, 299.
122 *NCFOM*, 55, 260.
123 *NCFOM*, 6–7, 60–63, 112, 292.
124 *NCFOM*, 53–58.
125 *NCFOM*, 46–47, 79, 134, 192.
126 *NCFOM*, 141, 175–78.
127 *NCFOM*, 173.
128 *NCFOM*, 161–62. This recalls Dostoyevsky's use of narratorial limitation in *The Idiot*.
129 John Cant, "Oedipus Rests: Mimesis and Allegory in *No Country for Old Men*," *The Cormac McCarthy Journal* 5, no. 1 (2005): 55.
130 Jarrett, "Genre, Voice and Ethos,'" 39; cf. *NCFOM*, 253.
131 *NCFOM*, 259–60.
132 *NCFOM*, 55–58.
133 Jay Ellis, "'Do You See?': Levels of Ellipsis in *No Country for Old Men*," in *Cormac McCarthy: All the Pretty Horses, No Country for Old Men, The Road*, ed. Sara L. Spurgeon (London: Continuum, 2011), 96; cf. 99.
134 *NCFOM*, 91, 127.
135 *NCFOM*, 156.

136 *NCFOM*, 108, 130, 136, 158.
137 *NCFOM*, 73, 131–32, 141.
138 *NCFOM*, 234; cf. 236–42.
139 *NCFOM*, 267.
140 *NCFOM*, 259.
141 And they also recur in *The Counselor*.
142 The phrase *cara y cruz*, literally meaning "face and cross," is the Spanish equivalent of "heads or tails."
143 *ATPH*, 236.
144 *TC*, 188–89.
145 A *corrido* is a narrative song with a moral, similar to a folk ballad; *TC*, 385, 391, 396.
146 *TC*, 207.
147 *TC*, 147.
148 *TC*, 191.
149 *TC*, 390.
150 *COTP*, 196–97.
151 *COTP*, 209.
152 In several plays Shakespeare probes the geographical and emotional elasticity of the Job story in different contexts, but *King Lear* is the most Joban. See Julia Reinhard Lupton, "The Wizards of Uz: Shakespeare and the Book of Job," in *Shakespeare and Religion: Early Modern and Postmodern Perspectives*, ed. Ken Jackson and Arthur F. Marotti (Notre Dame, Ind.: University of Notre Dame Press, 2011), 177; H. Hamlin, *The Bible in Shakespeare* (Oxford: Oxford University Press, 2013), 306; Paffenroth, *In Praise of Wisdom*, 70; Kenneth Muir, "Epilogue," in *King Lear: Critical Essays*, ed. Kenneth Muir (New York: Garland, 1984), 289; and S. Marx, *Shakespeare and the Bible* (Oxford: Oxford University Press, 2000), 162.
153 Alexander L. Barron, "'As Full of Grief as Age': *King Lear* as Tragic Ancestor to *No Country for Old Men*," *The Cormac McCarthy Journal* 10, no. 1 (2012): 24.
154 *NCFOM*, 147–48; cf. 114–22; 260–62.
155 *NCFOM*, 177.
156 *NCFOM*, 287.
157 *NCFOM*, 4.
158 *NCFOM*, 112.
159 *NCFOM*, 119–22.
160 *NCFOM*, 140.
161 Clines, *Job 38–42*, 1202–3.
162 Gordis, *Book of Job*, 560, 566; Gordis, *Book of God and Man*, 155.
163 Janzen, *Job*, 244–46.

164 A. Dillard, *Pilgrim at Tinker Creek* (Norwich, U.K.: Canterbury, 2011), 148: "Beauty itself is the fruit of the creator's exuberance that grew such a tangle, and the grotesques and the horrors bloom from that same free growth, that intricate scramble and twine up and down the conditions of time." Most sleepwalk through this theater of wonder, but those awake to reality encounter great beauty and great violence. A proper appreciation of creation requires the apprehension of this inherent paradox, the truth of which is that "you cannot have mountains and creeks without space, and space is a beauty married to a blind man. The blind man is Freedom, or Time, and he does not go anywhere without his great dog Death" (183).

165 J. Agee, *A Death in the Family* (London: Penguin, 2006), 140–41.

166 Newsom, *Job*, 602.

167 In Job 7:12 Job appears to recognize this, for he asks "Am I the Sea, or the Dragon, that you set a guard over me?"

168 K. Schifferdecker, *Out of the Whirlwind: Creation Theology in the Book of Job* (Cambridge, Mass.: Harvard University Press, 2008), 120; cf. Sylvia Huberman Scholnick, "The Meaning of *Mispat* in the Book of Job," *Journal of Biblical Literature* 101, no. 4 (1982): 521.

169 This notoriously problematic verse uses the verb נחם (*nḥm*), and exactly how this verb should be translated and what the meaning of Job's sentiment is are inextricably linked. Dhorme, *Commentary on Job*, 647; Gordis, *Book of God and Man*, 120, Rowley, *Job*, 342; Pope, *Job: Introduction, Translation and Notes*, 347; Habel, *Book of Job*, 576; and Longman, *Job*, 450 take it to mean "repent," although none of them states categorically what sin it is that requires Job's repentance. There is a suggestion that it is presumptuous and intemperate speech, but, as Wilson, *Job*, 206, points out, if 42:6 is the repentance of some vague spoken sin, it is curious that there is no declaration of subsequent divine forgiveness.

Although using the word "repent," Habel, *Book of Job*, 576, 583 takes its meaning to be "changing a course of action"; thus, Job ceases his lamenting stance toward God and chooses to leave grief behind. This is similar to the view of Hartley, *Book of Job*, 535–37 that Job withdraws his claim to innocence but without remorse, which leads him to prefer "recant." G. Gutiérrez, *On Job: God-Talk and the Suffering of the Innocent* (Maryknoll, N.Y.: Orbis, 1987), 86 notes that the verb *nḥm* with the preposition עַל (*'al*) usually means "change one's mind" or "reverse an opinion" (for example, in Exod 32:12, 14; Jer 18:8, 10; Amos 7:3, 6), and chooses that meaning, as does Wilson, *Job*, 16 for the same reason. Walton, *Job*, 432 concurs but suggests that Job is "moving on" from dust and ashes; in today's parlance, he is putting his sufferings out of his mind. Balentine, *Job*, 695 believes that Job sees his situation anew, presumably as a result of illumination from the divine speeches. Such a deliberate attitude on the part of Job is something that Clines, *Job 38–42*, 1208–24 wishes to highlight, so he translates it as "I accept consolation" for dust and ashes, preferring this to "repent." But Clines' Job is not determining to live out of fresh theophanic illumination. Rather, he is concessionary, believing he will never be heard. To Clines God's speeches are merely a reiteration of almighty sovereignty and bring no comfort.

Such fatalistic pessimism is in stark contrast to Gordis, *Book of God and Man*, 132, who insists that God's speeches are not a divine setting-aside of all Job's complaints, but a source of profound comfort to Job. Although using the language of repentance, he sees Job's words as reflecting neither a decision *in spite of* God's speeches nor even a decision *because of* God's speeches, but something far deeper. The speeches have not just changed Job's mind; they have touched his heart. It is most likely that the text of 42:6 has been left deliberately ambiguous. As Janzen, *Job*, 258 says, "The text ends in such an indeterminate way that the hearer or reader is drawn to complete the answer. That readerly act of completion will arise out of one's understanding of the book to this point and no doubt out of one's continuing engagement with the mystery of human existence and vocation in the world and before God."

This is a much more positive assessment than the dismissive conclusion that, because of the uncertainty of *nḥm*, 42:6 is corrupt, as Driver and Gray, *Critical and Exegetical Commentary*, 1.373; 2.347–48 allege. The inherent ambiguity of the verse is something that more recent commentators take seriously, as exemplified by Seow, *Job 1–21*, 72: "Virtually every word may be interpreted in different ways, thus effectively preventing closure." For Newsom, *Job*, 628–29, who gives five meanings to Job's words in 42:6 ("I repent upon . . ."; "I repent on account of . . ."; "I am consoled concerning . . ."; "I have changed my mind concerning . . ."; "I forswear . . ."), this ambiguity means that while one might choose a specific interpretation, which will be conditioned by what one perceives the book to be "about," one must recognize that others are also legitimate.

170 Cf. Rowan Williams, *On Augustine* (London: Bloomsbury, 2016), 83.

171 Alter, *Art of Biblical Poetry*, 137: "Job surely does not have the sort of answer he expected, but he has a strong answer of another kind."

172 In *TC*, 299 the blind man impresses on Billy the importance of realising that men like Wirtz exist: "Entienda que ya existe este ogro. Este chupador de ojos. Él y otros como él. Ellos no han desaparecido del mundo. Y nunca o haran." ("Understand that this ogre already exists. This eyesucker. Him and others like him. They have not fallen from the world. And they never will.")

5 THE POSSIBILITY OF HOPE

1 McCarthy, *Suttree*, 437.
2 Wrongly, as 42:16-17 attest.
3 Cant, *Myth of American Exceptionalism*, 80, 104, and 163 notes the similarities between McCarthy and T. S. Eliot, and this idea of the importance of movement is also found in the closing lines of T. S. Eliot's *East Coker*:

> Old men ought to be explorers
> Here or there does not matter
> We must be still and still moving
> Into another intensity
> For a further union, a deeper communion
> Through the dark cold and the empty desolation,
> The wave cry, the wind cry, the vast waters
> Of the petrel and the porpoise. In my end is my beginning.

T. S. Eliot, *Collected Poems: 1909–1962* (London: Faber and Faber, 1974), 203–4.
4 *COTP*, 293.
5 Brown, *Ethos of the Cosmos*, 374.
6 *TR*, 6.
7 As in Jer 4:22-29.
8 *TR*, 54.
9 Tim Edwards, "The End of the Road: Pastoralism and the Post-Apocalyptic Waste Land of Cormac McCarthy's *The Road*," *The Cormac McCarthy Journal* 6 (2008): 56. Steven Frye, "Life and Career," in *Cormac McCarthy in Context*, ed. Steven Frye (Cambridge: Cambridge University Press, 2020), 11 suggests that it is the result of a meteor strike.
10 *TR*, 13, 20, 23.
11 *TR*, 21.
12 *TR*, 29; cf. 187.
13 *TR*, 28, 33.
14 *TR*, 58.
15 *TR*, 60. Olivia Carr Edenfield, "Ernest Hemingway," in *Cormac McCarthy in Context*, ed. Steven Frye (Cambridge: Cambridge University Press, 2020), 62 and 67, n. 8 argues that her suicide is an act of maternal self-sacrifice that recognizes the father's primary responsibility as to his son, and enables him to fulfill that responsibility by removing from them the risk of her accompanying presence.
16 *TR*, 18–19, 22–23, 43–44, 54, 61, 191–92.
17 *TR*, 62–63.
18 *TR*, 68–74.

19 *TR*, 202; 119–20.
20 *TR*, 113–17.
21 *TR*, 139.
22 *TR*, 196; cf. 197, 272–76, 286–87.
23 *TR*, 14.
24 *TR*, 281; cf. 207–12. Yarbrough, "Tricksters and Lightbringers," 52.
25 *TR*, 300–307. Jacob S. Powning, "'Dreams So Rich in Color. How Else Would Death Call You?': An Exploration of the Ending in Cormac McCarthy's *The Road*," *The Cormac McCarthy Journal* 18, no. 1 (2020) argues that this is too simplistic and optimistic a reading. He has made a persuasive case for the novel's ending being the boy's dying dream.
26 Frye, *Understanding Cormac McCarthy*, 171.
27 Broncano, *Religion in Cormac McCarthy's Fiction*, 139.
28 Vanderheide, "Sighting Leviathan," 108–9.
29 Frye, *Understanding Cormac McCarthy*, 175 asserts that "it expresses with some force the value of belief as an essential ingredient of hope."
30 Michael Madsen, "'A Namelessness Wheeling in the Night': Shapes of Evil in Cormac McCarthy's *Blood Meridian* and John Carpenter's *Halloween*," in *Intertextual and Interdisciplinary Approaches to Cormac McCarthy*, ed. Nicholas Monk (Abingdon, U.K.: Routledge, 2012), 109 states that "it does become hard to argue, though, that the ending of *The Road* can be read as anything but hopeful." See too Frye, *Understanding Cormac McCarthy*, 175 and Alter, *Pen of Iron*, 179, for whom the ending's optimism is underscored in the prose's very rhythms: "Here at the very end, the background of biblical language for the first time strikes an affirmative note, with that background quietly marked by the decorous, slightly archaic subjunctive ('though it pass'), by the very idiom of the breath of God, and by the stately iambic cadence through monosyllables of 'it pass from man to man through all of time.'"
31 Allen Josephs, "The Quest for God in *The Road*," in *The Cambridge Companion to Cormac McCarthy*, ed. Steven Frye (Cambridge: Cambridge University Press, 2013), 140–41.
32 Jan Norbert Gretlund, "Cormac McCarthy and the American Literary Tradition: Wording the End," in *Intertextual and Interdisciplinary Approaches to Cormac McCarthy*, ed. Nicholas Monk (Abingdon, U.K.: Routledge, 2012), 49 says that "we do not know whether the hunter and the woman will eat the boy as soon as they need food." Gretlund is critical of the film adaptation, in which he accuses the director, John Hillcoat, of forcing a Christian ending on the work.
33 *TR*, 16.
34 *TR*, 22, 40–41, 126–31.
35 *TR*, 146.
36 *TR*, 140–65.

37 *TR*, 220.
38 *TR*, 236–61, 280–86.
39 Yarbrough, "Tricksters and Lightbringers," 53.
40 Daniel Luttrull, "Prometheus Hits *The Road*: Revising the Myth," *The Cormac McCarthy Journal* 8, no. 1 (2010): 20.
41 Yarbrough, "Tricksters and Lightbringers," 51.
42 *TR*, 51, 88–89, 171–85, 273–77.
43 *TR*, 277.
44 Erik J. Wielenberg, "God, Morality and Meaning in Cormac McCarthy's *The Road*," *The Cormac McCarthy Journal* 8, no. 1 (2010): 8.
45 Juge, "Road to the Sun," 24.
46 For references to ash, see *TR*, 2, 4–6, 11, 13, 15, 21–22, 24, 33, 40–41, 51–52, 62–63, 72–73, 79, 84, 90, 94–95, 104, 118, 129, 138, 140, 159, 186, 197, 215, 220, 225–26, 229–30, 293.
47 *TR*, 302–3; cf. 81, 108, 160.
48 Josephs, "Quest for God in *The Road*," 133; Russell M. Hillier, "'Like Some Supplicant to the Darkness over Them All': The Good of John Grady Cole in Cormac McCarthy's *Cities of the Plain*," *The Cormac McCarthy Journal* 14, no. 1 (2016): 27–28.
49 *NCFOM*, 309.
50 It is notable that the mistake Llewellyn Moss makes is in "fixin to go do somethin dumbern hell but I'm going anyways," by which he means returning to the scene of the gunfight in order to take water to a dying Mexican doperunner. See *NCFOM*, 24.
51 *NCFOM*, 299.
52 This is the argument of Walsh, "(Carrying the Fire on)," 344.
53 *NCFOM*, 306.
54 *NCFOM*, 307.
55 *NCFOM*, 308.
56 *NCFOM*, 295, 296.
57 *NCFOM*, 308.
58 Christopher T. White, "Dreaming the Border Trilogy: Cormac McCarthy and Narrative Creativity," *The Cormac McCarthy Journal* 13, no. 1 (2015): 128. See also Cormac McCarthy, "The Kekulé Problem: Where Did Language Come From?" *Nautilus* 19 (2017).
59 Cant, *Myth of American Exceptionalism*, 243.
60 Mundik, *Bloody and Barbarous God*, 262; cf. Kushner, "Cormac McCarthy's Apocalypse."
61 David Cremean, "For Whom Bell Tolls: Conservatism and Change in Cormac McCarthy's Sheriff from *No Country for Old Men*," *The Cormac McCarthy Journal* 5, no. 1 (2005): 22.
62 Barron, "'As Full of Grief as Age,'" 17; Flory, "Evil, Mood, and Reflection," 128.

63 *NCFOM*, 309.

64 This is what Potts, *Signs of Sacrament*, 78 fails to do in his identification of two biblical echoes in these dreams. He connects the first dream to the Parable of the Prodigal Son as Bell, the son, loses money belonging to his father. He associates the second dream with Gen 22:6, in which Abraham carries the fire necessary for the offering of Isaac as a sacrifice to God. Potts claims that Genesis records that Abraham carries fire in a horn as Bell's father does, but this is not what the Hebrew text suggests in its use of *bĕyādô* (בְּיָדוֹ), which means "in his hand." For Potts, the first dream concerns forgiveness and the possibility of beginning a new life undefined by the failures of the past. Similarly, the second dream evokes the possibility of new life in the midst of seemingly overwhelming deathliness. He recognizes that both dreams only *suggest* these things, and that their promise is by no means guaranteed.

65 *NCFOM*, 90.

66 *NCFOM*, 279.

67 *NCFOM*, 308.

68 *NCFOM*, 249.

69 *COTP*, 237.

70 Cant, *Myth of American Exceptionalism*, 221–23.

71 Hillier, "'Like Some Supplicant,'" 14. On John Grady Cole see also Cant, *Myth of American Exceptionalism*, 190.

72 Hillier, "'Like Some Supplicant,'" 9 says that in McCarthy's novels "striving to lead a live [*sic*] of moral worth and integrity, despite the tragedy and the loss, even though the attempt may be quixotic, is itself a thing of beauty in McCarthy's universe." See too Christian Kiefer, "The Morality of Blood: Examining the Moral Code of *The Crossing*," *The Cormac McCarthy Journal* 1, no. 1 (2001): 28.

73 *ATPH*, 62.

74 *ATPH*, 100.

75 *ATPH*, 74, 100, 132.

76 *ATPH*, 132.

77 *ATPH*, 34, 74, 88, 90, 284.

78 *TC*, 194.

79 *TC*, 286, 302, 422.

80 *TC*, 47, 137, 146–47.

81 *TC*, 436.

82 *TC*, 437.

83 Josyph, *Cormac McCarthy's House*, 171–74.

84 *TC*, 437; cf. Matt 5:45.

85 This is something in which the influence of T. S. Eliot may be felt: "Between the idea / And the reality / Between the motion / And the act

/ Falls the Shadow" ("The Hollow Men"). See Eliot, *Collected Poems*, 91–92.
86 *ATPH*, 16.
87 *ATPH*, 35.
88 *ATPH*, 241, 244.
89 *TC*, 5.
90 *TC*, 61.
91 *TC*, 65.
92 *TC*, 126.
93 *COTP*, 135.
94 *COTP*, 179–83, 201.
95 *COTP*, 230.
96 *COTP*, 288; cf. *TCo*, 146.
97 Potts, *Signs of Sacrament*, 147.
98 In *TC*, 299 the blind man tells Billy that "no one could speak for the origins of such men nor where they might appear but only of their existence."
99 *TC*, 299.
100 *TC*, 299.
101 *TC*, 287.
102 *TC*, 300.
103 *TC*, 300: "Ultimamente sabemos que no podemos ver el buen Dios. Vamos escuchando. Me entiendes, joven? Debemos escuchar."
104 *TC*, 302.
105 *COTP*, 196.
106 *COTP*, 270.
107 The double meaning of stabling is intended here. Billy, whose life has been lived with horses, is given a place in which he can rest, and in this his life is given stability by Betty's goodness.
108 *COTP*, 293.
109 H. Arendt, *The Human Condition* (Chicago: University of Chicago Press, 1958), 179.
110 *COTP*, 196.
111 See Chris Higgins, "Labour, Work, and Action: Arendt's Phenomenology of Practical Life," *Journal of Philosophy and Education* 44, nos. 2–3 (2010): 283–87 for a fuller discussion of what Arendt means by action.
112 Arendt, *Human Condition*, 184.
113 Arendt, *Human Condition*, 182.
114 Arendt, *Human Condition*, 184.
115 *TC*, 207.
116 Arendt, *Human Condition*, 190.
117 Arendt, *Human Condition*, 184.
118 Arendt, *Human Condition*, 192.
119 *TC*, 50, 137, 139, 243.

120 Potts, *Signs of Sacrament*, 150.
121 Potts, *Signs of Sacrament*, 79 says that in these novels "hope and redemption remain only murmured hints."
122 *BM*, 355.
123 Inevitably, some commentators read it as gnostic. Daugherty, "Gravers False and True," 169 sees in it a description of the mass of blind, barely living humanity who are little more than automatons and have no conception of the mystery inherent in life. The man striking fire is the revealer of gnosis, but most people are ignorant of any divinity. Mundik, *Bloody and Barbarous God*, 95–99 also reads it as gnostic, pertaining to the release of the divine spark from humanity. In her reading "those who search for bones" are those who adhere to scriptural dogma rather than personal experience, and "those who do not seek" are the irreligious. They are contrasted with the man who progresses even as their clockwork mechanism's motion is halting. He has escaped *heimarmene* (universally tyrannical fate), but they have not. These enslaved wanderers cross the man's tracks but cannot understand their significance, assuming them to be a natural phenomenon rather than something external. Although we disagree with Mundik's overall gnostic reading of the novel, we concur with her view that it is important that it does not close with the nakedly gamboling Judge Holden, but this progressing man, indicating that the book is *not* nihilist. In fact we suggest that the epilogue is quietly hopeful.
124 Melville, *Moby Dick*, 328.
125 I am grateful to the anonymous peer reviewer of the *Cormac McCarthy Journal* who alerted me to the central place of the word "cross" in a comment on a version of this section that was submitted for publication.
126 *BM*, 348.
127 We believe that the language here deliberately echoes Jesus' words from Matt 21:44.
128 Carson, "Drawing Fire from the Text," 20–25.
129 Carson, "Drawing Fire from the Text," 21.
130 *BM*, 150.
131 Carson, "Drawing Fire from the Text," 32.
132 *OD*, 246.
133 *OD*, 252.
134 Despite this apparent bleakness, Frye, *Understanding Cormac McCarthy*, 39 reads the ending hopefully, believing that Culla considers helping the blind man. This is a hugely optimistic reading, for the novel never even implies that Culla shows any tangible concern or kindness to the blind man. Moreover, the opposite is true: Culla tried unsuccessfully to conceal his presence from the blind man and then watched him potter "out of sight," with nary a word of warning (*OD*, 252). H. Boguta-

Marchel, *The Evil, the Fated, the Biblical: The Latent Metaphysics of Cormac McCarthy* (Newcastle upon Tyne, U.K.: Cambridge Scholars, 2012), 168 has a reading that is more plausible: Culla knows that someone should help, but refuses to display the necessary moral autonomy for he is "the forever inert," who remains "unchanged even by the horrid sacrifice of his son."

135 *OD*, 246, 251.

136 Grammer, "Thing against Which Time," 38 claims that the book "ends with the sinful pair wandering hopelessly and separately through the ruins of their fallen garden—with all the world before them, perhaps, but not the faintest hint of providential guidance."

137 Potts, *Signs of Sacrament*, 186.

138 There are shades of T.S. Eliot here too, for in Rinthy's end is the hope of a new beginning. The cart tracks in the woods recall "the deep lane / Shuttered with branches, dark in the afternoon" of Eliot's *East Coker*. See Eliot, *Collected Poems*, 196.

139 *OD*, 33.

140 Arnold, "Naming, Knowing and Nothingness," 52–54; Guillemin, *Pastoral Vision of Cormac McCarthy*, 71.

141 Arnold, "Naming, Knowing and Nothingness," 52 believes that for Culla "there is still the possibility for redemption."

142 *OD*, 248 (emphasis added).

143 *OD*, 5–6.

144 *OD*, 250.

145 Arnold, "Naming, Knowing and Nothingness," 53; Guillemin, *Pastoral Vision of Cormac McCarthy*, 56.

146 Although Cant, *Myth of American Exceptionalism*, 82 argues that Culla is linear time and his journey can only be terminated by death, whereas Rinthy is cyclic.

147 Cf. T. S. Eliot: Four Quartets; Burnt Norton I and Little Gidding V. See Eliot, *Collected Poems*, 189–90 and 221–23.

148 *OD*, 33.

149 *OD*, 220–35.

150 Clines, *Job 38–42*, 1241.

151 Brown, *Wisdom's Wonder*, 111.

152 Although Job is neither an Israelite nor bound by such legislation, it is likely that the book's Israelite audience would have heard this countercultural detail.

153 Davis, *Getting Involved with God*, 141–42; cf. Schifferdecker, *Out of the Whirlwind*, 110. See too Brown, *Wisdom's Wonder*, 130–31.

154 For example, Gordis, *Book of Job: Commentary*, 576; Janzen, *Job*, 267–68; Hartley, *Book of Job*, 542; Newsom, *Job*, 635; Wilson, *Job*, 209; and Longman, *Job*, 461.

155 Later on he states that he treated them well, attending to their complaints (Job 31:13-14).
156 However, Newsom, *Job*, 635 cautions that "it is difficult to say whether such 'outrageous' features are supposed to be accepted simply as part of the way one tells a story like this, or whether the author is subtly using this detail to make readers uncomfortable with a story that they would otherwise accept without question."
157 *TR*, 147.
158 *NCFOM*, 90–91, 133, 159–60, 265–66, 285, 300, 305; cf. 68, 136, 168.
159 *NCFOM*, 303.
160 Although the LXX translation of Job 2:9 is considerably expanded. In it, Job's wife, still unnamed, speaks of her own experience of what has befallen Job, and how she wanders about like a hired servant from place to place and from house to house, waiting for the sun to set. For a discussion of her function in the Joban prologue, see E. van Wolde, *Mr and Mrs Job*, trans. J. Bowden (London: SCM Press, 1997), 23–27.
161 *OD*, 233.
162 *OD*, 234.
163 *OD*, 246.
164 Bell, *Achievement of Cormac McCarthy*, 50 sees clearly that "her pain is *caused* by her choice to love and need, by her unwillingness to be less than human" (emphasis added).
165 *COTP*, 293; cf. Mark 9:41.

6 OF THEODICY AND TRANSFORMATION

1 McCarthy, *Suttree*, 437.
2 I take this as being the speech of Job, but Dhorme, *Commentary on Job*, xliv–liii; Rowley, *Job*, 221; Pope, *Job: Introduction, Translation and Notes*, xx; Gordis, *Book of God and Man*, 94–100; Habel, *Book of Job*, 37–39, 364–401; and Clines, *Job 21–37*, 548 all attribute this verse to Bildad. N. N. Snaith, *The Book of Job: Its Origin and Purpose* (London: SCM Press, 1968), 100–103; and A. Lo, *Job 28 as Rhetoric: An Analysis of Job 28 in the Context of Job 22–31* (Leiden: Brill, 2003), 127, 167 give useful summaries of further suggested reconstructions.
3 For example, *TR*, 10: "He descended into a gryke in the stone and there he crouched coughing and he coughed for a long time. Then he just knelt in the ashes. He raised his face to the paling day. Are you there? he whispered. Will I see you at the last? Have you a neck by which to throttle you? Have you a heart? Damn you eternally have you a soul? Oh God, he whispered. Oh God."
4 David Hume, "Dialogues concerning Natural Religion (1779)," in *The Empiricists: John Locke, George Berkeley, David Hume* (Garden City, N.Y.: Anchor, 1974), 493.

5 Eleanore Stump, *Wandering in Darkness: Narrative and the Problem of Suffering* (Oxford: Clarendon, 2010), 4.
6 For a helpful discussion of this area, see K. Surin, *Theology and the Problem of Evil* (Oxford: Basil Blackwell, 1986).
7 J. Swinton, *Raging with Compassion: Pastoral Responses to the Problem of Evil* (Grand Rapids: Eerdmans, 2007), 30–33. Such a viewpoint may also be detected in the assumption, widespread at the time of writing, that a vaccine for COVID-19 would be forthcoming and allow life to return to normal. While a vaccine has been engineered, which will hopefully allow life to more closely resemble what it did prior to the pandemic, such an outcome should not be considered to have been inevitable, and to assume that it was displays sheer human arrogance. Moreover, vaccine inequity means that in many parts of the world, normal life remains some way in the future.
8 Stump, *Wandering in Darkness*, xviii.
9 There is a clear movement from the Tennessee-based locales of his first four novels to the Southwest-Mexican borderlands of *Blood Meridian* and the Border Trilogy to the West Texas *No Country for Old Men* and then into the varied geography of *The Road*, although Cant, *Myth of American Exceptionalism*, 272–73 argues that this returns to East Tennessee, and thence onto the urban setting of *The Sunset Limited*.
10 Bell, *Achievement of Cormac McCarthy*, 1; Woodward, "Cormac McCarthy's Venomous Fiction"; Cant, *Myth of American Exceptionalism*, 11; Frye, *Understanding Cormac McCarthy*, 7.
11 Ronja Vieth, "A Frontier Myth Turns Gothic: *Blood Meridian: Or, the Evening Redness in the West*," *The Cormac McCarthy Journal* 8, no. 1 (2010): 59. For a discussion of the intertextual connections between McCarthy and Faulkner, see Jay Watson, "William Faulkner," in *Cormac McCarthy in Context*, ed. Steven Frye (Cambridge: Cambridge University Press, 2020).
12 Frye, *Understanding Cormac McCarthy*, 14.
13 G. M. Ciuba, *Desire, Violence, and Divinity in Modern Southern Fiction* (Baton Rouge, La.: Louisiana State University Press, 2007), 51.
14 Flannery O'Connor, "Catholic Novelists and Their Readers," in *Mystery & Manners*, ed. Sally and Robert Fitzgerald (London: Faber & Faber, 2014), 185.
15 Vieth, "Frontier Myth Turns Gothic," 62. For further reflections on McCarthy's use of Gothic, see too Guillemin, *Pastoral Vision of Cormac McCarthy*, and the excellent and penetrative investigation of Cooper, "McCarthy, Tennessee, and the Southern Gothic."
16 Within Southern Gothic an important motif is that of physical deformity, which implies emotional distress or moral ambiguity. In *Outer Dark* this deformity is represented by the incest-begotten nameless

child for whom Rinthy is searching. Also in the book there is an equivalence of Culla, the father, with darkness and shadow, while Rinthy, the mother, is associated repeatedly with light and grace. In this book, which echoes both Job and *King Lear* in its timelessness and nonspecific geography, McCarthy conjures a Gothic landscape in which evil is palpable yet undefined, present both in the characters and in the very landscape in which they reside. Vieth, "Frontier Myth Turns Gothic," 55 argues that the Gothic affect of *Blood Meridian*, in which "blood-curdling descriptions of violence are rendered in strikingly beautiful language to play on the sublime effects of attraction and repulsion," enables McCarthy to sound notes of warning about "an optimistically prosperous new nation."

17 This latter question is what the Caborcan asks the priest-hermit in *The Crossing*, and as already discussed, it cannot be answered by the hermit's priestly platitudes because they ignore the particularities of the Caborcan's situation.

18 Augustine, *Confessions*, trans. R. S. Pine-Coffin (London: Penguin, 1961), 148–49; Augustine, *Concerning the City of God against the Pagans*, trans. H. Bettenson (London: Penguin, 2003), 453–54.

19 D. Z. Phillips, *The Problem of Evil and the Problem of God* (London: SCM Press, 2004), 181–82.

20 *TC*, 47.

21 See Phillips, *Problem of Evil*, 181–82.

22 Alter, *Art of Biblical Poetry*, 127 speaks of this chapter's description of "the peculiar beauty of violence," that makes it "probably one of the most unsentimental poetic treatments of the animal world in the Western literary tradition."

23 *BM*, 88, 165, 122–25, 231; *ATPH*, 75, 178, 262; *TC*, 406–7; *NCFOM*, 98–99.

24 J. Hick, *Evil and the God of Love* (London: Macmillan, 1966), 93. However, the same charge has been made of Hick's Irenaean theodicy in Stephen T. Davis, ed., *Encountering Evil: Live Options in Theodicy* (Edinburgh: T&T Clark, 1981), 53.

25 Holmes Rolston III, "Does Nature Need to Be Redeemed?" *Zygon* 29, no. 2 (1994): 213.

26 C. Southgate, *The Groaning of Creation: God, Evolution, and the Problem of Evil* (Louisville, Ky.: Westminster John Knox, 2008), 14.

27 *CD* III/3, 297.

28 Arthur R. Peacocke, "God's Interaction with the World: The Implications of Deterministic 'Chaos' and of Interconnected and Interdependent Complexity," in *Chaos and Complexity: Scientific Perspectives on Divine Action*, ed. Robert John Russell, Nancey Murphy, and Arthur R.

Peacocke (Vatican City: Vatican Observatory Publications, 1997), 286; cf. *CD* III/3, 74.

29 *TC*, 46, 131, 152.

30 *TC*, 131.

31 *TC*, 152.

32 *TC*, 46.

33 H. McCabe, *God and Evil in the Theology of St Thomas Aquinas* (London: Continuum, 2010), 105.

34 John Polkinghorne, *Science and Creation: The Search for Understanding* (London: SPCK, 1988), 63.

35 In *An Enquiry concerning Human Understanding*, section VI, Hume asserts that "though there be no such thing as *Chance* in the world; our ignorance of the real cause of any event has the same influence on the understanding, and begets a like species of belief or opinion." See David Hume, *Enquiries concerning Human Understanding and concerning the Principles of Morals*, ed. L. A. Selby-Bigge (Oxford: Clarendon, 1975), 56.

36 Arthur R. Peacocke, *Creation and the World of Science: The Bampton Lectures, 1978* (Oxford: Clarendon, 1979), 90–91; cf. Peacocke, "God's Interaction," 277.

37 Katherine Sonderegger, *Systematic Theology*, vol. 1: *The Doctrine of God* (Minneapolis: Fortress, 2015), 230.

38 *TC*, 296. This is a God who allows five children to die of cholera (*OD*, 142), who does not save those barricaded for their lives inside a church (*BM*, 63), but does give rain to parched travelers (*BM*, 50). He is a God in whose hand resides all causes (*ATPH*, 28) but whose mind is closed to humankind and who is ultimately inscrutable and his ways unknowable (*TC*, 418; *COTP*, 25, 208).

39 Rowley, *Job*, 49.

40 Clines, *Job 1–20*, 103.

41 Phillips, *Problem of Evil*, 182.

42 These views are also all voiced by men. However, it is important to recognize that McCarthy's books, which are all set in male dominated worlds, contain a quiet female presence that often anchors and roots the male characters. This is most explicit in *NCFOM*, with Bell's frequently stated admiration for his wife, Loretta, but also seen in Carla Jean, who proves herself an equal match to Llewellyn Moss before being the sole character to stand up to Chigurh. In *COTP* it is Betty who rehabilitates Billy, and in *ATPH* Alejandra and the Dueña Alfonsa are integral to the fortunes of John Grady Cole. Furthermore, in *OD* it is Rinthy and not Culla who shows the greater strength of character and will. For further discussion see Linda Woodson, "'This Is Another Country': The Complex Feminine Presence in *All the Pretty Horses*," in *Cormac*

McCarthy: All the Pretty Horses, No Country for Old Men, The Road, ed. Sara L. Spurgeon (London: Continuum, 2011), 25–42.

43 *ATPH*, 226; cf. 291; *OD*, 234; *BM*, 20.

44 *ATPH*, 291.

45 Phillips, *Problem of Evil*, 185.

46 That is to say, their formative effect is not conveyed through propositional content (that would be locution aimed at the faculty of reason) but by the effects of the written word that exceed their semantic domain and do something to the reader through appealing to her imagination. For further details about locution, illocution, and perlocution, see P. Ricoeur, *Interpretation Theory: Discourse and the Surplus of Meaning* (Fort Worth, Tex.: Texas Christian University Press, 1976); Kevin J. Vanhoozer, *Is There a Meaning in This Text? The Bible, the Reader and the Morality of Literary Knowledge* (Leicester, U.K.: Apollos, 1998); and Kevin J. Vanhoozer, "What Is Everyday Theology? How and Why Christians Should Read Culture," in *Everyday Theology: How to Read Cultural Texts and Interpret Trends*, ed. Charles A. Anderson, Michael J. Sleasman, and Kevin J. Vanhoozer (Grand Rapids: Baker Academic, 2007).

47 Flannery O'Connor, "The Nature and Aim of Fiction," in *Mystery & Manners*, ed. Sally and Robert Fitzgerald (London: Faber & Faber, 2014), 75.

48 O'Connor, "Nature and Aim of Fiction," 75.

49 C. S. Lewis, *An Experiment in Criticism* (Cambridge: Cambridge University Press, 1961), 88.

50 C. S. Lewis, "The Literary Impact of the Authorised Version," in *Selected Literary Essays*, ed. Walter Hooper (Cambridge: Cambridge University Press, 1969), 142.

51 *BM*, 129–42.

52 *BM*, 314–15.

53 *BM*, 301, 304, 313; 322; cf. 328, 330.

54 Cf. Job 41:7.

55 And the *ciego* in *The Crossing*.

56 *TC*, 299.

57 These can be read as portrayals of straightforward Christian charity, for the Gospels clearly state the importance of neighbor love and the expanding of the concept "neighbor" to include everyone in need regardless of any human prejudice (Matt 5:42-47; 22:36-40; Luke 6:27-36; 10:29-37).

58 *TC*, 165. See too *ATPH*, 53–54, 79; *TC*, 307–8; and *COTP*, 291–93.

59 *COTP*, 36–37.

60 Cant, *Myth of American Exceptionalism*, 254.

61 *NCFOM*, 24.

62 *NCFOM*, 26.

63 *NCFOM*, 211; cf. 236–42.
64 *TC*, 189.
65 *TR*, 298–301.
66 *NCFOM*, 4.
67 *COTP*, 3.
68 *COTP*, 265; cf. *TC*, 327.
69 *COTP*, 267.

Bibliography

Agee, J. *A Death in the Family*. London: Penguin, 2006.

Agner, Jacob. "Salvaging *The Counselor*: Watching Cormac McCarthy and Ridley Scott's Really Trashy Movie." *The Cormac McCarthy Journal* 14, no. 2 (2016): 204–26.

Alonso-Schökel, Luis. "God's Answer to Job." In *Job and the Silence of God*, edited by Christian Duquoc and Casiano Floristán, 45–51. Edinburgh: T&T Clark, 1983.

Alter, Robert. *The Art of Biblical Poetry: Revised and Updated*. New York: Basic Books, 2011.

———. *Pen of Iron: American Prose and the King James Bible*. Princeton, N.J.: Princeton University Press, 2010.

Alter, Robert, and Frank Kermode. "General Introduction." In *A Literary Guide to the Bible*, edited by Robert Alter and Frank Kermode. London: Fontana, 1997.

Arendt, H. *The Human Condition*. Chicago: University of Chicago Press, 1958.

Arnold, Edwin T. "'Go to Sleep': Dreams and Visions in the Border Trilogy." In *A Cormac McCarthy Companion: The Border Trilogy*, edited by Edwin T. Arnold and Dianne C. Luce, 37–72. Jackson, Miss.: University Press of Mississippi, 2001.

———. "Naming, Knowing and Nothingness: McCarthy's Moral Parables." In *Perspectives on Cormac McCarthy*, edited by Edwin T. Arnold and Dianne C. Luce, 45–70. Jackson, Miss.: University Press of Mississippi, 1999.

Ash, C. *Job: The Wisdom of the Cross*. Wheaton, Ill.: Crossway, 2014.

Augustine. *Concerning the City of God against the Pagans*. Translated by H. Bettenson. London: Penguin, 2003.

——. *Confessions*. Translated by R. S. Pine-Coffin. London: Penguin, 1961.

Balentine, S. E. *Job*. Macon, Ga.: Smyth & Helwys, 2006.

Barnes, J. *Nothing to Be Frightened Of*. London: Vintage, 2009.

Barron, Alexander L. "'As Full of Grief as Age': *King Lear* as Tragic Ancestor to *No Country for Old Men*." *The Cormac McCarthy Journal* 10, no. 1 (2012): 16–26.

Barth, K. *Church Dogmatics I/1: The Doctrine of the Word of God*. Translated by G. W. Bromiley. Edinburgh: T&T Clark, 1975.

——. *Church Dogmatics II/1: The Doctrine of God*. Translated by H. Knight, W. B. Johnston, T. H. L. Parker, and J. L. M. Haire. Edinburgh: T&T Clark, 1957.

——. *Church Dogmatics III/3: The Doctrine of Creation*. Translated by G. W. Bromiley and R. J. Ehrlich. Edinburgh: T&T Clark, 1956.

——. *Church Dogmatics IV/1: The Doctrine of Reconciliation*. Translated by G. W. Bromiley. Edinburgh: T&T Clark, 1961.

——. *Church Dogmatics IV/3.1: The Doctrine of Reconciliation*. Translated by G. W. Bromiley. Edinburgh: T&T Clark, 1961.

——. *Church Dogmatics IV/3.2: The Doctrine of Reconciliation*. Translated by G. W. Bromiley and T. F. Torrance. Edinburgh: T&T Clark, 1962.

Barton, John. "Déja Lu: Intertextuality, Method or Theory." In *Reading Job Intertextually*, edited by Katharine Dell and Will Kynes, 1–16. New York: Bloomsbury, 2013.

Basselin, T. J. *Flannery O'Connor: Writing a Theology of Disabled Humanity*. Waco, Tex.: Baylor University Press, 2013.

Bell, Madison Smartt. "A Writer's View of Cormac McCarthy." In *Myth, Legend, Dust: Critical Responses to Cormac McCarthy*, edited by Rick Wallach, 1–12. Manchester. U.K.: Manchester University Press, 2000.

Bell, V. M. *The Achievement of Cormac McCarthy*. Baton Rouge, La.: Louisiana State University Press, 1988.

Bernhoft, Iain. "'Some Desperate Entrepreneur Fleeing from a Medicine Show': Judge Holden in the Age of P. T. Barnum." *The Cormac McCarthy Journal* 10, no. 1 (2012): 27–45.

Bimson, John. "Fierce Beasts and Free Processes: A Proposed Reading of God's Speeches in the Book of Job." In *Wisdom, Science and the Scriptures: Essays in Honour of Ernest Lucas*, edited by Stephen Finamore and John Weaver, 16–33. Oxford: Bristol Baptist College and Regent's Park College, 2012.

Bimson, John J. "Who Is 'This' in 'Who is This . . . ?' (Job 38:2): A Response to Karl G. Wilcox." *Journal for the Study of the Old Testament* 25, no. 87 (2000): 125–28.

Boguta-Marchel, H. *The Evil, the Fated, the Biblical: The Latent Metaphysics of Cormac McCarthy*. Newcastle upon Tyne, U.K.: Cambridge Scholars, 2012.

Brinks, C. L. "Who Speaks Words without Knowledge? A Response to Wilcox and Bimson." *Journal for the Study of the Old Testament* 35, no. 2 (2010): 197–207.

Broncano, M. *Religion in Cormac McCarthy's Fiction: Apocryphal Borderlands*. New York: Routledge, 2014.

Brown, D. *God and Mystery in Words: Experience through Metaphor and Drama*. Oxford: Oxford University Press, 2008.

Brown, F. *A Hebrew and English Lexicon of the Old Testament, with an Appendix Containing the Biblical Aramaic: Based on the Lexicon of William Gesenius as Translated by Edward Robinson*. Oxford: Clarendon, 1952.

Brown, W. P. *The Ethos of the Cosmos: The Genesis of Moral Imagination in the Bible*. Grand Rapids: Eerdmans, 1999.

———. *Wisdom's Wonder: Character, Creation, and Crisis in the Bible's Wisdom Literature*. Grand Rapids: Eerdmans, 2014.

Cant, John. *Cormac McCarthy and the Myth of American Exceptionalism*. New York: Routledge, 2008.

———. "Oedipus Rests: Mimesis and Allegory in *No Country for Old Men*." *The Cormac McCarthy Journal* 5, no. 1 (2005): 47–58.

Carson, Jordan. "Drawing Fire from the Text: Narrative and Morality in *Blood Meridian*." *The Cormac McCarthy Journal* 12 (2014): 20–38.

Carver, R. *All of Us: The Collected Poems*. London: Harvill, 1997.

Ciuba, G. M. *Desire, Violence, and Divinity in Modern Southern Fiction*. Baton Rouge, La.: Louisiana State University Press, 2007.

Clines, D. J. A. *Job 1–20*. Nashville, Tenn.: Thomas Nelson, 1989.

———. *Job 21–37*. Nashville, Tenn.: Thomas Nelson, 2006.

———. *Job 38–42*. Nashville, Tenn.: Thomas Nelson, 2011.

Cooper, Lydia R. "McCarthy, Tennessee, and the Southern Gothic." In *The Cambridge Companion to Cormac McCarthy*, edited by Steven Frye, 41–53. Cambridge: Cambridge University Press, 2013.

Coulson, J. *Religion and Imagination: "In Aid of a Grammar of Assent."* Oxford: Oxford University Press, 1981.

Cremean, David. "For Whom Bell Tolls: Conservatism and Change in Cormac McCarthy's Sheriff from *No Country for Old Men*." *The Cormac McCarthy Journal* 5, no. 1 (2005): 21–29.

Crews, Michael Lynn. *Books Are Made Out of Books: A Guide to Cormac McCarthy's Literary Influences*. Austin.: University of Texas Press, 2017.

———. "The San Marcos Archives: *Blood Meridian* and the West." In *Cormac McCarthy in Context*, edited by Steven Frye, 288–99. Cambridge: Cambridge University Press, 2020.

Dacus, Chris. "The West as Symbol of the Eschaton in Cormac McCarthy." *The Cormac McCarthy Journal* 7, no. 1 (2009): 7–15.

Daugherty, Leo. "Gravers False and True: *Blood Meridian* as Gnostic Tragedy." In *Perspectives on Cormac McCarthy*, edited by Edwin T. Arnold and Dianne C. Luce, 159–74. Jackson, Miss.: University Press of Mississippi, 1999.

Davis, E. F. *Getting Involved with God: Rediscovering the Old Testament*. Plymouth, Mass.: Cowley, 2001.

Davis, Stephen, T., ed. *Encountering Evil: Live Options in Theodicy*. Edinburgh: T&T Clark, 1981.

Detweiler, Robert. "Theological Trends of Postmodern Fiction." *Journal of the American Academy of Religion* 44, no. 2 (1976): 225–37.

Dhorme, É. *A Commentary on the Book of Job*. Translated by H. Knight. Nashville, Tenn.: Thomas Nelson, 1967.

Dillard, A. *Pilgrim at Tinker Creek*. Norwich, U.K.: Canterbury, 2011.

Dillistone, F. W. *The Christian Understanding of Atonement*. Welwyn, U.K.: James Nisbet, 1968.

———. *The Novelist and the Passion Story*. London: Collins, 1960.

Dorson, James. "The Judaeo-Christian Tradition." In *Cormac McCarthy in Context*, edited by Steven Frye, 121–31. Cambridge: Cambridge University Press, 2020.

Dowd, Ciaran. "The Santa Fe Institute." In *Cormac McCarthy in Context*, edited by Steven Frye, 33–44. Cambridge: Cambridge University Press, 2020.

Driver, S. R., and Gray, G. B. *A Critical and Exegetical Commentary on the Book of Job: The International Critical Commentary*. Edinburgh: T&T Clark, 1921.

Edenfield, Olivia Carr. "Ernest Hemingway." In *Cormac McCarthy in Context*, edited by Steven Frye, 59–67. Cambridge: Cambridge University Press, 2020.

Edmondson, T. *Priest, Prophet, Pilgrim: Types and Distortions of Spiritual Vocation in the Fiction of Wendell Berry and Cormac McCarthy*. Eugene, Ore.: Pickwick, 2014.

Edwards, Tim. "The End of the Road: Pastoralism and the Post-Apocalyptic Waste Land of Cormac McCarthy's *The Road*." *The Cormac McCarthy Journal* 6 (2008): 55–61.

Eliot, T. S. *Collected Poems: 1909–1962*. London: Faber and Faber, 1974.

Ellis, Jay. "'Do You See?': Levels of Ellipsis in *No Country for Old Men*." In *Cormac McCarthy: All the Pretty Horses, No Country for Old Men, The Road*, edited by Sara L. Spurgeon, 94–116. London: Continuum, 2011.

Evenson, Brian. "Embodying Violence: The Case of Cormac McCarthy." *The Cormac McCarthy Journal* 14, no. 2 (2016): 135–48.

———. "McCarthy and the Uses of Philosophy in the Tennessee Novels." In *The Cambridge Companion to Cormac McCarthy*, edited by Steven Frye, 54–64. Cambridge: Cambridge University Press, 2013.

Fiddes, Paul S. "Concept, Image and Story in Systematic Theology." *International Journal of Systematic Theology* 11, no. 1 (2009): 3–23.

Flory, Dan. "Evil, Mood, and Reflection in the Coen Brothers' *No Country for Old Men*." In *Cormac McCarthy: All the Pretty Horses, No Country for Old Men, The Road*, edited by Sara L. Spurgeon, 117–34. London: Continuum, 2011.

Fretheim, T. E. *Creation Untamed: The Bible, God and Natural Disasters*. Grand Rapids: Baker Academic, 2010.

———. *God and World in the Old Testament: A Relational Theology of Creation*. Nashville, Tenn.: Abingdon, 2005.

Frost, Robert. *A Masque of Reason*. Oxford: Alden, 1948.

Frye, Steven. "Histories, Novels, Ideas: Cormac McCarthy and the Art of Philosophy." In *The Cambridge Companion to Cormac McCarthy*, edited by Steven Frye, 3–11. Cambridge: Cambridge University Press, 2013.

———. "Life and Career." In *Cormac McCarthy in Context*, edited by Steven Frye, 3–12. Cambridge: Cambridge University Press, 2020.

———. *Understanding Cormac McCarthy*. Columbia: University of South Carolina Press, 2011.

Gilbert, Scott. "Discourse Theory in *The Crossing*." *The Cormac McCarthy Journal* 1, no. 1 (2001): 38–43.

Giles, James R. "*Outer Dark* and Romantic Naturalism." In *The Cambridge Companion to Cormac McCarthy*, edited by Steven Frye, 95–106. Cambridge: Cambridge University Press, 2013.

Glatzer, Nahum N. "Introduction: A Study of Job." In *The Dimensions of Job: A Study and Selected Readings*, edited by Nahum N. Glatzer, 1–48. Eugene, Ore.: Wipf and Stock, 2002.

Gordis, R. *The Book of God and Man: A Study of Job*. Chicago: University of Chicago Press, 1965.

———. *The Book of Job: Commentary, New Translation, and Special Studies*. New York: Jewish Theological Seminary of America, 1978.

Grammer, John M. "A Thing against Which Time Will Not Prevail: Pastoral and History in Cormac McCarthy's South." In *Perspectives on Cormac McCarthy*, edited by Edwin T. Arnold and Dianne C. Luce, 29–44. Jackson, Miss.: University Press of Mississippi, 1999.

Gray, J. *The Book of Job*. Sheffield, U.K.: Sheffield Phoenix, 2010.

Gretlund, Jan Norbert. "Cormac McCarthy and the American Literary Tradition: Wording the End." In *Intertextual and Interdisciplinary Approaches to Cormac McCarthy*, edited by Nicholas Monk, 41–51. Abingdon, U.K.: Routledge, 2012.

Guillemin, G. *The Pastoral Vision of Cormac McCarthy*. College Station: Texas A&M University Press, 2005.

Gunkel, Hermann. "The Influence of Babylonian Mythology upon the Biblical Creation Story." In *Creation in the Old Testament*, edited by Bernhard W. Anderson, 25–52. London: SPCK, 1984.

Gustafson, Hans S. "Sacramental Spirituality in *The Brothers Karamazov* and Wendell Berry's Port William Characters." *Journal of Literature & Theology* 27, no. 3 (2014): 345–63.

Gutiérrez, G. *On Job: God-Talk and the Suffering of the Innocent*. Maryknoll, N.Y.: Orbis, 1987.

Habel, N. C. *The Book of Job: A Commentary*. London: SCM Press, 1985.

Hamlin, H. *The Bible in Shakespeare*. Oxford: Oxford University Press, 2013.

Hartley, J. E. *The Book of Job*. Grand Rapids: Eerdmans, 1988.

Hauerwas, Stanley. *Dispatches from the Front: Theological Engagements with the Secular*. Durham, N.C.: Duke University Press, 1994.

Hick, John. *Evil and the God of Love*. London: Macmillan, 1966.

Higgins, Chris. "Labour, Work, and Action: Arendt's Phenomenology of Practical Life." *Journal of Philosophy and Education* 44, nos. 2–3 (2010): 275–300.

Hillier, Russell M. "'Like Some Supplicant to the Darkness over Them All': The Good of John Grady Cole in Cormac McCarthy's *Cities of the Plain*." *The Cormac McCarthy Journal* 14, no. 1 (2016): 3–36.

———. *Morality in Cormac McCarthy's Fiction: Souls at Hazard*. Cham, C.H.: Palgrave Macmillan, 2017.

———. "'Nor Hell a Fury': Malkina's Motivation in Cormac McCarthy's *The Counselor*." *The Explicator* 72, no. 2 (2014): 151–57.

Holloway, David. "Modernism, Nature, and Utopia: Another Look at 'Optical Democracy' in Cormac McCarthy's Western Quartet." *The Southern Quarterly* 38, no. 3 (2000): 186–205.

Hume, David. "Dialogues concerning Natural Religion (1779)." In *The Empiricists: John Locke, George Berkeley, David Hume*, 431–517. Garden City, N.Y.: Anchor, 1974.

———. *Enquiries concerning Human Understanding and concerning the Principles of Morals*. Edited by L. A. Selby-Bigge. Oxford: Clarendon, 1975.

Janzen, J. G. *Job*. Atlanta: John Knox, 1985.

Jarrett, Robert L. *Cormac McCarthy*. New York: Twayne, 1997.

———. "Genre, Voice and Ethos: McCarthy's Perverse 'Thriller.'" *The Cormac McCarthy Journal* 5, no. 1 (2005): 36–46.

Jasper, D. *The Study of Literature and Religion: An Introduction*. London: Macmillan, 1989.

Josephs, Allen. *On Cormac McCarthy: Essays on Mexico, Crime, Hemingway and God*. Wickford, R.I.: New Street Communications, 2016.

———. "The Quest for God in *The Road*." In *The Cambridge Companion to Cormac McCarthy*, edited by Steven Frye, 133–48. Cambridge: Cambridge University Press, 2013.

Josyph, P. *Cormac McCarthy's House: Reading McCarthy without Walls*. Austin: University of Texas Press, 2013.

Juge, Carole. "The Road to the Sun They Cannot See: Plato's Allegory of the Cave, Oblivion and Guidance in Cormac McCarthy's *The Road*." *The Cormac McCarthy Journal* 7, no. 1 (2009): 16–30.

Jüngel, Eberhard. "Metaphorical Truth: Reflections on the Theological Relevance of Metaphor as a Contribution to the Hermeneutics of Narrative Theology." In *Theological Essays 1*, edited by John B. Webster, 16–71. Edinburgh: T&T Clark, 1989.

Keegan, James. "'Save Yourself': The Boundaries of Theodicy and the Signs of *The Crossing*." *The Cormac McCarthy Journal* 1, no. 1 (2001): 44–61.

Keller, C. *Face of the Deep: A Theology of Becoming*. Abingdon, U.K.: Routledge, 2003.

Kiefer, Christian. "The Morality of Blood: Examining the Moral Code of *The Crossing*." *The Cormac McCarthy Journal* 1, no. 1 (2001): 26–37.

Kierkegaard, S. *Fear and Trembling; Sickness unto Death*. Translated by W. Lowrie. New York: Doubleday, 1954.

Kissane, E. J. *The Book of Job: Translated from a Critically Revised Hebrew Text with Commentary*. Dublin: Richview, 1939.

Koehler, L., and Baumgartner, W. *The Hebrew and Aramaic Lexicon of the Old Testament*. Translated by M. E. J. Richardson. Leiden: Brill, 2001.

Kushner, David. "Cormac McCarthy's Apocalypse." *Rolling Stone*, 2007.

Larrimore, M. *The Book of Job: A Biography*. Princeton, N.J.: Princeton University Press, 2013.

Levi, A. H. T. "The Relationship between Literature and Theology: An Historical Reflection." *Journal of Literature & Theology* 1, no. 1 (1987): 11–18.

Lewis, C. S. *An Experiment in Criticism*. Cambridge: Cambridge University Press, 1961.

———. *A Grief Observed*. London: Faber & Faber, 1961.

———. "The Literary Impact of the Authorised Version." In *Selected Literary Essays*, edited by Walter Hooper, 126–45. Cambridge: Cambridge University Press, 1969.

Lilley, James D. "'The Hands of Yet Other Puppets': Figuring Freedom and Reading Repetition in *All the Pretty Horses*." In *Myth, Legend, Dust: Critical Responses to Cormac McCarthy*, edited by Rick Wallach, 272–87. Manchester, U.K.: Manchester University Press, 2000.

Lo, A. *Job 28 as Rhetoric: An Analysis of Job 28 in the Context of Job 22–31*. Leiden: Brill, 2003.

Longman, T. *Job*. Grand Rapids: Baker Academic, 2012.

Luc, Alex. "Storm and the Message of Job." *Journal for the Study of the Old Testament* 25, no. 87 (2000): 111–23.

Luce, Dianne C. "The Archives and the Tennessee Years II." In *Cormac McCarthy in Context*, edited by Steven Frye, 273–80. Cambridge: Cambridge University Press, 2020.

———. "Cormac McCarthy and Albert Erskine: The Evolution of a Working Relationship." *Resources for American Literary Study* 35 (2010): 303–38.

———. *Reading the World: Cormac McCarthy's Tennessee Period*. Columbia: University of South Carolina Press, 2009.

Lupton, Julia Reinhard. "The Wizards of Uz: Shakespeare and the Book of Job." In *Shakespeare and Religion: Early Modern and Postmodern Perspectives*, edited by Ken Jackson and Arthur F. Marotti, 163–87. Notre Dame, Ind.: University of Notre Dame Press, 2011.

Luttrull, Daniel. "Prometheus Hits *The Road*: Revising the Myth." *The Cormac McCarthy Journal* 8, no. 1 (2010): 20–33.

MacKenzie, Cameron. "A Song of Great Order: The Real in Cormac McCarthy's *The Crossing*." *The Cormac McCarthy Journal* 13, no. 1 (2015): 100–120.

Madsen, Michael. "'A Namelessness Wheeling in the Night': Shapes of Evil in Cormac McCarthy's *Blood Meridian* and John Carpenter's *Halloween*." In *Intertextual and Interdisciplinary Approaches to Cormac McCarthy*, edited by Nicholas Monk, 100–111. Abingdon, U.K.: Routledge, 2012.

Marx, S. *Shakespeare and the Bible*. Oxford: Oxford University Press, 2000.

McCabe, H. *God and Evil in the Theology of St Thomas Aquinas*. London: Continuum, 2010.

McCann, J. Clinton, Jr. "The Book of Job and Marjorie Kemper's 'God's Goodness.'" In *Reading Job Intertextually*, edited by Katharine Dell and Will Kynes, 285–96. New York: Bloomsbury, 2013.

McCarthy, Cormac. *All the Pretty Horses*. London: Picador, 1993.

———. *Blood Meridian*. London: Picador, 1985.

———. *Cities of the Plain*. London: Picador, 1999.

———. *The Counselor*. London: Picador, 2013.

———. *The Crossing*. London: Picador, 1995.

———. "The Kekulé Problem: Where Did Language Come From?" *Nautilus* 19 (2017): 22–31.

———. *No Country for Old Men*. London: Picador, 2005.

———. *The Orchard Keeper*. London: Picador, 1965.

———. *Outer Dark*. London: Picador, 1968.

———. *The Road*. London: Picador, 2006.

———. *The Sunset Limited*. London: Picador, 2010.

———. *Suttree*. London: Picador, 1980.

McCosker, Philip. "Blessed Tension: Barth and Von Balthasar on the Music of Mozart." *The Way* 44, no. 4 (2005): 81–95.

Melville, H. *Moby Dick*. New York: Norton, 2002.

Mills, Luke William. "American Faerie: Medieval Fairy Lore in Cormac McCarthy's *Blood Meridian*." *The Cormac McCarthy Journal* 17, no. 1 (2019): 27–42.

Moos, Dan. "Lacking the Article Itself: Representation and History in Cormac McCarthy's *Blood Meridian*." *The Cormac McCarthy Journal* 2, no. 1 (2002): 23–39.

Muir, Kenneth. "Epilogue." In *King Lear: Critical Essays*, edited by Kenneth Muir, 281–93. New York: Garland, 1984.

Mundik, P. *A Bloody and Barbarous God: The Metaphysics of Cormac McCarthy*. Albuquerque: University of New Mexico Press, 2016.

Newsom, Carol A. *The Book of Job: A Contest of Moral Imagination*. Oxford: Oxford University Press, 2003.

——. *Job*. Nashville, Tenn.: Abingdon, 1996.

Nielsen, K. *There Is Hope for a Tree: The Tree as Metaphor in Isaiah*. Sheffield, U.K.: Sheffield Academic, 1989.

Oberhänsli, Gabrielle. "Job in Modern and Contemporary Literature on the Background of Tradition: Sidelights of a Jewish Reading." In *Reading Job Intertextually*, edited by Katharine Dell and Will Kynes, 272–84. New York: Bloomsbury, 2013.

O'Connor, Flannery. "Catholic Novelists and Their Readers." In *Mystery & Manners*, edited by Sally and Robert Fitzgerald, 169–90. London: Faber & Faber, 2014.

——. "The Nature and Aim of Fiction." In *Mystery & Manners*, edited by Sally and Robert Fitzgerald, 63–86. London: Faber & Faber, 2014.

Paffenroth, K. *In Praise of Wisdom: Literary and Theological Reflections on Faith and Reason*. New York: Continuum, 2004.

Parrish, Timothy. "History and the Problem of Evil in McCarthy's Western Novels." In *The Cambridge Companion to Cormac McCarthy*, edited by Steven Frye, 67–78. Cambridge: Cambridge University Press, 2013.

Pastore, Stephen. "Judge Holden: Yahweh on Horseback." In *They Rode On: Blood Meridian and the Tragedy of the American West*, edited by Rick Wallach, 108–11. Miami: Cormac McCarthy Society, 2013.

Peacocke, Arthur R. *Creation and the World of Science: The Bampton Lectures, 1978*. Oxford: Clarendon, 1979.

——. "God's Interaction with the World: The Implications of Deterministic 'Chaos' and of Interconnected and Interdependent Complexity." In *Chaos and Complexity: Scientific Perspectives on Divine Action*, edited by Robert John Russell, Nancey Murphy, and Arthur R. Peacocke, 263–88. Vatican City: Vatican Observatory Publications, 1997.

Peebles, Stacey. "Cormac McCarthy: A Critical History." In *Cormac McCarthy in Context*, edited by Steven Frye, 316–25. Cambridge: Cambridge University Press, 2020.

Pelham, A. *Contested Creations in the Book of Job: The World-as-It-Ought-and-Ought-Not-to-Be*. Leiden: Brill, 2012.

Perdue, L. G. *Wisdom in Revolt: Metaphorical Theology in the Book of Job*. Sheffield, U.K.: Almond, 1991.

Phillips, D. Z. *The Problem of Evil and the Problem of God*. London: SCM Press, 2004.

Phillips, Elaine A. "Speaking Truthfully: Job's Friends and Job." *Bulletin for Biblical Research* 18, no. 1 (2008): 31–43.

Pinker, Aron. "A Friend's First Words in Job 4:2." *Vetus Testamentum* 63 (2013): 78–88.

Plato. *The Laws*. Translated by T. J. Saunders. London: Penguin, 1975.

Ploskonka, Mitchell. "'See the Wild Man Two Bits': James Robert, Disability and Personhood in *Blood Meridian*." *The Cormac McCarthy Journal* 16, no. 1 (2018): 55–72.

Polasek, Cassie. "'Books Are Made Out of Books': Herman Melville's Moby Dick and Cormac McCarthy's Judge Holden." In *They Rode On: Blood Meridian and the Tragedy of the American West*, edited by Rick Wallach, 82–94. Miami: Cormac McCarthy Society, 2013.

Polkinghorne, John. *Science and Creation: The Search for Understanding*. London: SPCK, 1988.

Pope, M. H. *Job: Introduction, Translation and Notes*. New Haven, Conn.: Yale University Press, 2008.

Potts, M. L. *Cormac McCarthy and the Signs of Sacrament: Literature, Theology, and the Moral of Stories*. London: Bloomsbury, 2015.

Powning, Jacob S. "'Dreams So Rich in Color. How Else Would Death Call You?': An Exploration of the Ending in Cormac McCarthy's *The Road*." *The Cormac McCarthy Journal* 18, no. 1 (2020): 26–36.

Prather, William. "'Like Something Seen Through Bad Glass': Narrative Strategies in *The Orchard Keeper*." In *Myth, Legend, Dust: Critical Responses to Cormac McCarthy*, edited by Rick Wallach, 37–54. Manchester, U.K.: Manchester University Press, 2000.

Ricoeur, P. *Interpretation Theory: Discourse and the Surplus of Meaning*. Fort Worth, Tex.: Texas Christian University Press, 1976.

Rolston, Holmes, III. "Does Nature Need to Be Redeemed?" *Zygon* 29, no. 2 (1994): 205–29.

Rowley, H. H. *Job*. London: Thomas Nelson, 1970.

Ryken, L. *Triumphs of the Imagination: Literature in Christian Perspective*. Downers Grove, Ill: InterVarsity, 1979.

Sansom, Dennis. "Learning from Art: Cormac McCarthy's *Blood Meridian* as a Critique of Divine Determinism." *The Journal of Aesthetic Education* 41, no. 1 (2007): 1–19.

Schifferdecker, K. *Out of the Whirlwind: Creation Theology in the Book of Job*. Cambridge, Mass.: Harvard University Press, 2008.

Scholnick, Sylvia Huberman. "The Meaning of *Mispat* in the Book of Job." *Journal of Biblical Literature* 101, no. 4 (1982): 521–29.

Scott, N. A. *The Broken Center: Studies in the Theological Horizon of Modern Literature*. New Haven, Conn.: Yale University Press, 1966.

Seow, C. L. *Job 1–21: Interpretation and Commentary*. Grand Rapids: Eerdmans, 2013.

Sepich, John E. *Notes on Blood Meridian: Revised and Expanded Edition*. Austin: University of Texas Press, 2008.

——. "'What Kind of Indians Was Them?' Some Historical Sources in Cormac McCarthy's *Blood Meridian*." In *Perspectives on Cormac McCarthy*, edited by Edwin T. Arnold and Dianne C. Luce, 123–44. Jackson, Miss.: University Press of Mississippi, 1999.

Shaviro, Steven. "'The Very Life of the Darkness': A Reading of *Blood Meridian*." In *Perspectives on Cormac McCarthy*, edited by Edwin T. Arnold and Dianne C. Luce, 145–58. Jackson, Miss.: University Press of Mississippi, 1999.

Shaw, Patrick W. "The Kid's Fate, the Judge's Guilt: Ramifications of Closure in Cormac McCarthy's *Blood Meridian*." *Southern Literary Journal* 30, no. 1 (1997): 102–19.

Simon, U. *Atonement: From Holocaust to Paradise*. Cambridge: James Clarke, 1987.

——. *Story and Faith: In the Biblical Narrative*. London: SPCK, 1975.

Smith, James K. A. *On the Road with Saint Augustine: A Real-World Spirituality for Restless Hearts*. Grand Rapids: Brazos, 2019.

Snaith, N. N. *The Book of Job: Its Origin and Purpose*. London: SCM Press, 1968.

Sonderegger, Katherine. *Systematic Theology*. Vol. 1: *The Doctrine of God*. Minneapolis: Fortress, 2015.

Soskice, J. M. *Metaphor and Religious Language*. Oxford: Clarendon, 1985.

Southgate, C. *The Groaning of Creation: God, Evolution, and the Problem of Evil*. Louisville, Ky.: Westminster John Knox, 2008.

Spencer, William C. "Cormac McCarthy's Unholy Trinity: Biblical Parody in *Outer Dark*." In *Sacred Violence: A Reader's Companion to Cormac McCarthy*, edited by Wade Hall and Rick Wallach, 69–76. El Paso, Tex.: Texas Western Press, 1995.

Stinson, Emily J. "*Blood Meridian*'s Man of Many Masks: Judge Holden as Tarot Fool." In *They Rode On: Blood Meridian and the Tragedy of the American West*, edited by Rick Wallach, 95–107. Miami: Cormac McCarthy Society, 2013.

Stump, Eleanore. *Wandering in Darkness: Narrative and the Problem of Suffering*. Oxford: Clarendon, 2010.

Surin, K. *Theology and the Problem of Evil*. Oxford: Basil Blackwell, 1986.

Swinton, J. *Raging with Compassion: Pastoral Responses to the Problem of Evil*. Grand Rapids: Eerdmans, 2007.

Treier, Daniel J. "Theological Hermeneutics, Contemporary." In *Dictionary for Theological Interpretation of the Bible*, edited by Kevin J. Vanhoozer, Craig G. Bartholomew, Daniel J. Treier, and N. T. Wright, 787–93. London: SPCK, 2005.

——. *Virtue and the Voice of God: Toward Theology as Wisdom*. Grand Rapids: Eerdmans, 2006.

Tsumura, D. T. *The Earth and the Waters in Genesis 1 and 2: A Linguistic Investigation*. Sheffield, U.K.: Sheffield Academic, 1989.

Vance, Norman. "George Eliot and Hardy." In *The Oxford Handbook of English Literature and Theology*, edited by Andrew Hass, David Jasper, and Elisabeth Jay, 483–98. Oxford: Oxford University Press, 2007.

Vanderheide, John. "Sighting Leviathan: Ritualism, Daemonism and the Book of Job in McCarthy's Latest Works." *The Cormac McCarthy Journal* 6 (2008): 107–20.

———. "Varieties of Renunciation in the Works of Cormac McCarthy." *The Cormac McCarthy Journal* 5, no. 1 (2005): 30–35.

Vanhoozer, Kevin J. *Is There a Meaning in This Text? The Bible, the Reader and the Morality of Literary Knowledge*. Leicester, U.K.: Apollos, 1998.

———. "What Is Everyday Theology? How and Why Christians Should Read Culture." In *Everyday Theology: How to Read Cultural Texts and Interpret Trends*, edited by Charles A. Anderson, Michael J. Sleasman, and Kevin J. Vanhoozer, 15–62. Grand Rapids: Baker Academic, 2007.

van Wolde, E. *Mr and Mrs Job*. Translated by J. Bowden. London: SCM Press, 1997.

Vieth, Ronja. "A Frontier Myth Turns Gothic: *Blood Meridian: Or, the Evening Redness in the West*." *The Cormac McCarthy Journal* 8, no. 1 (2010): 55–72.

Wallace, Garry. "Meeting McCarthy." *Southern Quarterly* 30, no. 4 (1992): 134–39.

Wallach, Rick. "Editor's Introduction: Cormac McCarthy's Canon as Accidental Artifact." In *Myth, Legend, Dust: Critical Responses to Cormac McCarthy*, edited by Rick Wallach, xiv–vi. Manchester, U.K.: Manchester University Press, 2000.

———. "Judge Holden: *Blood Meridian*'s Evil Archon." In *Sacred Violence: A Reader's Companion to Cormac McCarthy*, edited by Wade Hall and Rick Wallach, 125–36. El Paso, Tex.: Texas Western Press, 1995.

Walsh, Richard. "(Carrying the Fire on) No Road for Old Horses: Cormac McCarthy's Untold Biblical Stories." *Journal of Religion and Popular Culture* 24, no. 3 (2012): 339–51.

Walton, J. H. *Job*. NIV Application Commentary Series. Grand Rapids: Zondervan, 2012.

Warren, Craig A. "Drawing a Blank: Illustrating 'the Kid' in Cormac McCarthy's *Blood Meridian*." *The Cormac McCarthy Journal* 18, no. 1 (2020): 3–25.

Watson, Jay. "William Faulkner." In *Cormac McCarthy in Context*, edited by Steven Frye, 47–58. Cambridge: Cambridge University Press, 2020.

Wharton, J. A. *Job*. Louisville, Ky.: Westminster John Knox, 1999.

White, Christopher T. "Dreaming the Border Trilogy: Cormac McCarthy and Narrative Creativity." *The Cormac McCarthy Journal* 13, no. 1 (2015): 121–42.

Whybray, N. *Job*. Sheffield, U.K.: Sheffield Phoenix, 2008.

Wielenberg, Erik J. "God, Morality and Meaning in Cormac McCarthy's *The Road*." *The Cormac McCarthy Journal* 8, no. 1 (2010): 1–19.

Wiesel, E. *The Trial of God (as It Was Held on February 25, 1649, in Shamgorod)*. New York: Schocken, 1979.

Wilcox, Karl G. "'Who Is This . . . ?': A Reading of Job 32:2." *Journal for the Study of the Old Testament* 23, no. 78 (1998): 85–95.

Williams, Rowan. *Dostoevsky: Language, Faith, and Fiction*. London: Continuum, 2008.

———. *The Edge of Words: God and the Habits of Language*. London: Bloomsbury, 2014.

———. *On Augustine*. London: Bloomsbury, 2016.

———. *On Christian Theology*. Oxford: Basil Blackwell, 2000.

Wilson, L. *Job*. Grand Rapids: Eerdmans, 2015.

Wood, R. C. *The Gospel according to Tolkien: Visions of the Kingdom in Middle-Earth*. Louisville, Ky.: Westminster John Knox, 2003.

———. *Literature and Theology*. Nashville, Tenn.: Abingdon, 2008.

Woodson, Linda. "McCarthy's Heroes and the Will to Truth." In *The Cambridge Companion to Cormac McCarthy*, edited by Steven Frye, 15–26. Cambridge: Cambridge University Press, 2013.

———. "'This Is Another Country': The Complex Feminine Presence in *All the Pretty Horses*." In *Cormac McCarthy: All the Pretty Horses, No Country for Old Men, The Road*, edited by Sara L. Spurgeon, 25–42. London: Continuum, 2011.

———. "'. . . You Are the Battleground': Materiality, Moral Responsibility and Determinism in *No Country for Old Men*." *The Cormac McCarthy Journal* 5, no. 1 (2005): 4–13.

Woodward, Richard B. "Cormac Country." *Vanity Fair*, 2005.

———. "Cormac McCarthy's Venomous Fiction." *The New York Times Magazine*, 1992.

Yarbrough, Scott D. "Tricksters and Lightbringers in McCarthy's Post-Appalachian Novels." *The Cormac McCarthy Journal* 10, no. 1 (2010): 46–55.

Author Index

Subject Index

Scripture Index